HE GOES BEFORE

Stories of

A MEDICAL MISSIONARY IN AFRICA

OLIVE RAWN with Cheryl Hersh

Photos of artifacts:
Lynn Wichmann: 6–9, 87, 141, 199
Ed Surrey, Facebook.com/Edward Surrey photography: 2, 289
Cover design: Mark Haines, diluvium.com

All scripture taken from the New King James Version®. Copyright © 1982 by Thomas
Nelson. Used by permission. All rights reserved.

Proceeds from this book will be donated to Bethany Bible Fellowship Church and
Africa Inland Mission.

ISBN-13 9781790249855

CONTENTS

PREFACE

At one time, Olive Rawn traveled the world and experienced a life of extraordinary adventure in service of her precious Lord and Savior Jesus Christ. As we began this project in the summer of 2017, her physical world had shrunk to one room in a nursing home, yet her spirit had not. Her story, it seems to me, reaches across both distance and time. I invite you to walk along with Aunt Olive (as she is known to everyone) through her joys and her fears, her successes and failures. Thanks to her mother's foresight, most of Aunt Olive's weekly letters have been preserved, and the stories that follow were taken from that correspondence. This book is not meant to be an exhaustive discussion of the history of the times, but simply Aunt Olive's observation and interpretation of events as they unfolded before her.

I knew Aunt Olive from church, and figured she must have some good stories to tell. I thought it might be interesting to write them down, picturing perhaps ten pages photocopied and dispersed to interested folks. Olive's niece Karen Fluck generously shared the letters with me, and I began meeting with Aunt Olive once a week from the summer of 2017 until her death at the age of ninety–six in January of 2018. As is often the Lord's way, He gently expanded my tiny idea into the book you hold today. In her letters, Aunt Olive often remarked on the nature of God's leading in her life. She loved to say that God knew all about the thing before her and her job was to simply take the next step. She went step by step with Him and counted the taking of each step as everything. I can only agree.

To sit beside Aunt Olive each week and talk about what I had read in her letters was a great joy in my life. Sometimes her memories were clear and other times she would turn to me in surprise and ask, "Did I really do that? I don't remember that at all." Once when our conversation turned from a difficult event in the past to difficult current events, she shook her head and remarked that maybe the Lord would return soon. Then she suddenly sat up tall and turned to me with a great big smile and said, "Maybe today!" Through all our conversations, her love for her Lord and her hope and desire to be home with Him never dimmed.

Please know that if you are reading this story, I have prayed for you—that walking for a time beside Aunt Olive might speak wisdom and encouragement into your own journey.   —Cheryl Hersh

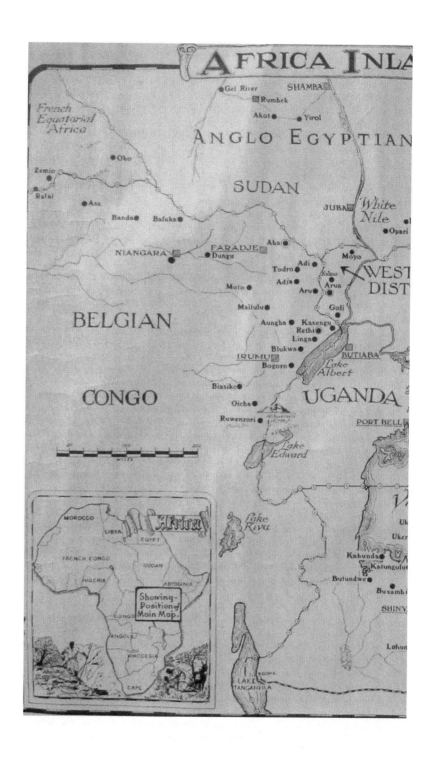

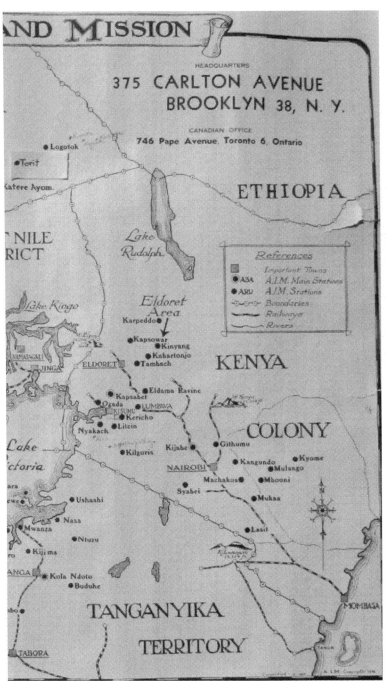

Map used by permission of AIM

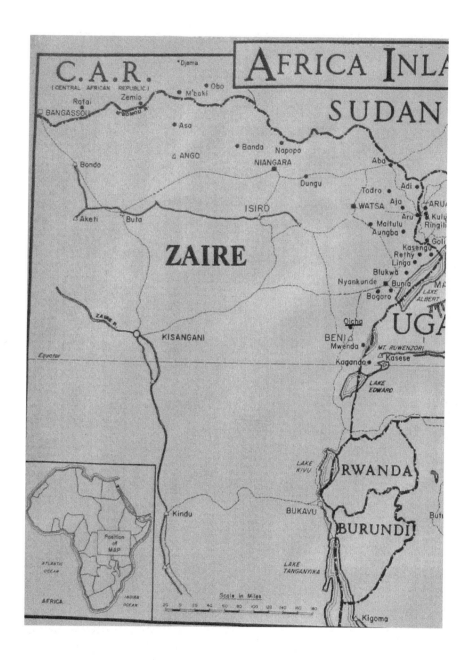

8

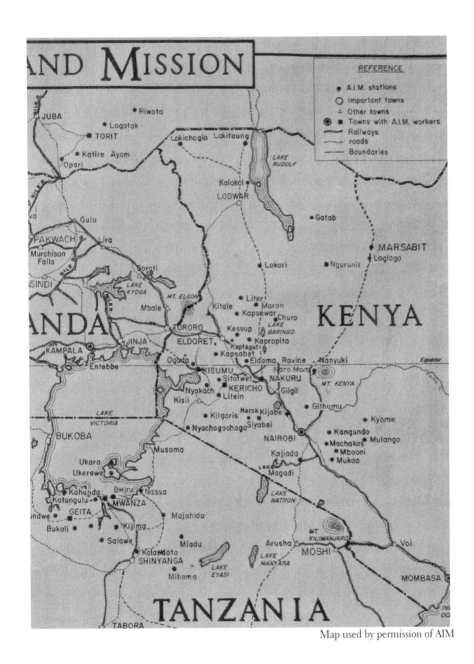

Map used by permission of AIM

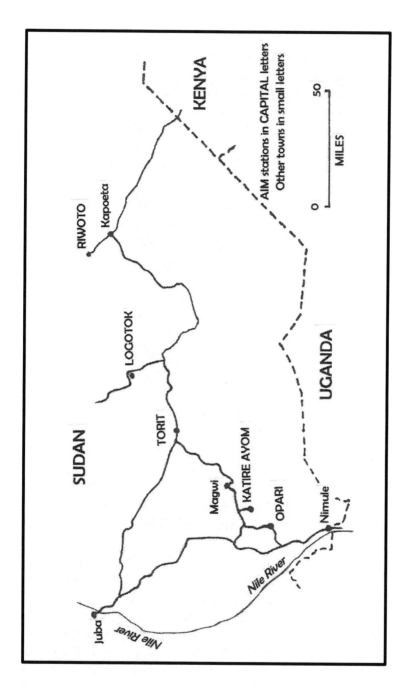

SUDAN

KENYA

UGANDA

RIWOTO

Kapoeta

LOGOTOK

TORIT

KATIRE AVOM

Magwi

OPARI

Nimule

Juba

Nile River

Nile River

AIM stations in CAPITAL letters
Other towns in small letters

0   50

MILES

Cartography by Russ Noble

Term One
1949 - 1954

1949

*Commit your way to the Lord, trust also in Him, and He
shall bring it to pass. (Psalm 38:3)*

I was on my way. On Tuesday, March 22, 1949 at 5:20 pm, I and eleven other passengers sailed out of New York towards the continent of Africa on the S.S. Talisman, a Norwegian freight ship with forty-two crew.

As the Lord leads, he had guided me step by step to this place. My family always went to church. If the doors were open, we were there, and I received Jesus as my personal Savior when I was a little girl. Missionaries were always before us. Mission Sunday! We couldn't wait to hear about another place where people were working. We couldn't wait to hear another story from a missionary. We couldn't wait to see the pictures. Missionaries came home on furlough and I'd hear all about them.

I trained as a nurse at Grandview Hospital then felt led to go to Bible school. My parents didn't have money to help me, so I worked at Hahnemann Hospital while attending classes at Philadelphia School of the Bible (now Cairn University) and managed to graduate debt free. I knew I wanted to serve the Lord but felt the foreign field was too far away. After all, I was just a Pennsylvania Dutch country girl. I'd never be able to do something like that. I wrestled with what the Lord would have me do, and nothing seemed clear. Finally, I yielded my ALL—yes, even to the foreign field if that was where God wanted me. Only then did I have peace. The leaders of my church prayed with me, and in May of 1948, I began the process of applying to Africa Inland Mission (AIM).

By early March of 1949, I was traveling to the Mission house in New York for last minute preparations before beginning my assignment in Sudan, Africa. So many had helped me get to this point. Some prayed, some gave gifts, some built crates, and some helped me pack.

When I walked into the mission house that first day, I had to turn around and go right out for my yellow fever shot, which for some reason was only given at 1:45 p.m. each day. From there, I went to get my visa.

Nine months later, when I tried to leave Congo for Sudan, I discovered that they had issued me a visa for only three months. This caused no end of a paperwork fuss, but at the time I picked it up, I took no notice of the dates.

I met Bill and Dorothy Beatty, fellow members of the new Sudan team, for the first time. They were leaving for Africa in a few days and wished they could find a corner to stick me in so we could all travel out together, but we would meet up again by the end of April.

My sending denomination, Mennonite Brethren in Christ (now called Bible Fellowship), had held a farewell service on March 4 at the

Mother and Olive in New York

Allentown Bethel Church. Before sailing, I spent my days at home with final rounds of seeing loved ones, visiting churches, and one last goodbye on March 20 with my home church family in Hatfield. Folks there wrote letters for me to open, one each day of the trip. As I recall, I followed that direction and the letters encouraged me along the way.

How wonderful the Lord was to me. I didn't want to go away from home, yet now, at twenty-seven years old, I was on my way and He made the way easy. My desire was to be willing for His path at all times. I didn't know what the future held. Whether my time in Africa was long or short, I wanted to be willing for it. Was I really willing? Or did I have big ideas of my own I wanted worked out? No! By His Grace I wanted His way.

The ship was scheduled to sail on March 21, but that morning I had notice of a delay until noon the next day. Pastor and Mrs. Kratz, Sister Didden and Charles Toro, all from my home church, came to see me off on the twenty-first because I couldn't get word to them in time. Unfortunately, they were unable to stay until the next day. Pastor Bean and Aunt Sara also came to the dock as well, but I missed them completely. I couldn't see the reason for the delay, but I wrote in a letter home that "in all things the Lord has something to teach us. I am willing to take His way for His ways are best. We can only go a step at a time but that step with Him is everything." When the ship finally sailed, it was a tearless leaving as I had no one to see me off.

Eleven of the twelve passengers were missionaries, three of us bound for Congo (myself, Mrs. Davies, and Edythe Gant) and the others to Nigeria (Dr. and Mrs. Faust and their two sons Gerald, twelve years old, and Arnold, sixteen; Thelma Lauderton; Miss Henderson; Mr. Ratzloff; and one other). The twelfth passenger was a retired captain. At that time, we traveled on freighters so our things went with us on the same ship and didn't cost as much.

My cabin room was cute, with a combination desk/bureau, a lounge chair, and a high bunk with room underneath to store things. I had two drape-covered portholes, a wine–colored leaf design rug, and a pretty aluminum thermos pitcher for water in a rack on the wall. All the comforts of home and more than I was used to!

The next day brought a surprise. We anchored off Philadelphia to take on gasoline for Port Gentil, Gabon, and passengers could go ashore on a launch and see the sights of Philadelphia! I bought six pairs of stockings that day, because my three extra pair were somewhere in a trunk in the hold of the ship. As I was re-boarding, my shopping bag tore and the stockings almost dropped into the water. Our quick-thinking captain stepped on them and saved them going overboard. Leave it up to me to do something like that!

Finally, on that Friday at 12:30 p.m., the S.S. Talisman left foggy Philadelphia, sailing the Atlantic towards the west coast of Belgian Congo. I lost some pride as I learned my sea legs. First breakfast, then dinner; thereafter, I could sympathize with others who suffered more. By Sunday I was enjoying the excellent meals. As it was a Norwegian ship, we were served some form of fishes at each meal in addition to the main course. I even started to enjoy the pickled herring. Each afternoon, we all met for tea time.

The nine adult missionaries seemed to be all of one mind. We gathered for Sunday services as well as each day for a time of Bible study and prayer, with each of us taking a turn at leading. At the end of our trip, the captain remarked on how well we all got along which apparently wasn't the case on all his trips.

We traveled about 400 miles with a half hour gain each day as I continued learning about my fellow passengers. We played table tennis (Arnold, our sixteen–year–old, won the tournament), saw porpoises and a whale at a distance. I crocheted, embroidered, read, walked, memorized scripture, wrote letters, and talked well into the evenings. Re-studying obstetrics took up some of my time and I read several things I couldn't remember ever being told before. I opened my daily letters, filled with encouraging messages and clippings. Edythe Gant became a great friend to me. We kept in contact through all the years. She was returning to Congo with her trousseau to be married and had some advice to give the two or three of us new missionaries.

The captain of our ship was a jolly fellow and kept us laughing. He joined us some evenings for games and snacks and told of the time he spent in a German prison camp during WWII. He also gave us tours of the ship, up to the bridge and down to the engine room. What a place! Fourteen pistons as tall as my waist and grease everywhere and on everything, causing us to slide as we tried to walk.

Four of us formed a quartet and practiced songs to sing in the Sunday service. We had no instruments but found that each of us could sing a part. As we neared Africa, I followed the example of those returning and began taking quinine to prevent malaria.

I wasn't a bit homesick during this time, and I didn't intend to be either (although, that thinking hadn't worked so well for the seasickness). I knew the Lord would help me. I had asked my parents to pray for me as they knew the discouragement that had been in my life when the way was hard. I knew there would be hard places, but I also knew the Lord would be with me.

On April 7, the ship crossed the Equator, and I didn't even feel the bump! The following day, after thirteen days on board, I caught my first real glimpse of Africa at Port Gentil. Black folk didn't look much different than in America, except they were barefooted. I had to laugh at the chatter because I couldn't understand any of it. Once, as I sat at my desk typing letters, three Africans stopped and peered into the porthole, watching me, which made me feel a little like a monkey in a cage. Mrs. Davies remarked that it was only beginning, for they liked to watch the white person.

On April 9, 9:45 a.m., I stepped ashore in AFRICA. It was a beautiful day with a hot sun, a pretty blue sky, and the land so green. We wandered around the town and stopped at the post office to mail our letters. There was such a crowd, so I stuck my hand in like everyone else to get waited on. There were cars and trucks, but no one saw two motor cars alike. We really had to watch and move out of the way of the drivers. Walking around the market reminded me of a farmers market at home with different stands showing their wares.

The unloading at Port Gentil was slow. The men were working hard, but . . . there's always another day. The returning missionaries assured us it was just the African way. I thought it good to see how they worked now so I would be better prepared when I finally settled in Sudan.

After eight days at Port Gentil, the men finished unloading and left with great singing—another African way. We joked that having been at the port so long, we probably put down roots and wouldn't be able to get the anchor up. What a sensation to be moving again. On Easter the next morning, we had our sunrise service. I felt a little off because of the movement, but I wasn't sick. I felt better after tea time, although I didn't want to see, let alone eat any of the Easter candy the girls pulled out.

With the river pilot on board, we made our way up the Congo River to Matadi. The number of ships filling the harbor caused us a delay of four days until there was space to get in. So near and yet so far! Still, it was beautiful on the Congo, waiting, anchored between two mountains and green everywhere. I heard the frogs calling in the evening just like on the farm at home.

Finally, on April 24, I officially entered Belgian Congo at Matadi, leaving most of my ship friends after six weeks together. Mr. Waltander, from the Swedish mission, met those of us getting off at Congo and took us up to the mission. Praise the Lord for the local missionaries to help with the details of customs and paperwork. I slept under a mosquito net for the first time that night. I also bought a sun helmet, which was a very important item in that day.

Things went along well, yet I felt so helpless when I couldn't understand the language. I watched the people. Here the women wore long dresses in bright colors. I thought it a wonder they never dropped their babies as they carried them sitting on an extra piece of material on their back. One day I saw a woman walking up the hill carrying a basket with four long neck bottles in it on her head, her baby on her back, and a cooking pot on the palm of one hand.

After a week, Bill and Dorothy Beatty and their thirteen–month old son Barry met me in Matadi, and we boarded a train for the eleven–hour, 300 mile trip to Leopoldville (Kinshasa). The train, smaller than those in the United States, made many stops. We stared out the windows as we followed the Congo River for a little while, then went on through villages and beside beautiful hills and mountains. We finally arrived at the Baptist Mission in Leopoldville black with soot and so happy for hot water to bathe and wash our hair. Leopoldville was very modern. I saw 1949 cars everywhere. The home where we stayed had many beautiful flowers. Dorothy and I talked of what our new place might be like in Sudan and thought we would want flowers too.

I had seven letters held for me in Leopoldville. When people met me, they remarked that they were waiting to see who this person was that was getting so much mail. They thought for sure that I must be corresponding with a "someone special" back in the USA.

The next leg of our journey to the interior of Africa was by DC-3 plane—my first time in the air. To avoid causing my parents worry or concern, I didn't tell them that I was flying until after I landed in Irumu. We traveled over 1,000 miles, and it was beautiful. I could see the winding Congo River. Roads looked like narrow brown streaks in the forests, and with the clouds casting shadows, the land was all shades and patterns of green. Once in a while, I could see a clearing and a few grass roof houses. As our plane approached Irumu, a rainbow appeared.

The Rethy (Rethi) station, site of a school for missionary and African children, was only 100 miles away from Irumu, and Mr. VanDuesen (head of the entire Congo work) thought we should wait there instead of sitting in a hotel room. That car trip took about four hours on dirt roads (including a ten–minute stop to change a flat tire). Betty Wilson, who would also join us in the Sudan work, met up with us in Rethy. We ate in different missionaries' homes. I attended my first native service, walked around the native stores, and caught my first glimpse of a native hut, with a woman cooking amid clouds of smoke. I began some Kingwana (Swahili) language study with one of the missionaries and learned much of African ways and missionary work.

We had three weeks in Rethy until the Beattys and Betty Wilson would go to the Aru station for orientation, and I to Oicha for medical training. I knew I would miss them all until we finally met again in Sudan. They were so nice and Bill Beatty was like a brother to me with all his teasing. Before the Beattys departed, we met with the Congo Field Counsel. Their advice was to get the language good, take our quinine, wear a helmet in the hot areas, and boil water–then we would have good health. They showed us the place on the map where our station might be

Ready to travel

located in Sudan and informed us the government was eager to do all they could to help us get started.

The Beckers

I left Rethy bright and early at 5:15 a.m. on Friday, May 27, riding the 200 miles to Oicha with Mr. and Mrs. Bell. Dr. Becker, who was in charge of the station, and his wife met me and were just as nice as everyone said they would be. I discovered that Dr. Becker was a man of prayer, his lantern lit at 5 a.m. each morning. When he prayed, you knew he knew the Lord.

The Oicha station had a church, a school through fourth grade, and a large medical work. Africans, missionaries, Belgians (in the Belgian government service or in business), and Greek merchants (who ran local food

Waiting for a diagnosis

stores and other businesses) all brought their families for medical needs. I was amazed to see all the buildings Dr. Becker had built in his thirteen years there.

The next Monday, Mrs. Becker took me to Beni to complete the government paperwork required when entering the country and to do some shopping. I bought a lantern and kerosene because Oicha had electricity, but only from 6–9 p.m. Just as I was leaving the store, I remembered the matches!

Dr. Becker was eager to help me prepare for the work in Sudan and my learning began quickly. A worker from another mission arrived to have her eyes examined, but the next day took ill with dengue fever, a different type of malaria. By the next day it turned into blackwater fever—that dreaded disease of Africa. I began to special her (became her private duty nurse) during the day and continued to care for her until she was able to leave several weeks later. I am happy to say that in all my years in Africa, I never came down with a bad case of malaria.

I studied the Kingwana language with Mrs. Becker and had medical class with Dr. Becker, who gave three of us new missionary nurses all the classes he taught his national students. Learning to use a microscope challenged me greatly. I followed Dr. Becker on morning rounds in the wards and saw heart conditions, burn cases, skin grafting, and care for ulcers. The national staff taught me so much as well. First I observed,

Oicha dispensary

then I practiced. There were so many new things. It was all new. I had no time to be homesick because I was busy learning to do things I had never done at home.

Jewell Olson, another nurse who arrived to work at Oicha, and I set up housekeeping in half of a brick building made to care for patients. We would live in that house until I left for Sudan. On moving day, she unpacked one of her files and I heard a scream and a jump. A mouse! I wasn't going to run, but I didn't want to kill it either. We called the native man, who found four more baby mice and took care of it all. They must have gotten in while the box was stored in the Beckers' garage. Jewell and I remained as sisters through the years even though we only saw each other in Africa.

My first Fourth of July in Africa started as any other day with a language lesson in the morning and then work in the dispensary (that day I assisted with a skin graft). Later, eight adults and four children plus a few of the Africans drove to the forest for a picnic. We played games like in the USA. Then, when it was time to eat, it rained just like the USA. We strung canvas from car to car and thoroughly enjoyed the feast including fire roasted corn, baked beans, potato salad, sandwiches, peanuts, and banana cake. We sat together in Africa representing the states of Minnesota, Nebraska, Arkansas, Ohio, Michigan, and Pennsylvania and the continent of Africa, all celebrating the independence of the USA.

Over my months at Oicha, I continued learning, and maternity work kept me busy. Dr. Becker felt I should deliver about fifty babies in order to be considered properly trained. Both missionaries and Africans delivered at the station, and back then mothers stayed in bed for several days after giving birth.

Olive, Esther, Jewell

American Style   *African Style*

Once, a call came for a mother needing help in a village. I wanted to go along, so we set out walking. After about twenty minutes, asking everyone we saw where this woman was, someone said it was over two kilometers further. I didn't want anyone to think I was afraid to walk, so I went on with them. When we got there, the bank was so high and steep I had to climb up using the stretcher. The Africans were barefooted, so they could climb by digging in their toes. By the time we arrived, the baby had been born and was lying on a banana leaf. The maternity girls took over, wrapping him in covers we had brought with us, and they let me carry the baby while others brought the mother. African babies didn't wear diapers—you just had to be quick and hold them to the side. The African girls in training were also trying to get their turns with the babies, but by the end of August, I had managed to deliver six babies.

Mr. John Buyse, leader for our new work in the Sudan, and Bill Beatty drove through Oicha with their new trucks that they had just picked up from the coast. I wanted to go on with them to Sudan at that time, but it was thought best for me to stay and continue my training while the men went ahead to see the government and begin building

Heading into the forest

houses. I was disappointed, but Mrs. Becker encouraged me, saying I was really being saved a lot because it would be hard to not have a place to set up or put things. So I waited patiently and continued with training to be as prepared as possible.

During October and November, my training continued. Jewell worked in the operating rooms, Miss Edna Amstutz did the leprosy work, and Esther Mogenat, a mid–wife from Europe, gave me good help and instruction. I worked with Benjamin, a male nurse, seeing patients in the dispensary and took time in the laboratory learning the symptoms of different illnesses.

Miss Edna pushed for more and more experience for me because in Sudan, the nearest hospital would be sixty miles away. I helped in an operation so I could learn to suture skin. She told me that I must learn to sew! I really had to push the needle, because the skin was tough. Seth, another of the African nurses, helped me learn to give intravenous medicines. For some reason, those with difficult veins suddenly disappeared from the line when I was the one giving needles.

I was encouraged to go with missionaries to other places in the area. Often, on Sundays, we attended services in the leprosy camp. I also visited a Pygmy village in the forest, seeing for myself the distance people walked to teach others about Jesus.

The staff met daily for prayer as well as chapel services on Sundays. Mrs. Becker led a women's Bible study for a large group once a week, and I was glad to attend and learn all the ways of giving forth the Word of God in a medical work.

Years ago, Miss Edna had built up a work on her own and she gave me good advice for my preparations. I began gathering the items I would need in Sudan. I collected bottles for lab work, sewed cloths for under sterile materials, and gathered supplies. I didn't have a microscope and Dr. Becker felt I should make it a matter of prayer. It would be necessary because there would be no place to send specimens for examination.

One night, a call came that a native school teacher's wife was having trouble. Jewell and I went together, and Dr. Becker came out in his pajamas to see us off. As we were walking, Jewell remarked that she finally felt like a missionary. We hadn't gone far when we found the woman by the side of the road and the baby already born. We brought her to the hospital, then back to bed for us. The next morning, Dr. asked how things went and suggested I use my conscience to know if I ought to count it as one of my fifty deliveries!

A Pygmy mother and child

Never a dull moment at Oicha. One afternoon, I was so tired that I laid down to sleep in the afternoon. Do you think I could? First, Jewell came in singing. She stopped as soon as she saw me and then took calls at the door. Next, someone came selling something. Then, one of the boys arrived with candy, but it turned out he was at the wrong door. Next, two kiddies from the Shuitt family stopped by and were talking with Jewell. Things finally quieted down when Mrs. Becker came to the door with a rather loud "Hodi" (the native word used instead of a knock). By that time, I couldn't do anything but laugh! I tried to rest again, but fifteen minutes later, another "Hodi!", this time from Miss Edna. I never did sleep that afternoon, but at least my legs got a break.

One day towards the end of October, Mrs. Becker called me over to entertain guests while she prepared supper. Who was there? Bill and Dorothy Beatty! Bill hadn't been well, having had amoebic dysentery since before he even got off the boat, so was in Oicha for treatment. I learned I was to go with them to Aru when they returned there after a few weeks of rest. That was the plan, although things changed so often out here, you never really knew where you stood. The Lord knew all about it and so I just let him lead. Hearing about the work in Sudan excited me and I started learning some of the Acholi language spoken there.

Early November I scrambled to learn all the last bits I might need to know. Mrs. Becker generously shared bandages and medicines to help me begin, and Miss Edna taught me more details for starting a new work. One morning, Dr. Becker walked into the pharmacy where I was helping Mrs. Becker and asked what I had done about a microscope. Of course, I hadn't done anything yet. He informed me, just so I wouldn't go duplicating it, that they had sent for one as a gift to begin the work in the Sudan. I could hardly believe it, but it was true. It is just like the Lord to answer our every need from a place where we aren't even looking.

The count was twenty-eight delivered babies to my credit, but as I had a way to journey to Sudan, I said my goodbyes. In Africa, you traveled when there was a ride. I was glad to go in a way, yet I hated to leave. It felt like home and seemed strange to go. Dr. and Mrs. Becker had become and would remain my African parents.

Early on November 22, I set off with the Beattys. One hour out and a tire had a blowout. Now with no spare, the next flat took longer to repair. We stopped at various stations traveling north, a different bed each night, from Beni to Rethy then heading to the Aungba station. At Rethy, we were told to drive out the way we came in to get to Aungba. Well, either we didn't hear right, or we came in a different way. Dorothy told Bill he was going the wrong way, but Bill didn't listen. The one–hour trip turned into two as we just kept driving on and on and on.

From Aungba we traveled next to the Adi station, and by the end of November we arrived at the Aru station. The Beattys went on to Sudan to prepare and the single missionaries, Betty Wilson and I, would follow through Arua, Uganda, then by Nile river boat in time for Christmas. A letter came from the girls at Oicha saying they hadn't delivered any babies since I left, and all the children were asking where I was. I delivered my twenty-ninth baby at the Aru dispensary.

Dr. Williams, at the Arua Hospital in Uganda, gave me more medicines and equipment with the advice that people would come quickly and I needed to be prepared to help. On December 16, Betty and I boarded the Nile River steamer and arrived the next day at Nimuli, Sudan. The Buyses and the Beattys met us, and we all traveled on to Opari, Sudan.

The six of us, John and Mabel Buyse, Bill and Dorothy Beatty (plus their son Barry, only one and a half years old), Betty Wilson, and I, under the Africa Inland Mission, began our work in Anglo-Egyptian Sudan (ruled at this time by Egypt and Britain). Opari had been an outpost work of the Church of England, so there was one grass-roofed stone building on site for when their missionaries visited, as well as some small huts. Britain had pulled out of that work, so that left the door open for AIM to take over.

Uncle John and Aunt Mabel (about seventy years old) were like dad and mom for these young kids coming into the work. They led the team and did survey work for new sites. The Beattys ran the church work. Betty started up the new girls' school. A boys' school, led by national teachers and paid by the government, was nearby. I began the medical work.

I settled into my mansion of a little round mud hut. It reminded me a lot of living in a tent at Camp Meeting! George, my little brother, asked if I had to stoop to get into my hut. Yes! It was well furnished with a washstand made of bamboo poles and a piece of wood, a bed with a large mosquito net, two chairs, two tables, two mats as well as all the medical supplies covering half the floor. My clothes hung from a rod of the roof at the foot of my bed. The roof peaked in the middle and the door was a woven grass work to stand over the doorway with a pole on either side to keep it there. Unfortunately, my first night's sleep in my new house was disrupted by the noise of a scurrying mouse.

Betty had a similar mansion next to mine. Mr. Buyse said both huts would be for my medical work once we moved into the stone building, nicknamed the Egg by Aunt Mabel for its oval shape. At this point, the married couples were staying in the Egg until their homes were built.

After treating my very first case the next morning, we took a quick break on Monday to travel the dirt road to Juba to register with the Anglo-Egyptian Sudan government and to customs to get our freight cleared. We stayed until Wednesday, then left for home at 4:30 p.m. (to avoid the heat). Five miles from home, we got stuck in sand and finally arrived at 11 p.m.

By the end of December, I was really into the work with an average of thirty-seven patients a day, and it was hard to get letters or anything else done. I minded very much that I couldn't treat the people the way I should as I didn't have the medicines, or even a microscope to be sure of the treatment. I was impatient to move and have the huts for my dispensary. At this time, I worked under a tree and had to take out the boxes of medical supplies from my home only to return them at the end

Standing in front of my home

of the day. Praise the Lord, some folks did know English and a teacher interpreted for those patients who didn't. Looking back, I see how God does time things, for learning the Acholi language was difficult enough in addition to setting up living. If I had had to get a dispensary building going and do lab work (I was so slow with the microscope), I wouldn't have had time left for anything else. The Lord knows best.

1950

Wait on the Lord; be of good courage, and He will strengthen your heart; wait, I say, on the Lord.
(Psalm 27:14)

The year began with many, many patients. One day I saw ninety-four cases, and twenty-three of those were completely new. So many very sick people, sick so long that there was not much I could do for them. I used my pressure cooker over a fire to sterilize things for the dispensary. More than once, my helpers let the fire get too hot and it blew a gasket! Some had told me it would take time to build up a medical work, but Dr. Williams from Arua was correct and word spread quickly. My total for January was 1,474 visits. The African who helped me said it was not just a dispensary, for the people called it a hospital. If out here under a tree was a hospital, I wondered just what the work in a building would be like. Of course, some people came solely to check me out. It was the dry season, no garden work, so why not come and see what this nurse does. Eventually the crowds did slow down, although Mondays remained as the busiest day.

One Sunday evening a man came from a distance with his little girl, about eight years old, who had burned her arm back in September. Her hand healed with some deformity, but the top of her arm was awful, caked with some sort of native medicine/mud and pus underneath. I didn't know how to get it clean that late in the day, so I covered it with a wet dressing overnight. The next day I set out my sterile things, scrubbed up and called them over. The father and child took one look at everything and the father yelled: "RUN". She ran. There I was, the poor thing left with only a rag over the open wound. Dorothy could hardly stand it, but what could we do? How I was made to feel again my helplessness. I put the things away thinking of that poor child and the pain she must be having from the open wound. Back to the dirt she went. How often that is true in the lives of men and women. They come to the way of truth and are ready to accept, but they decide to go back to their own sinful ways and the end is worse than the beginning.

That January, the entire Beatty family came down with fevers, then Betty as well. I moved a cot into her hut and slept there to care for her. I was glad for my daily naps during that time, something I never thought I needed at home. Praise the Lord, I didn't get sick.

Because it was still the dry season, we had many local folks working to build our homes and storage before the spring rains. Once the rainy season started, the men would not be as available to build for us as they would be tending their own gardens. I also began training helpers for the medical work, including how to use the pressure cooker to sterilize, how to read a thermometer, and how to keep patient records. Monwelli, who stayed with me many years, began in February. He was faithful and learned well. I also trained Erasto who had begun as my house helper. He was a good worker (when he came) but was not as steady as Monwelli. What can you do?

The country was beautiful with blue skies, pretty sunrises and sunsets, and lovely full moons. I noticed so much more in the sky without city lights. My days were filled with medical work, finally opening my boxes of freight that had been packed nearly a year before, and studying the Acholi language. Everything I did was so new.

God was gracious as we worked things out. Missionaries have different temperaments and each of us had different ideas on how things should go in this new work, so—a matter of prayer. In the beginning, we all ate meals together. The Buyses and Beattys were sharing the three–room Egg until their houses could be built. Aunt Mabel and Dorothy were complete opposites. The Beattys experienced some frustration trying to parent their son in the midst of so many people. Betty and I were not alike in many things either. Uncle John was the leader, so we were to do what he said, but he focused on the big picture and pushed to expand the work further, so Bill ended up handling details of everything else. I prayed and trusted God that we would get along and glorify the Lord.

We all came from different church traditions as well. The Buyses were Baptist and the Beattys were from a reformed Episcopalian background which was more formal than my Mennonite Brethren in Christ upbringing. I had grown up in a tradition with very strong standards of behavior including no smoking or drinking or dancing. I guess I was a little old fashioned because even when my Bible College had shown a movie from Moody Bible Institute, I didn't attend. Each of us different, but as long as the Word was preached and we were serving the Lord, it was all for His glory. After all, we would all have to get along in heaven.

I eagerly set out on my first maternity case and returned confused and overwhelmed. Their customs were nothing at all like in the USA, or even in Oicha. By the time I arrived in the village, four other women were already there trying to stage the show, and I had to be careful to not do too much different than what they insisted on or was their custom. I did require they come in the house for the actual delivery, but they really wanted her outside. The women there squatted, resting on their heels for delivery and another woman supporting her in back, so I had to do the best I could without being able to understand the talk, examine the woman properly, or keep a sterile field. I just stood there thinking, "Why did you have me come here if you don't want to follow what I say?" Nothing was as I would have liked it to be, but the child was safely delivered.

In a letter home, I wrote: "We praise the Lord for His guidance in a strange land with strange customs and strange language, not yet understood. May the Lord give wisdom and strength to do for these people just what He has purposed for us when He sent us forth. "

My second call came from a village a mile out. I was so disappointed because by the time I arrived, baby Mae had already been born to Lydia and Andreya (who later was ordained our Pastor for the work).

In my white uniform with the pins and my cap on my head as my helmet in the sun, I moved forward, building the work. My helper felt important when I made him a smock to wear. We began prayers and reading the book of Matthew with the workers each day at 6:45 am. I took the first day. Reading from the Acholi Bible—I managed okay; praying—I quickly scribbled down three sentences in Acholi and prayed that day with one eye open.

By February, the married couples moved into their homes and I into the Egg. I settled in with my bed (it had been too big for the hut), pictures up and doilies out. I made a wash table from a packing crate — well, Uncle John did most of it. They think girls are so helpless! But, I do admit it was better made than what I had thought of. I could have my treadle sewing machine out and it was wonderful to open it and sit right down and sew in comfort. Betty and I each had our own room, with the front room shared as a living room. Eventually we also had a hut for cooking. Erasto slept in the mud hut to guard the medical things. I wrote home to my brother Raymond that I had running water — the men ran, carrying water in five-gallon tins on top of their heads from the river to the barrel at the back door.

The evening of the first spring rain, Sudanese young and old rejoiced. With flares and buckets they went to the ant hills to catch the flying ants emerging. They were a delicacy. My lamp outside attracted those ants as well, so I caught some too. I gave them to others, but did taste a few (just to say I did!)

In April, I was called to see a school boy. He had a sore tummy which didn't get better. They say you don't have appendicitis out here and yet

The Egg

it's found. Bill and I left with the child at 10 p.m. for the hospital in Torit. While in Torit, we met up with Major Wright, who knew a place a few miles out for getting game. He went, and in one hour came back with two small animals, two birds and a large animal which he claimed was the best eating in Africa. It looked something like a cow and must have weighed 500 pounds. Since it was his first, he wanted the head and we brought the rest home. School boys, teachers, missionaries, and workmen alike had a big feast.

We canned the leftover so that each household had three cans of steak, five of hamburger, and four of regular meat. Dorothy and I worked at it, but oh, what a time! I had to get the canner out—bottom of a huge box. Then, I couldn't remember what I did with the Book of Instructions. I looked and looked, and finally after opening about every box in the house, I found it in my duffel bag. I had gotten ten cans out, and then decided we needed more, so back to the bottom of the big box again. I hauled out my meat grinder for the hamburger. We ran both my pressure cooker and Dorothy's for five loads. Finally finished at 7 p.m. and I slept well that night I can tell you.

In Africa, adjustment was the way of life. Handling situations that arose became a matter of much prayer and thought. I had a cook, another man who cleaned and did the wash, and eventually third man to help in the garden. Most of the men working in my house were honest, but some needed to be encouraged. I learned to keep peanuts and sugar out of sight and to put my pen away. In the eyes of the Africans, we had so much, so why not take the good things? It was true, we had plenty. It came to me again when my brother Raymond graduated from high school that year. I saw the boys here having to try and learn everything in just four years of school and those in America had so much.

In addition, we were not always sure the Africans who said they were Christian were true. Many of them smoked. In England and Europe, the Christians had different standards and the missionaries who were here before us also smoked. Were we to judge or change with them? The school would celebrate by beating the drums and dancing, although they told us they were just exercising. What was to be done? It was hard to know where to draw the line. What they had done for years, we thought of as wrong, and yet it seemed different to them. We all struggled and prayed as we faced the need for wisdom each day.

Building continued and by May the site for the new dispensary was staked out. We bought poles, bamboo, stone, cement, and dry season grass for the roof. By July, the grass roof was on, and then came the walls. Bamboo was tied between the upright poles inside and outside and filled in between with stones. Then, a good mud pie: they stamped the ground and slung mud on both sides to fill the wall. When it was dry, more mud to plaster the cracks and make it smooth. Like Noah's ark, there was an opening between the wall and roof—giving us the best way to watch and discourage the trail of ants climbing toward the roof.

In regard to money, one received an allowance and unless you were a person with a lot of extra gifts, you just did what you could with the money and trusted the Lord to help with the rest. Since there wasn't a church behind the work of our station, it was up to us to build it up as well as teach the local Africans to do what they could. So, I continued putting money into the work at Opari, building and buying medicines. I knew it would not be a loss if the Lord wanted it. If I moved elsewhere, either the Africans would take over, or it would become a place to visit. That is the way things went. We did what we could with what the Lord provided and then waited until He showed we could do more.

Putting on the roof

By this time Dorothy was about three months pregnant. I planned on going to Oicha with them for the delivery, but at this point, she was not telling others and we didn't think anyone knew. However, the Acholi women on the station tackled her on the matter. They called me right down afterward and told me as well. She tried to push them off, but finally admitted to four of them and asked them not to say anything to the other missionaries. She told them if they knew so much, they should tell her how many months. Three, they informed her. Bright people!

May was busy with training my medical helpers: what is dirty, clean, and sterile; what it means to be sick and how the body will fight illness; why we boil things for twenty minutes. Patients continued to come for care at a steady pace—wounds, ulcers, broken bones, pulling teeth (takes strength!). May was also the month my Christmas package finally caught up with me. Betty and I sat right down and enjoyed a chocolate bar.

One Wednesday morning at 1:30 a.m. I got a call through the window to come to a distant village for a mother who had been in labor since Saturday. I asked Bill for the car as it was a distance and he decided to come along as the car was not in the best condition. When I got there, the people around the woman said the baby was dead already. I examined her to make my own observation and what a thing I found! I was just sick for a little but got courage and went on. The baby's head had been cut while still in the mother. Why, I didn't know. Whether they knew the child had died and then cut for the spirit to come out, that was my guess. Anyway, I went right ahead and put the forceps on and took the baby. I had never used forceps before, but after I got the position right it was no trouble at all. I asked the husband (who had done cement work for us) why he didn't call me sooner, but he said he was away and had just come back. In the meantime, Bill returned with penicillin for the mother. The older women of the village were with the baby in the hut afterward and were making some motions over it and talking, but I wasn't sure exactly what the procedure was. There was a fresh mound by the side of the house when I went back the next night to check on the mother. We said a word of prayer even though only one or two understood Acholi. I prayed it would open the village and hearts to the Gospel. The mother was so cooperative and did eventually recover. I made several trips back to check on her and would have liked to bring her in, but there just wasn't any room.

A much happier delivery came in June for Joanna, the wife of teacher Elijah. He called me about 7 p.m., and I readied my things and dashed off. All of a sudden, he shouted, "Run Madam!" I ran and found her outside her hut with no one else around. I set my things down just in time to catch her little boy before he hit the ground. She always seemed to be a sort of loud, contrary person, but now I saw a different side, a nice side. She had worked in the rice field that morning then went ahead and carried a large load of wood home after she began feeling funny. How's that for working it! These Acholi women knew how to get their labor going. I also learned yet another new thing—keep a sterile pack always ready!

I planted a garden: lima beans, string beans, corn, carrots, beets and tomatoes as well as peanuts and potatoes. One Sunday evening I went to the garden to get some carrots for salad and found the monkeys had come during the day and ate up all the corn. It was just beginning to get ears and they stripped them all. I was so glad I had picked the green beans the day before. They went through the lima beans as well, eating the bean and leaving the shell on the ground.

By this time I had chickens too. They liked to scratch in the garden, and what do you know, they lived in the living room. Some even began

Grass mats protect my garden from the sun

delivering their eggs right in the house. They loved to climb all over the cupboards and scratched so hard on the table cover, I thought it would tear. It became tiresome to chase them. We needed screens and doors but had no lumber to do it right then. I decided to use the dispensary doors on the house, then, worry about the dispensary later. I knew the Lord knew all about it and would supply if I was careful how I used what he sent.

Once, I took a trip to Juba where there are lots of shops with all sorts of things if you have the money. But me—so much of my money went out to the building projects and medicine that I was broke. I could only buy the bare necessities. No luxuries at all. During that visit I stayed with some British missionaries—so much bread and tea. They had tea three times a day in addition to breakfast, lunch and dinner. Also, the women dressed up in long gowns for dinner. Needless to say, I didn't have evening wear, so I wore my floor length housecoat to dinner and even received a compliment on it from a gentleman at the dinner. Did Dorothy, Bill, and I ever laugh afterwards.

By the end of June, the inside of the dispensary had been mudded. Our church was almost finished as well and it looked beautiful. It had a stained table, benches made of bamboo, and a motto on the wall in Acholi saying "Jesus died for me."

I should have had a bookkeeper. Keeping the books straight was a job for me because there were many expenses of medicine, materials for the dispensary, and my personal expenses. Fifty dollars a month went much further in 1950, but I was thankful I had a reserve account to draw from. Once, Uncle John had some small gifts come in for the work that they were using to pay for some of the building on the station. Bill suggested helping me with the dispensary, so I got back all the money for the labor, the grass for the roof, and wood for the door. Most of the money went right out to pay for an order of drugs from Khartoum. But I was thankful that at least I did not have to take anything out of my reserve account.

Around the end of July that year, we got the sad word that the Shuitts, from the Oicha station, had lost their two–year–old son. He was found unconscious and they thought he may have gotten the hose used for gasoline. No one could revive him. Some have to give a lot to serve the Lord in a far land.

By August, Uncle John was taking many trips surveying for the new Logotok station and for one in Katire Ayom (Katere Ayom). Dr. Reitsma and his wife Kim were planning to come out and work at Logotok as well as a nurse, Martha Hughell. Martha stayed at our station briefly in August until she received her permits to go into Congo for training.

We all celebrated when Bill and Dorothy got a radio. Although not able to talk with other stations, we could hear them and just having that contact felt good. About this time, Major Wright and the Americans in Torit were suddenly recalled and I was happy to receive some of their offered medicines and other medical supplies which they did not want to transport back to the USA.

I did not leave the station as often as the others did because of the medical work. I planned to go back to Oicha with the Beattys for the birth of their second child at the end of October. We were also hoping to have a turn to go to Ruwenzori to Mother Stauffacher (who ran the rest home there) for a few days before continuing back north again. However, one day towards the end of August, the Beattys, Betty, Martha, and I took time off to go to the game park near Nimuli. We decided to look for the rhinos, and we found them. Dorothy (pregnant), Barry, I, and one native with his spear stayed at a tree and waited for the others to go further. Eventually we found a seat for ourselves in the tree thinking if something

Sister carries water, mother carries wood and straw for a patient's bed.

came near, it would be safer to be there already than to try and scramble up at the last minute! And sure enough, we saw white rhinos the distance of about two city blocks. Later on our way out, a mother rhino with her baby didn't get our scent, so we passed safely by. Naïve new young missionaries; the Lord protected. Crossing back over the Nile, our boat had mud packed in the holes so the water wouldn't come in too fast. And so it went.

In September, I finally moved into the finished dispensary. Monwelli continued learning more of the inpatient work. Once, a grandmother with a very sick small child had to stay overnight, and I set the alarm for Monwelli to get up during the night to give the child her medicine. I sure would like to have been a mouse to see his first reaction to this new concept of an alarm clock. Monwelli had just been taken into the church and seemed to want to serve the Lord. I was praying that he would be the one to continue doing the work for me. I didn't want to set my hopes too high but let the Lord have His way in each life, including mine.

My time was filled. I was busy each morning in the dispensary. Sunday school classes began in the fall as school children returned. Yunia, my cook's wife, helped me with the girls' class. Moyi was a good cook. I had been canning vegetables as well as meat (if someone shot game), so he learned to do the canning. We had celebrations with meals for birthdays and holidays and when guests passed through the station. I also expanded my musical skills and began to learn on Dorothy's accordion. It went well, but I couldn't brag because my arm tired so easily from pulling the thing. One day in the village, Bill played his horn and I the accordion.

Our Oicha trip started with much prayer that our passports and visas would arrive in time, otherwise, we all would have to apply for emergency ones. Such a bother. With so many countries so close together, one needed passports and visas to cross borders. God answers prayer, and our papers arrived in the last possible mail before we left.

So, with Obadiah (also training for medical work) and Monwelli taking over the dispensary, we left in the beginning of October, working our way down, stopping at stations along the way. Two Africans came along and often they laughed and covered their mouths in surprise as they saw so many people, stations, and large churches in the Congo.

We arrived in Oicha on October 18. As I got out of the car, Dr.

Becker called my name and the sound of his voice was like coming home. Greetings everywhere. They really laughed at me as I confused Acholi and Swahili words. The Beattys and I began the wait for either Judy or David to arrive. I wrote letters, visited with Jewell, and learned more at the hospital. To be at the station once again was a joy and a spiritual blessing. When I heard the African workers in the lab sing hymns as they worked, I was filled with joy and in my heart, I aimed for the same back in Opari.

David Beatty was delivered on November 2.

After giving birth on a Thursday afternoon, Dorothy put her legs over the side of the bed on Friday and on Saturday she stood up. By Monday she was cleared by Dr. Becker to go up to lunch. I wrote home, "Nothing to having a baby these days!!!" Dorothy and I had read in *Reader's Digest* about a new thing called natural childbirth, so she tried it. And she went through with it too. She didn't have the book for the exercises beforehand, but she read Dr. Becker's copy. We were surprised to find him willing to try this way. He was more inclined to give something for

the pain. Mrs. Becker could hardly get over the idea, but she was always encouraging Doctor to give something as she must have had an awful time with her two. Dorothy was a good patient with no complications, and it ended well.

We headed back at the end of November and spent Thanksgiving in the Ruwenzori station at Mother Stauffacher's rest home. While there we took a trip to a nearby park at the plains and lake. We saw so many animals — elephants, hippos, buffalo, antelope, wild pigs, and birds. Some close, some far away. We saw a mama elephant and baby nearby, and it was so cute to

Boy wearing a hat made of a melon shell

watch her throw her trunk up and the baby imitate the motion. The beauty of this land was wonderful. Most of the way back, we could see all the peaks of Mt. Ruwenzori. The only disappointment of the day happened when Bill lost his glasses (he was always breaking or losing them). And yes, the baby went along to the park.

December 7, we returned to Sudan via Aba to bring Martha Hughell back from her hospital orientation. She began learning Latuka, a difficult language which was spoken at Logotok. Martha was a swell girl with red hair, and it was great to have an extra hand in the new dispensary.

The men had done well while I was gone. They only broke two thermometers and one small bottle of cod liver oil. The second day I was back, I broke another thermometer when it fell out of a man's mouth. I sort of forgot it and left it in too long and of course when it hit the cement floor—that was the end.

My heart was burdened for the people. On market day, many of the folks drank too much. They were loud and got in fights. I was praying on my knees and thought maybe someone would have to give their life for the people here. If the Lord wanted it to be me, I was willing. The

Acholi children

burden seemed so great. I believed God would help, but there just wasn't change in lives. I asked the Lord to show me each day what to say and how to say it so that I might be used to awaken these people from their sin.

December passed, work continued. I planned for a few more patient huts behind the dispensary, treated the sick, and continued depending on Divine guidance to meet the challenges.

Praise the Lord for our first full year in Sudan

1951

Not by might nor by power, but by my spirit, says the Lord. (Zechariah 4:6)

The new year began with new paths. We struggled a bit in our interactions with the Africans. We had so much, they had so little. We wanted to help, yet simply giving things always caused problems. In the medical work, I began charging a small fee (28¢ for the year and 14¢ for a group of needles). All the other stations did the same. I hadn't charged the first year as I often didn't have enough medicine to even help. However, the people didn't accept this change and almost no patients came in during the first two weeks of January. I had planned to go to Rethy in a few weeks for the AIM conference, so I decided to wait until I returned from that trip and deal with it all then. I didn't know what else to do.

At 2:45 a.m., January 12 the pickup truck, loaded with four adults and two babies, left for the Congo—one flat tire, trouble at customs into Congo and we arrived at Aru station by 4 p.m. We traveled on to Rethy the next day. The biennial conference, with missionaries from Congo, Uganda, Central Africa, and Sudan was a highlight for everyone. We had speakers, business meetings and prayer meetings. On Sunday night, each worker new within the last two years gave his/her testimony. Mr. Pierson dedicated six babies, including David Beatty. David cried before and afterward, but not when he was in Mr. Pierson's arms. We ended the conference with communion.

Showers of blessing both inside and out as Rethy had oddly cool and rainy weather during the dry season. But more important, the Lord was with us to bless and enrich our lives for His glory. I had some time with Dr. and Mrs. Becker, and what a joy to see them. Their advice always pointed me back to the Lord, telling me to know what the Lord wanted first of all. I talked with Dr. Becker concerning the drop in numbers at my dispensary due to charging a fee. When he heard I had it on for just two weeks, he burst out laughing and told me to give it time and stick to it; people would come if they were really sick.

Monwelli and the microscope

We returned from Rethy with a lot of cabbage, so Martha and I took a stab at making sauerkraut—that is, a stab in the dark. At the end, it didn't look or smell right. It is awful to say I helped and watched Mother, yet didn't know how to do it myself. So it goes. Anyway, we tried.

My microscope finally arrived. Martha worked with it in the dispensary hut and the poor girl was eaten alive with bedbugs. What a time! We cleaned and cleaned. From what my helpers said, the bugs were there for the entire time I had lived in the hut. Apparently the bedbugs just didn't like me.

By mid-February, numbers in the dispensary began picking up. I had an average of eighteen to twenty a day: not as many as before, but enough as I had to do the microscope work as well as teach my helpers to use it. I was so happy to have my microscope. No more puzzling over whether to treat hookworm (with a terrible, horrible smelling medicine) or Belharzia (which meant twenty needles, three a week). I pulled a few teeth (the second time went better). One woman was brought in with a head wound down to the skull. It was the dry season and water was not plentiful, so it had a very dirty look. In addition, six hours had passed since the injury. I treated it but didn't sew it up, as too much time had gone by for stitching.

One day, Obadiah came in and told me there was smallpox in the village and his child had it. I didn't know what I was going to do. Martha and I went to investigate. Neither of us had ever seen smallpox, yet on examining the child we felt confused. It looked more like measles to us. I checked back in my book, and then found out they had heard the name "smallpox" and had given it to measles. Children out here often died from the measles because they weren't strong and it went to their chests. On top of that, mothers wouldn't wash the children because they thought it would make the rash go inside. I told them such cases could come in for medicine and not die. So my smallpox scare was over. Lesson— always good to find out the proper word in a strange language.

At the end of February, we had no one to work or carry water for they all wanted to work their gardens back in the village and do other things. Our African workers were not used to working steadily, so if they had food, that's all that mattered. It was discouraging, and I never knew what the next day would bring, but I tried to keep my eyes on Him and know that all things work together for good to them that love the Lord, and that all things help to make us more like Himself.

About this time, Monwelli's wife had a child. I didn't really understand their customs, but apparently, if a man asked for a girl and the father said yes, she was his wife. However, until he paid for her, she couldn't live with the man. If a child came along, many times the father would let her go on a smaller amount or maybe let her go but keep asking for the rest of the money. Monwelli was trying to earn the money for his wife.

Monwelli gave me money to make a romper for his baby boy because there was no place around to buy something like that. I used some of the feed bag material I had brought out with me. I sewed it up but didn't add the buttons as the babies out here didn't wear diapers. It turned out nice, and the only thing he thought wrong was that the material had flowers. I told him Dorothy made suits for Barry out of her dresses that wore out on the top and he seemed better satisfied after that.

Dr. Douglas Reitsma arrived in March, ahead of his wife-to-be Kim who would come out at the end of June after she finished her schooling. Because she was a new Christian, the mission determined she should get more training before they married and she came to the field. Dr. Doug seemed like a grand fellow and really knew his stuff, although I suppose I was able to teach him a few things.

One day he and Bill came in about 8 p.m. I was settled down to letter writing when I heard the Dr. Doug call, "Come on down, Olive." The summons of a doctor, and what could a nurse do then? I went and found them carrying two men who had been injured by a buffalo during a hunt. The Africans hunted in the dry season by burning the grass and trapping the animals. A buffalo attack is an awful thing. One man was gored in three places with the wound on his leg straight through. Martha and I cleaned them up and Doctor treated them. Too much time had passed for stitches (you'd only run into trouble later); therefore, we only packed them with iodoform gauze. Both men eventually recovered.

The work went on. We continued giving out the Word of God even though sometimes it seemed like hitting a stone wall. We pressed on, knowing His Word would not return void, desiring only to be faithful.

Dr. Doug decided to travel out to Logotok to see the site and the buildings going up. Was he surprised when we all went along. We teased him that out here in Sudan we did things together, and he might find that when he and Kim stopped their truck on their wedding trip, they would find us all in the back!

Logotok[1] was a lovely area with pretty mountains nearby. The folks there were a strong people and nice, even though they wore no clothing. I knew I would miss Dr. Doug when he moved there. It had been nice to work with him and throw a little bit of the responsibility off on him for a while.

March and April passed with some difficult and sad cases and many with a good outcome. My work with patients remained public, everyone standing around watching. Of course sometimes I would chase them out, but it was best not to if I didn't have to. I wanted them to see I was not doing something to hurt them. Seeing what was done gave confidence to continue treatment or bring others in.

We had visitors coming through to see this new work, including the British government. I was always busy with patients, making medicines,

---

[1] Since Aunt Olive's time, the orthography in this language has changed as follows: Logotok to Lohutok (place), Latuka/Latuko to Lotuho (people), Latuka to Otuho (language). In this book, references to this people group will reflect the spelling consistent with the original letters.

writing letters, and sewing for house and medical needs. But yes! There was always time for making a pie or birthday cake or hosting the visitors.

I experienced some homesickness and eagerly waited for the letters from home. Usually mail from the USA arrived with about a two–week delay. I wrote at least one letter a week to Mother and Daddy and they sent the same. I also wrote to my sister Esther and my brothers and replied to letters others wrote to me. I had gotten used to sending birthday or Mother's/Father's Day greetings early so they would be received on time. Mail delivery to the stations depended on one of us traveling to Torit and picking it up. Outgoing mail went with anyone going to any town and we all finished letters in a big rush whenever someone announced they were heading out. Mail from home always refreshed and encouraged me.

In May, we had a visit from another missionary and three African pastors from the Congo. They seemed to make a big impression on the men here. It was amazing to see the different village men come out. Hearing from a fellow African meant something to them. Two of the pastors could speak Alur and that was close to Acholi. Our men learned some Alur and the pastors picked up some Acholi. It was wonderful to hear them talk away. Those men carried weight with the people and we hoped we could get them to come back again.

Communicating medical directions to folks did not always go smoothly. A man came in who had been hit on the head with a small ax that had cut deep! I noticed the pulsing of the brain when I dressed it. From what I could gather, he received the injury in a fight at a dance over his young wife. I wanted him to stay quiet for a time to make sure his speech came back, but every time I checked on him—he was up sitting in a chair. They just couldn't understand when I said "rest in bed."

A woman came in with a huge ulcer on her leg and only a little girl to care for her. How that girl cried when I dressed her mother's leg. What some of these little girls have to go through so early in life. So much sadness out here. I had another woman who came in to deliver a baby that was already dead. Things weren't going well, and we gave her sleeping pills to relax her and make her deliver. It was her ninth pregnancy and only two children alive. Her father was there praying and seemed to think calling out louder and louder would make God hear. He was praying in Madi, so I couldn't understand most of it. I did hear God and Mary, but never Jesus. He quieted down once the baby was out, but then we had to wait so long for the placenta that he began praying all over again. The other woman with her made some motions, threw grass, and rubbed her stomach. Finally, when it was all over, the father, a rather old man, laid down right there and slept. I felt my burden for the people sitting in darkness.

The measles left and a whooping cough epidemic arrived. The villagers didn't seem to see the danger of it and couldn't understand isolation. I suppose because no rash or anything else showed up, they just called it a bad cold. It sure was bad. An eight–month–old baby came in and I could hear and diagnose right away. I treated him, but the next day he had a convulsion. It didn't last long and when he could swallow again, I gave him more medicine and said they should stay so I could keep my eye on him. After another really bad convulsion the following day, he began breathing again but was unconscious. The mother mourned and cried and thought he was too far gone as his "voice was dead". I tried to persuade her to stay, but I guess they had never seen someone unconscious get well again. She left with him and I wept as I thought I might have been able to help if they stayed, but leaving—almost certain death.

Girl caring for her sister

I began having cases of diarrhea come in. They got bad so quickly. Eventually everyone recovered except for one school boy. He was carried in with severe aching and tightening of his muscles. Martha and I were with him all afternoon and had a long talk about it. We read books and thought it had all the signs of cholera—or was it poison? We couldn't be sure without a laboratory examination and he soon died. We felt the boy knew the Lord, so we were comforted by that. Bill was able to talk with the family when they came to take the body. In spite of fears that more cases would come in, after five days passed with no more like it, I felt we were in the clear. I was never sure of that diagnosis.

The Africans were not my only patients. One morning about 4 a.m., Aunt Mabel came up calling out to me in great pain. It had been so dark that she didn't see a scorpion on her washcloth and those tails whip around fast. I gave her an injection of Emetin as Uncle John said that takes the pain away, but it stayed swollen and so painful. She couldn't even describe the pain. Thirty years in Africa and this was her first. That sting didn't stop her from driving off later in the day for an education meeting in Torit.

About this time, I was having trouble finding time for more classes for my helpers. Then, I had to have a class of a different kind when I found sixty sulfathiazole tables missing in one month. I knew I had to confront them, and I dreaded it. I had to trust the Lord to guide my tongue and say the right thing and do the right thing.

On June 26, Dr. Douglas Reitsma and Margaret Kimble (Kim) were married at Opari, Anglo-Egyptian Sudan. It was quite the event for our little station. The Africans wondered if the money was taken care of in the USA or here. We carefully explained that was not how we did things. "Oh," they all said, "Your land is good!"

We worked to make a wedding that was really special. It was a beautiful day and everything went off smoothly, although the ceremony did start fifteen minutes late because we girls took so long finishing the flowers. It was a garden wedding on the front lawn of the Egg with zinnias marking the path for them to march.

I played the pump organ for music and the Wedding March. (A missionary needs to be prepared for anything.) Dorothy attended Kim and Martha sang a solo for the first time. She laughed saying, "Wait until my mother hears about this!" Uncle John gave the bride away, Bill officiated, and Betty did the flowers and took pictures. Aunt Mabel with Barry, David, and the African teachers and wives sat in the audience.

The bride wore a street length dress of white lace and a white lace hat fitted to her head with a veil that turned back and looked like a crown. She carried red oleander which looked somewhat like roses. Dorothy carried white frangipani, a little white flower as well as purple ones something like it. The groom wore a light–colored suit.

It didn't take long to marry them off. The reception was served buffet style with roast pork (brought in and butchered the night before by the groom and the other men [the original plan was spam]), rolls, potato salad (with a first tomato to give it color), ice cream, and a three–tiered cake made by Dorothy. Kim had brought out Kool-aid from home for the punch.

Kim wore a teal colored seersucker dress when they left for Juba (just the two of them), then on to the Aba station for their wedding trip. We heard on the radio that they arrived safely and looked back in remembrance of a beautiful day.

Uncle John Buyse, Dorothy Beatty, Kim and Dr. Reitsma, Hank Senff,
Bill Beatty, Barry

July marked some changes for the Opari station. Only four of us were there to celebrate July Fourth with corn on the cob, spaghetti and meatballs, ice cream, and popcorn. The Reitsmas and Martha were busy setting up the Logotok station. I felt bad for Kim having so much to do in arranging the house, training helpers, and learning the language. Dr. Doug did check back in at Opari from time to time. One of our many other visitors that month was Ruth Johnson from the Home Office in

New York. What a joy for her to come out and see the work. Also, Mr. Hank Senff began looking into moving here to help with our Sudan team.

The end of the month brought yet another change to our routines when the Beattys moved the eighteen miles to the Katire Ayom station. Bill had to return a second time on moving day for another load and to get the forgotten screws for David's bed. We always knew the work was going to expand, but it was a hard adjustment. I missed my daily chats with Dorothy.

Betty Wilson moved into the Beattys old house and I had the Egg all to myself. I spent some time setting up and moving things around. Previously, I had noticed some of the food I had canned tasted funny. I had eaten it and didn't become ill, so I had figured it was ok. Now, since I had more space, I dug my bread box out of one of my storage boxes. Moyi, my cook, made nice fresh bread and put it in the bread box. When I ate a piece, oh my, did it taste bad, just like the stuff in the cans. So one mystery solved—apparently my containers absorbed the packing material smell and caused the food to taste bad.

The medical work went on. A woman who had been hit by a bicycle was brought in with a fracture above the ankle. She had a splint on when she came in. But, I had to redo it because the man who had splinted the leg to bring her in wanted his wood back. I redid it several times trying to get it right, then Dr. Doug came and put plaster on it along with the splints. After that I felt better about the whole thing. Another man came in with a spear wound through from ear to eye.

About this time, things became difficult when I had to ask Obadiah to leave the work. He would not commit himself to listen and do the work as I asked him. Monwelli was sick and in the hospital so I was on my own. Martha came back to assist and the Lord helped me carry on.

Twins nearly a year old were brought in. The girl weighed 9 lbs. 8 oz. and the boy 11 lbs. 4 oz. One had measles and a fever, the other a badly infected ear. Twins were very unusual in that area. Moyi told me that usually they starve one because they think if both live, the father will die. I asked him if his wife had twins would he think that. He quickly answered, "I don't want that!" I would never wish twins for any of them. How hard it was for even the Christians here to overcome fears bred into them.

By the end of August, the Logotok station was about ready to start up. Martha was busy sewing for the work, and I prepared some supplies for them. I also collected some things for Katire Ayom as Dorothy was finding people coming for medical help as well. I almost felt like Mrs. Becker, gathering things together to send out for other dispensaries.

My garden began to produce and I had my first tomato, five inches by three and a half inches by four inches. I always picked the tomatoes at the first sign of turning red to stay ahead of the birds. All the time something wanted my garden food: if not the birds, then the rats or chickens or monkeys.

August had the top record so far with 1500 visits. Whooping cough was still whooping. It was starting to lessen in the Opari area but just moving up into Katire Ayom. I gave whooping cough shots to several including David Beatty, who did not see me as a friend for a time after that. I assisted when Uncle John filled two teeth for Dorothy. (He was on the field a long time and had learned how to do so many things. He did the dental work for many people as he traveled around.) I was having trouble finding people to learn the medical work. Monwelli was still not strong and I had a sore and painful finger. I was so tired!

Betty and the Beattys took me to Juba for my birthday in September. That evening, Bill began with stomach pain from malaria. They just couldn't seem to come up here without one of them being sick. I consulted with Dr. Wheaton, the British doctor at Juba, about Bill and then also about Monwelli's ongoing illness. To my shame, I found out I was not giving Monwelli the correct dose of medicine. How humbling to report a mistake to a doctor I had never met before. Dr. Wheaton was kind about it and went on to ask me to make some reports of my cases for the government, telling me, "You are hiding your light!" Bill recovered and we traveled home in heavy rain without incident, passing right by the deep marks where we skidded on the trip up.

The Buyses came back from a two–week trip to Congo and we eagerly heard all the news, good and bad. In this land you couldn't telephone, you just had to wait until the next news came along. We found out that Congo was sadly lacking medical workers. The Beckers were on furlough. Rethy didn't have a nurse and Zola Smith began filling in there for a month. She would then hand things over to Esther who would cover until a new person could come to the field. They told Uncle John that we didn't need so many for the medical work up here! Well, we had them and would not give them up. Even if I could have been happy in the work there, so much was needed here.

Monwelli eventually regained his health and then learned to use the sewing machine. He always wanted me to sew, and I didn't have the time, so I told him if he wanted to learn, he could sew for the dispensary and do his things too. He had quite a time figuring out how to make his feet work the treadle to make the machine go forward and not break the thread, but he got over that. He eventually even made a dress for his wife with only a little direction and some help from me for the finishing touches.

The folks from Logotok came down for a visit, and what a time they were having to find Africans to work. Martha was quite busy as she was the one who could speak Latuka, so she was the preacher, teacher, and interpreter. They were hoping to finish the dispensary building by Thanksgiving. Even though it was only October, Betty and Martha began planning their vacation to Kenya in January. I didn't want that kind of trip, so I planned to spend my vacation down with Zola. She said she didn't mind playing second fiddle for sometimes that wasn't

Doug, Kim, Martha

as hard as first! Buyses would take vacation in February or March, so we wouldn't all be gone at the same time.

About this time, the Arab man in charge of the store in Opari came in with a very sore finger. I gave him sulfa and medicine for the pain so he could sleep, but the next morning things were worse. The swelling moved up his arm, and I had to send him off to the hospital. He was very nice to us and I was sorry I couldn't help him at the station. I almost made him faint that morning when I put a needle in for Novocain to examine the finger. (Just like all the men the world round.) After he left, Monwelli told me the name I wrote down on his card was the Arab word for "shopkeeper," not his actual name. I asked Monwelli why he didn't tell me, and he responded that I never remembered words he told me anyway, so he didn't always correct my language. Hmmm.

One day in October I had 105 visits, and I really hit the jackpot with a total of 1944 for the month. A few new helpers started in medical work, and I needed them. Sometimes I had as many as sixteen inpatients needing to be checked. I also hoped to start giving the workers at least one day off each week. Then there were the records. I would have much rather done the work and let someone else do the books, but being the head means doing many things you wouldn't have to do otherwise.

Aunt Mabel came down with some kind of dysentery, Betty was not feeling well, and I started with a scratchy throat. The Beatty family was on the blink again with fevers and colds. Early in November, I passed out at midnight on my way to our outhouse. I came to just fine, but Betty did help out in the dispensary the next day so I could sit while I worked. I ran low on medicine and had to spread out what I had. Many times I dispensed with a song on my lips like a prayer—little is much when God is in it. And we depended on God.

Mr. Senff arrived at our station. He, Bill, and Uncle John made many trips amongst our stations and Torit. It seemed like they were always on the road. One day Uncle John came home with nineteen packages, and seven of them were for me. The cars and trucks broke down and got stuck with regularity. Aunt Mabel never panicked if Uncle John didn't get back at the expected time. I guess after all those years she was used to it. Travel was always an adventure. Where a road crossed a stream, usually there was cement across the bottom of the stream bed. If it rained, you just had to stop and wait until it was safe to travel over. Once, the Buyses and the Beattys got stuck in the mud overnight. Four adults and two under four years old slept in the car. Aunt Mabel said, "Dorothy's a good African mother with her bottles ready anytime David cried!"

With extra rains in November, I was able to store up rain water in quart jars for making medicine in the dry season. My total attendance at the dispensary rose to 2,069.

Packages coming from afar didn't always make it through the mail. While I got my Christmas package on time this year, I am sorry to say it didn't come through well. I never knew if it was customs or the mail that gave it the rough time. A lamp globe was broken in thousands of pieces with tapioca all through the glass. Two pounds of cornmeal broke, and I thought I could scoop it out and use it until I looked closely. Something else was in it. I noticed another broken box, and found that I had a grand mixture of cornmeal and Epsom salts. I saved about a half pound of the cornmeal that I thought I could safely use. Dorothy and Barry were visiting at the time, so Barry played with the unusable mixture like sand. Bandages that folks made for us from their worn–out sheets always came through fine.

As we approached Christmas I enjoyed oranges and grapefruit from my trees. Grapefruit for breakfast, dinner, and supper, and what a treat. We didn't have American products, but I did find my favorite shredded wheat and how I enjoyed it—even if I had to pick out the weevils. What can you do? Those bugs—flour often needed lots of sifting! I did what I had to do.

One day, Moyi tried to make a red velvet cake on his own and ended up putting in twice the amount of flour required. It was so heavy we could hardly eat it. I told him he would learn by doing and I made mistakes too. Actually, he had very few mistakes considering he couldn't go to a book and read a recipe. A cake won't hurt anyone if it fails.

Hank Senff was back in Congo in December trying to get permission to bring in his goods and some brick machines so we

Mr. Senff and the Beattys

could get to building in Logotok. We also needed to put up a new church building at Opari as ours was falling and we were hopeful to make it brick.

Medical work continued in December. I had to again confront my medical helpers about missing medicine. I treated so many cases of pneumonia that I ran out of sulfa drugs and had to use injected penicillin. I broke my 2cc syringe and added a P. S. appeal to a letter to Dr. Doug. I was always asking him for something and really couldn't remember what I had done the previous year without him.

I couldn't help everyone. One girl, sick with pneumonia and meningitis was taken home and died on the way. I could help her brother who had come in as well, but the girl was too far advanced. Oh, the people needed to know the peace of God. The fear of death was awful. I gave the family words as I found them and prayed with them before they left but didn't get an Amen from them. I could only point them to the one who comforts.

I attended a special service with the nationals singing on the Sunday before Christmas, then all the Sudan workers met at Katire Ayom with the Beattys for Christmas day. It was a long day, but passed quickly. We had turkey with all the trimmings. The Beattys put a large board over their table, so we could all eat together. They had a nice tree and we all

Betty, Olive, Uncle John, Aunt Mabel

exchanged gifts. So many changes throughout this past year, yet we looked forward to the new things God would bring to us in the New Year.

1952

And the life which I now live in the flesh I live by faith in
the Son of God, who loved me and gave Himself for me.
(Galatians 2:20)

We can plan, but only God knows the way. Betty and Martha planned to vacation together on the Nile river boat, but Uncle John's car broke down, and they had no way to get to the boat. In this delay, the mail came with news that Martha's father had died. I had planned to go with the Beattys on vacation and Bill had the car ready to go, but since no one knew when Betty and Martha could leave, Hank Senff suggested that we three girls vacation together. He offered us his pickup truck. We could go anywhere we wanted as long as we had the money for gas. Because I had the license for both Sudan and Congo, I drove, and on January 3 we headed out via Juba, Sudan to Aba, Congo. In Juba we ran into Doug and Kim getting their truck which had arrived from home. What a disappointment—windshield cracked, the generator stolen, and all the tools gone. What can you do?

We three girls got our manifest and had no trouble leaving Sudan. Entering Congo we found quite a sticker at customs and had to open every suitcase. Then, because I didn't own the truck, they wanted collateral paid. On top of it all, Betty and Martha had no visa for the Congo. They were finally given one month in the country. On January 5, Mr. Senff came through with delegates for a Bangala conference being held at Adi, and eventually managed to straighten out the whole matter concerning the truck. We didn't know why all the delay, but we were that far and at least had gotten a little rest out of it.

Many were traveling to the Bangala language conference at the Adi station. While at the Aba station we learned that Mr. Sidney Langford's car had broken down and people needed rides to the conference, so some traveled with us to Adi. In spite of large crowds, there was a room for us so we stayed there a day. What a thrill to see such a large African Conference.

As we left Adi, we came across an accident. The wife of one of the men from Torit had been hit by a bicycle and broke her leg, so we first played ambulance to the Arua, Uganda hospital where they could set it. Then, while driving on to the Aru station, we almost had a blowout, but Betty noticed a funny noise so we stopped before the tire actually burst. The Lord was good and each day saw us to the next step.

While at Aru, I saw the work, washed the dust out of clothes, and rested. I came down with a minor case of malaria so I didn't mind spending a bit of time alone while the others went off to different places.

On the twelfth, we drove on to the Rethy station for a week. Many missionaries lived there, and we stayed in one home and ate in turn with many others. Rethy abounded with vegetables, which we canned and ended up with 128 cans among us. A broken mainspring delayed our departure, but on the nineteenth, we started out to Oicha.

I thought we'd never get there. I wanted to get in before dark but didn't make it. I knew the road, but it seemed to go on and on and I thought maybe I made a mistake. In addition, the truck started smoking and we had to stop to add oil. I could drive, but didn't know much about repair. We knew how to measure with the dip stick and struggled to slowly add the oil into that tiny hole. Clauden Stauffacher (Mother Stauffacher's son, who was also a missionary), normally a quiet person, couldn't stop laughing when I asked him about it later. He taught me the real place to add oil for the next time.

At Oicha, Dr. Stevens was filling in for the Beckers, who were just coming back from furlough. I had hoped they would be back in time for my visit, but they arrived after I had already returned to Opari. I did enjoy my time with Jewell as well as refreshing and learning more for my medical work. I tried to think of all my questions so as to not think of some later that I might wish I had asked. I still felt a part of Oicha. Betty and Martha, having few connections there, went to Ruwenzori for a few days while I stayed and visited and recovered my full strength from the malaria.

On the twenty-eighth we began making our way back via Rethy, Aungba, Aru, then Aba. Leaving Congo involved unloading everything in the truck for them to see, then packing it all back up again. Back in Juba, we took one night in luxury at the hotel. After all that dusty traveling on dirt roads, a bath in a big white tub with running water felt wonderful.

First I washed myself, then I washed the ring off the tub. The food there tasted delicious, yet in looking around we found ourselves back in the world again, seeing all the drinking, a woman wearing a strapless gown, and her companion with a goatee right alongside two archdeacons.

We left Juba at 2:30 p.m. the next day, waited a half hour for the ferry to cross the Nile to the east side, and arrived back at Opari by 8 p.m. After a good night's sleep, I unpacked the truck, cleaned the cobwebs out of my house and put everything away. Reading the mail caused a little homesickness. It was hard, but then I thought of the many people praying for me. I had a surprise that evening on my visit to the "little house." Even with a bright moon, I was glad for my flashlight when I found a small foot-long snake right inside the door. The Lord protects all along the way. Praise His Name.

Monwelli had carried the medical work well in my absence and Aunt Mabel said he was on the job. He only had 156 visits during the month, but some of them were bad, including a school girl with diarrhea, a woman with a very bad chest, and a man with burns on his legs from a grass fire (which were healing nicely). I was glad I had left some of the drugs out for him to use and was pleased with the way he had carried on. Now, it was his turn for time off. I gave him three weeks but knew he would probably take more because he wanted to go far. I prayed that the Lord would work in his heart. There seemed to be an unrest in the people that we thought to be a spiritual need, and we prayed that the people would be willing to give themselves wholly to the Lord.

And so February went. We had British visitors one night. I had supper for eight and finished off the meal with an Orange Chiffon pie. Medical work was slow which gave opportunity for teaching new helpers, and there was the usual dry season hunting for meat. Dr. Constandine (a British doctor in the area) came around for the first time in almost a year. The British had three months of vacation a year, so some time might pass until they would stop by again. I liked when doctors came through as it was a chance to consult on any cases I had, even if the advice was to keep on doing what I was already doing.

Most of our news came to us from people passing through the station. However, when King George of England died, Bill heard about it on his radio and sent a runner with a letter to tell us at Opari. The British government men all began wearing black arm bands, and many told us that Elizabeth (who was visiting Africa at the time) would become a good Queen, though I thought it sad to see a good man gone.

John and Mabel Buyse, our leaders, finally had their turn for vacation in March. While they were gone, I replaced the roof on my house—and what a dirty mess. As the men worked the grass and dirt fell in, so I had to cover everything. Then they might skip a day before they did more and so it went. Of course, it rained when part of the roof was off. It never fails even in the dry season when a roof is off!

Dorothy, invited by the District Commissioner's wife, went with the children up to Gelo (about 100 miles away; it was high and cool and we hoped to build a rest home there one day). Bill came down to Opari to help Hank for a few days, so Betty and I took on preparing the meals for both men. At this time, we had no potatoes, so we always served spaghetti. Betty switched it up once and made macaroni instead. Then, I found about four cans of potatoes hidden away and happily opened one to give us a change. One day, Bill and Hank took four patients to Torit and didn't get back for supper until about 10 p.m. The Buyses had a gas refrigerator that we all could use, and we had made strawberry ice cream for dessert. Both men were such teases and told us there was a party going on with the government people and they were tempted to stay but then thought of the ice cream waiting back here for them.

Another day, Bill and Hank went hunting, and returned at 9 p.m. with two antelope. They hadn't eaten yet and wanted the liver cooked. After cooking, we put the remainder of the meat in the refrigerator overnight and I finally got to bed by 11:30—so much for my plan of turning in early that night. The next day Moyi was able to do up six cans of meat and three of hamburger each for Betty and me.

Fewer patients showed up, so I again had more time for teaching my staff. Monwelli was not back yet. I needed patience to show my helpers their responsibility to the work and to God. Many could only think about the money. These were a people without a care and no worry about tomorrow, which is good as far as the physical goes, but what about eternity?

We had news of additions to our Sudan group. Barbara Battye and Dallas and Winnie Green were coming out soon to join the Logotok work. The Greens were expecting, and we weren't sure if they would try to travel before the birth of their baby or wait. Often babies did better if they were born here rather than adjusting to the climate change afterward, but we would wait and see. There was also another couple, Dan and Jean Olsen, who were waiting to see if they could come. As well, both Dorothy and Kim were expecting. We would increase the workers in Sudan one way or the other.

During this dry season, the water at Opari seemed like mud. When I washed my hair, I didn't know which was dirtier, the water or my hair. I figured it might even dye my hair dark. Aunt Mabel liked to say that she just put the light in the far corner and closed her eyes to wash her face! After water was boiled and it stood and settled, it was still the color of light tea.

The government said water had to be found at the Katire Ayom site in order for building there to begin. They sent prisoners out to dig for water, but it was not found easily. I wondered—was this God's spot, or were we failing in some way so He couldn't answer. We were discouraged that many professed Christ but did not live it. I prayed that their eyes would open to Christ. I wanted to be Christ-like and led by him, but so many things so easily came in and took time away from real study. I didn't want to be a hindrance by allowing my work to be first instead of Christ.

In the beginning of April, four of us crammed into the cab of Uncle John's truck for a very hot ride to the Beattys' to celebrate Barry's birthday. John wanted to check in anyway, so we managed two things in one. David was really traveling around by this time and wore out his shoes before new ones could arrive. Birthdays were always special times for us.

We had lots of company around Easter. That year, the Langfords of Aba station came with one child, the Amstutzes of Arua came with their grown boy before he left for college and Mr. Lloyd of Britain came with the Vollers. Mr. Sidney Langford preached on Good Friday and Mr. Voller preached on Easter. I had eight folks for dinner and Moyi, my cook, put supper on the stove then disappeared. Later I found out he had been looking for food for his kiddies and yielded to temptation for a drink. He left his cooking and went into the bush and passed out. When he came to, three hours later, he came back repentant.

With so many people on the station, I moved into Betty's house and the Langfords stayed in my house. I had quickly sewn up another mosquito net and worked so fast that the seams were not as nice and even as I would have liked. I told Dorothy that whoever was under it was to sleep and not examine it too closely. Betty made cushions for her couch and did a very neat job. I found medical and garden work more my line than sewing.

Dr. Doug and Kim Reitsma arrived back from a trip to Uganda. He had not been well, and they found he still had malaria in his blood, so he started on a good course of treatment. He came back with Typhoid and Tetanus shots which left each of us with quite sore arms. It was good to have him help and give direction in medical work.

At the end of April, Monwelli came back from vacation but not to stay. He was restless and wanted three things: a house for his wife, guarantee of food, and higher wages. We missionaries had to work together so as not to show partiality in the wage scale. We paid workers at the end of the month and it was always difficult. They really didn't earn much, but we didn't have much to give. Due to all the hunger, we did add food every month which was like a pay raise. Because of lack of schooling, Monwelli couldn't get into training schools, so it was hard for him to find other work to get a higher wage. In the end, he decided to continue on with me and did a great work.

In May, we had another company spree with visitors three Sundays in a row. Dr. Ted Williams and his family came for a week from Arua, Uganda, and he helped me with some tough cases in the medical work. We had the Stoughs visit as well as two nurses, Ada Rury and Alice Winsor, who had been visiting in Kenya and were going home by way of Opari. Whenever we had British visitors, we always had to remember *tea time*. If the guest house filled, I took folks into my house.

Ada stayed with me and went along late one Friday to help with a maternity case. I thought I heard two heart beats! I didn't tell them. Saturday passed quietly, then, on Sunday when the woman in labor finally seemed to be getting somewhere, the other women with her took her away while we ate dinner. Her husband got mad and found her and brought her back. Things went faster, and by the time they called me back at 11:30 p.m. I found the first baby born dead and the second one fine. Before delivery, I hadn't heard a second heartbeat, so I didn't think they had done anything to the baby but that it simply was a hard labor and too much for the baby. By the time we got the woman settled and went back to my house, Miss Rury couldn't sleep for all the excitement. She told me, "I could never take such a strain as out here!" The family left the next day, I thought because they couldn't run their affairs here like they wanted to. That poor woman after about five days of labor and then a hard delivery had to walk at least a mile. I never heard more, so I guess she was alright.

The site at Katire Ayom remained uncertain. They had been working on the well since January and were down 50 feet with still no water. Uncle John was very concerned. He felt the Lord gave us that place, as it was in the midst of the Acholi tribe. But the government said we needed water and even with blasting and the prisoners digging, we couldn't get to water. We wondered if the Lord had something better for us that we couldn't see right then. We didn't know the outcome but kept trusting the Lord.

At the end of May, we had the affair of the snake hunt. Earlier in the month, it had been after my chickens, and we searched but couldn't find it. It came back a second time at night and climbed up the pole into the chicken house. That snake had a good time until we got him. I took my light out into the dark, and the boys finally speared it—a python of 107 inches. Exciting times!

My cook cut his toe with the hoe and missed work so I helped a younger boy with the garden. The child figured that since we had people to work here, we must have had people working for us at home. He was surprised I knew how to do such work! No, I enjoyed the gardening, but I rarely had time between my medical work and teaching the workers there. I was busy and quite glad for help.

Always something new happening. Monwelli got bilharzia and had to take the twenty-one needles. The grist mill for the school boys broke down and they had to grind by hand. Betty's work with the girls was growing and we began to see changes in the girls who attended school. Barbara Battye arrived to work with Martha in Logotok. Monwelli recovered and got 81% on his digestive system test. My brother Raymond and his fiancée Evelyn wrote to me of their engagement.

One morning at 5:30 a.m., the teacher Elijah called that his wife Joanna was having her baby. I HURRIED! Too late again. By the time I got there, she was holding her baby boy.

Susan Elizabeth Reitsma arrived June 20 at 1:30 p.m. Doug told us the Latukos were full of questions. They said, "Soo-sie! Why does she have clothes? Why don't you give her more hair?" Kim wanted to have her baby at Logotok so she would be "Latuko." She was a sweet baby but caused some anxiety to Mama with her crying in between feedings. Their helpers thought she should be fed every time she cried—just the African way.

Betty and I took a break to go to Logotok to see Susie and the work. On Sunday, they had ten out for their service under a tree. Everyone was still learning the language and Martha did most of the translating. While there, Martha and I went with Mr. Senff to a Lokora village to buy grain. They were a picturesque people and painted their bodies with an oily red mixture from plants and wore lots of beads and metal ornaments, but no clothes. When we got out of the car, they flocked around and many reached out to feel my hair. A few understood Acholi so we could communicate a bit. While at Logotok, we visited a Latuko village as well. So interesting to see how different groups build their homes in different ways.

Monwelli again did well in my absence. Akim, who was new and still learning, helped out, but on the side, Monwelli told me to watch him because he hadn't done too well while I was away. Betty's school girls didn't come back to school at their usual time. Why not? The girls were used in the grain fields to holler until hoarse to keep the birds from eating the ripening grain. I tried to plant a small patch of wheat, small compared to the big fields Daddy planted on the farm, but it didn't grow.

Towards the end of July, Uncle John drove his truck with the four from Opari and a few Africans to the Beattys for dinner. He thought we'd get there by 1 p.m. About eight miles out, we ran out of gas, so

Latuko hut - crawl on your knees to get inside

we pushed the truck into the shade and sent runners ahead to get gas from Bill. We finally arrived at 3 p.m. That truck gave the mission in Sudan more headaches. It was supposed to be the one to haul heavy things and help with the building and here it was—a wreck. Every time you went out in it, you never knew if you'd get where you were going or not. Coming home, I stood in the back with two of the Africans, because the driving in the mud was hard enough without four people in the front. Uncle John hit a stump and gave the truck a jar—and there was one of the boys lying on the road. He had a sore arm, but thankfully nothing was broken. What can I say about traveling in Africa?

Once, when the Beattys drove in from Katire Ayom after a heavy rain, the roads were so muddy they had to drive fast to avoid getting stuck. They did slip around and turn sideways whenever they hit a slick spot. Of course, David and Barry just laughed. The Africans said that Bwana could pass any test after that trip in.

Bill was in charge of selling two cars from the Congo and I drove one to Juba for him. I was glad for a chance to be behind the wheel again! That night in the Juba Hotel, I had a bath in a real tub with running water. On returning from Congo we met up with Myrtle Wilson and Rose Mary Hayes, who were in Juba on their way to visit Opari for a week. Driving Myrtle's '48 Chevy was like going on air over those bumps. It was my reward for driving the truck to Aba and feeling the bumps the whole way. Bill, driving ahead of us, stopped to wait and when I saw him, I slowed into second gear to stop but then couldn't shift back into high— only reverse or second. Bill got under the car and found a cotter pin missing and the screw holding the gears lost. Only one hour to find something the right size to fix it.

When we arrived back in Opari with Myrtle and Rose, Akim, my medical helper, couldn't get over that white women get so old and have never married. For an African woman it is a shame to never marry. He thought we must have left our husbands at home.

I had hoped Dorothy could come to Opari before they went to Oicha for the birth of their child, but Bill said no, the roads were too bumpy. I guess Daddy's word goes. Then, I had the thought that I could get at least one more visit before the baby if I went up there with my microscope to help with the folks who were coming in to Dorothy (those worms gave the school children such stomach aches). I made the trip and stayed for a few days.

I wrote to my twelve-year-old brother George suggesting that he be glad he didn't have such things as worms. The children couldn't eat before drinking the medicine or afterward until evening. I also reported to my brother about seeing comet planes (the first commercial jet airliners) flying over. Sometimes we could hear them, but sometimes they were just a dot and smoke trail in the sky with no sound reaching us.

Back at Opari, the Buyses had a special dinner when the Gibsons came from Juba to visit. I wore my good brown dress and white high heeled pumps. Of course, while we were eating, the heavy rain began. Neither Betty nor I had thought to bring a raincoat or boots, so at the end of the evening the gathering of clothes began. Betty got Aunt Mabel's old hat and Uncle John's raincoat with an old pair of shoes left behind by Mrs. Uhlinger. I got Aunt Mabel's boots and her raincoat with a hood. I wasn't able to close the boots, so I couldn't run up the hill. The raincoat kept flapping open. By the time I got home, I was so dripping wet that I went ahead and closed the windows (grass mats across the screens on the outside). Then since I was wet anyway, I put out the dishes to collect the rainwater to use in the dispensary.

We started to have many elephants around, looking for food. The game warden killed two and the people were happy for the meat. Monwelli came back early after going home, telling me that there were too many elephants around. Because the grass was so tall at the time, you couldn't always see what might be near the path.

Dorothy and Bill headed down towards Oicha for the birth of their baby. Aunt Mabel thought they were cutting it close, but the other two hadn't come early, so I supposed they would be ok. Bill had been gone most of the week before, getting the car fixed for the trip and Dorothy told us she thought he had gone for the baby without her! I wished I could go with them, but just wasn't able to leave my work at that time.

Moyi's wife Yunia gave birth to her third child, and I went out to her. She had a prolonged time of it, and because of their different delivery customs, I ended up quite stiff from all the stooping and kneeling. I told her the next day that at least she had something to show for her stiffness; I didn't. Their practice meant she could stay in her house resting with other women preparing her food for four days until the official naming, then she's back to work, except one woman will carry water for her one more day. She asked me to come to the feast and naming of the baby.

The village women (non-believers) planned a dance afterwards. Even though Yunia may not have been in agreement, she couldn't stop the villagers. Uncle John advised me to take Betty along and go and have a few songs, a portion of scripture, and a prayer thanking God for the baby and tell them that was the Christian way. When I talked to Yunia, she agreed right away. I prayed that I could be a witness to the women.

On the USA Labor Day, I had ninety patients and called it Labored Day instead of holiday. Uncle John worked on the big truck we now called "the lemon". Whenever he went to fix one thing, something else showed up. Then, he went from fixing cars to fixing teeth. We were surely glad for someone to be the dentist.

Uncle John had to go to Rethy to care for the children's teeth, so we celebrated Aunt Mabel's seventieth birthday before he left. My first try at the cake was delicious. Unfortunately it crumbled when I tried to ice it, so I made a second. My description of Aunt Mabel at seventy years: "She doesn't seem that old and is well able to do everything. Entertains all the time as people come through. Not handy at cooking, but does a good job of talking wisely for different people's lives. Well–read and up on everything. "

The Beattys had left one of their cats with Betty during their trip to Oicha. The cat moved to my house where she spent nights hunting lizards or rats or bats in the grass of the ceiling of my rooms. I wasn't sure which, but I had all three. I thought maybe she decided to come to the "doctor's" house to have her babies. She beat Dorothy by two days and had four wild cats. Hank got rid of all but one. I didn't think I'd take

Moyi, Yunia, and children

too much interest in it, but one day the mommy went off and the poor thing looked like it was cold, so I took it in my lap. That was that, and I hoped it might be a nice kitty after all.

Barbara Jean Beatty was delivered September 22. They didn't have to hurry after all.

My birthday rolled around again on the twenty-seventh. In the morning I got a card asking me to come to high tea at 5 p.m. Because the medical work was so busy I arrived fifteen minutes late, yet nothing seemed ready. Aunt Mabel said, "the table's all set," picked up the flint gun and out the back door we went. We had a picnic of hot dogs and potato salad at the top of some large rocks. The rain came and after the break for everyone to run and shut windows, we came back and enjoyed cake and talk. My thirty-first birthday. I thought thirty-one must be for tablecloths because I got three. How everyone laughed as each time I opened a present I found another tablecloth. (Usually our gifts were something stored away in our boxes that we thought the person could use.) I needed one tablecloth, but three would certainly keep me for quite some time.

I had to let Akim go at the end of the month due to drinking. Erasto came back and was helping again in the medical work, so I continued classes with Monwelli and Erasto. Medical work went on with close to 2000 visits in October. The Beattys stopped by with baby Barbara on their way home and to my delight brought Jewell Olson along for a vacation and a short time with me.

November was filled with many things. We learned that Eisenhower was elected our president back in the States. Sunday school topped out at 186. Monwelli began to give needles and did well. His father-in-law was making him nervous, perhaps by pushing for more dowry to be paid. My eye became inflamed and swollen, and when Dr. Constandine came through he told me to take sulfa drug, which helped. Uncle John gave the Thanksgiving message talking about the three pictures of ourselves in the Word—the old, the new, and what we shall be. November ended with 2194 medical visits, the highest ever.

Although I dreaded to think of the three mile walk to get there, I looked forward to our upcoming baptism for the believers. Moyi, my cook, was refused baptism because he still had a drinking problem, and he wanted to leave and get baptism somewhere else. We talked with him for quite some time and explained it wasn't because we didn't want to, but because he wasn't walking straight and the devil wouldn't leave him just because he went somewhere else. He said he'd think about it. Many felt a change to a Christian name at baptism meant everything, and it didn't matter whether you changed your ways or not. I wept and kept praying for him. We ended up baptizing twenty-six and had baby dedication and communion when we returned to the station.

Medical work kept me busy. I had to do a spinal tap and Dr. Constandine came back through to give advice for treatment. We had many cases and Monwelli remained faithful and steady and there was hardly ever a hard word from him. I prayed he would remain true, following the Lord.

We celebrated Christmas at Opari on the twenty-third with a roast chicken and presents. Drums started up at 6 a.m. for the local celebrations, but on the station, we had church and communion followed by games and football. On the twenty-sixth, we traveled to Logotok for Sunday service. School children sang Christmas carols and Martha gave a flannelgraph, battling the wind. Uncle John dedicated

Baptism

Susan. The Reitsmas wanted it done there for a Christian testimony before the people.

My medical totals: 17,131/year; 674 new patients; 1,472/monthly average and 47/daily. What would the New Year be?

1953

And lo, I am with you always even to the end of the age.
(Matthew 28:20)

Having woken up at 6 a.m. on January 1, I felt like I was seeing the New Year in with folks at home due to the time difference.

Erasto's pal in Juba called and told him to come quickly as there were good jobs there. His mother and others pleaded with him to stay, but to no avail and he left the medical work for the city. I eventually found out that he did get a job on a fishing boat.

In January, political talk sprang up from the native women during our Sunday school prep time. Sudan wanted independence, but the southern end was not really as ready as the north. In the north, the Arabs wanted freedom, but the south remembered what the Arabs had done before. They didn't want Arab rule; they still wanted the British to help. Time would tell the outcome.

This was the year for our mission conference in Rethy. Paul Stough, of the British field council, and Mr. Richardson brought Sir Arthur (President of the British Council of Africa Inland Mission) and Lady Smith to visit Opari for the weekend. It was something addressing a "Sir" and "Lady." His official title was Lieutenant General Sir, but you would never have known it for they were very easy to be with. They were touring the AIM work and he was to be speaking at our conference as well as at the Kingwana African Conference to follow at Oicha.

Praise the Lord my passport and Congo visa arrived in time to attend the Conference. I prepared the drugs ahead for Monwelli so he could carry on the medical work while I attended the conference and then took my yearly vacation in Oicha.

I rode in the back of the pickup truck to Arua, Uganda. We left Arua at 9 a.m. the next morning and lost some time at customs on the Congo border, finally crossing over at 5:30 p.m. Once we arrived at Rethy, I was pleased to find I could share a room with Jewell in Evelyn Kuhnle's home.

The conference made me feel like I was back in the USA at camp meeting with seeing the families and all the children. Boys will be boys—yes even MKs. They stirred up a bunch of bees! Yet I was richly blessed by hearing from God's Word. Sir Arthur Smith spoke on our Foundations in Christ—Faith, Freedom, Fellowship and Fruitfulness. We need freedom from the bondage of sin and from being overcome with temptation. The thing worse than falling is not getting up again, and only a worm can't stumble. Another day, he spoke on Joy. He stressed Philippians 4:4 saying we don't always want to rejoice in circumstances but should remember our higher calling to rejoice in the Lord always and everywhere. The hotter the fire, the purer the gold. Metal is pure when the workman is able to see himself and our trials bring us to the place that Christ can see Himself in us. The three men in the fiery furnace were not touched by the fire—only their bonds. I was encouraged with the Word of God.

And so the conference went. I helped with salads, though most of the catering was done by the African staff from the children's school. I watched Susan for a night when Dr. Reitsma was ill, and Barbara when Dorothy played the piano. The week ended with the North Congo versus South Congo baseball game. (North won again, 41–13, but a good game just the same.) We closed the Conference on the last Sunday afternoon with baby dedication and communion.

I traveled on to Oicha with the Reitsmas for my vacation. Tire trouble caused a stop overnight at the Bogoro station, but we arrived at Oicha on the twenty-first in time for the African Kingwana Conference.

The theme for this conference was "Our Warfare in the Christian Life." Thirty-one different tribes with 451 delegates from mission stations attended. A Pygmy man from Biasika, one of the first two baptized, gave his testimony. They were so hard to reach because they always moved around. Then, a Pygmy from Oicha couldn't be left out and went to the platform to give his greeting too. A Christian chief from near Rethy gave his testimony, then another chief, unsaved, gave his greeting. After he sat down, the leader said, "We want to pray for this chief that he will get saved." Think of doing that at home after a mayor welcomed you to his area.

I didn't attend all the services due to the strain of understanding the language, but I did help with the food. This time, the missionaries did the work and let the nationals go to the services. I learned to make Thousand Island dressing and found it to be the only dressing I didn't care for so much. The men washed the dishes and the women dried. We had everything finished and the tables cleaned in one hour and the Africans were amazed we could do dishes so quickly.

The conference wasn't all meetings. One afternoon, a Pygmy man climbed a tall tree for us to get pictures. He climbed right up a heavy vine to the top in about three minutes and slid down in about half a minute. Claudon Stauffacher went out to try to get fresh meat for the Africans and came back with three buffalo. It seemed like he could always get something when he wanted it. I enjoyed buffalo liver for dinner.

I stayed in Oicha going around to learn more for my medical work. One evening, while I was writing to Mother and Daddy, the Reitsmas stopped by for a visit. Kim told me to tell my mother she had very good taste for the doll she had sent for Susie. Susan liked it and so did the Latukos, who always wanted to handle it and make it cry.It was getting so dirty that Kim decided to put it away for a time until Susie could hang on to it herself.

On February 14, I traveled back to Rethy with the MacIntoshes. The truck radiator had a hole, so we had to stop everywhere there was water to fill our containers, which were too small to hold much. We arrived at 7:45 p.m., and by 9:15 I had washed and eaten dinner, and with the time difference I was ready to "attend" my brother Ray and Evelyn's wedding back in Emmaus, PA. I would have liked to attend in person but settled for sending money home to mother to buy a present so I could at least be a little part of their day.

I left Rethy with fresh vegetables, some of which spoiled by the time I got home. I thought I had packed them well enough, but the heat got to them. On the way back, we stopped in Gulu, Uganda. Betty and I walked around the town, and as I followed her on a narrow sidewalk I heard her say, "watch out for the hole." By the time it registered, I was in it. My left leg ended up with a nice cut, but no permanent damage.

I had just arrived back in Opari when Hank drove up with the new missionaries, the Greens, and came right to my house. They had first gone to Dorothy and Bill at Katire Ayom, but when Dorothy saw how sick their baby was she hurried them in to me. I attended to the baby and gave her some medicine and kept her with me for several nights. Poor Winnie Green was just so worn out she hardly knew what she was doing. They had all been sick when they arrived and didn't have even one night of full sleep. Because they came out to Africa by plane, they had left home in the awful cold and landed in the awful heat—all in just a few days. They probably got some sort of flu on the way and it was too much for them. The baby began showing signs of recovery, so they didn't have to travel further to a doctor. After a few nights sleep, Winnie, Dallas, and the other two children, Carol and Kenny, were back to themselves. I just marveled at the way the Lord allowed me to be used at such a time.

I took on a new helper, Onesimo, and two days later Monwelli told me he desired to leave. We talked a long time, but there was no stopping him. He told me he couldn't leave when Erasto did, then the Greens came for help and he didn't want to tell me then either. Food and wages were an ongoing problem. And with the temptation of people always asking him for extra medicine, he was afraid he would fall. I told Monwelli that I couldn't stop him, but if he felt he made a mistake, he should come back and we'd talk business. I was glad it hadn't happened one or two years ago. With three years behind me, I felt more stable in the work and could take it better. So it went, I had my new helper of just two days and as green as they come, but I thought he would learn fast and we'd get along somehow. Monwelli did eventually return to work for me again.

The next morning, Dr. Constandine arrived with small pox vaccinations for everyone. There were some cases spreading in the area from someone who thought they had chicken pox and it really was smallpox. Two boys in the school contracted it and had to stay in a hut by themselves. Contagious diseases were difficult to treat; just try keeping someone in one place. They simply didn't see the need and would mix as much as they liked. I could keep an eye on the boys because they were near the dispensary and they listened to me very well.

As the Beattys were busy packing for furlough, the Sudan Army had maneuvers in our area for a few days and the English captain came and joined us for tea. The Greens planned on moving into the Beattys' home at Katire Ayom while they were away, then eventually go on to Logotok.

So the month of March began with people coming and going and many arrangements. I dreaded the time I would have to pack to go on furlough. I had remade most of my crates into other things. But I decided to wait for that bridge; I had enough to think about without beginning down that line of thought.

I planted some tomato seeds in boxes. We were starting to get some rains and I looked forward to getting the garden going. The seeds in boxes worked very well and I eventually ended up with more than 200 tomato plants, enough to supply to anyone who wanted them.

On Saturday, March 21, the Beattys left for furlough, the first of our party to go. They came down to Opari the Sunday before. I had decided to have supper about 6 p.m. so the children could get to bed, but as usual, nothing went off as planned. Dallas had gone to Katire Ayom with the big truck to bring the Beattys' ducks and chickens to Betty. Dorothy rode back with him, and they arrived about 5 p.m. only to discover that nine of the chickens had died from the heat. We finally ate at about 7 p.m. with no sign of Bill. By the time he got in and set up Barbara's bed he was so tired, he could hardly eat. About 9 p.m., after the children were in bed, we gathered at the Buyses' and had a time almost like a watch night with singing and a service. Uncle John spoke a bit. He was leaving the next day, so this was our farewell service. We stayed up later and later and no one seemed to want to leave. Poor Bill had so much upon him that week, and I hoped he could have the strength until they could get the boat at Nimuli and rest. Three sheep were brought down from Logotok for help in feeding all the people at Opari that week. Bill and Dorothy were well organized in their packing. It was quite something to see that you have everything you need for the family for all kinds of weather. The children were so good and I figured their grandparents would have the time of their life once the children arrived back in the USA.

In the end, Dr. Constandine took them to the boat as there was no one else around to do it. He stayed on the station overnight, taking over my house, and since Uncle John was gone, I went and slept in his bed. That's how things went on the station. We moved around to fit everyone in. Because Dr. Constandine had to hurry back to Torit, and we didn't want to hold him up, we said our goodbyes at Opari thinking "goodbye" probably wouldn't dawn on us until at least a month later when we no longer had them dropping in to Opari.

A short time later, our pastor's mother died. Pastor Andreya's mother was a believer, but few of the family were. I didn't see her often for she came in so seldom because she couldn't walk well. Betty and I went to the burial and read the Word and prayed, but I couldn't stay long because of the medical work. Once again I saw the different customs. People cried and howled, then the next minute were as quiet and calm as could be, smoking their pipes. That seemed to be the way they paid respect to the dead.

Pastor Andreya and family

Our days passed with not only goodbyes and deaths but fun as well. Some of the Africans knew about April Fools day and were working on Betty and me. I was caught once, but not the second time.

Onesimo took to the work very well and had a good spirit. I would like to have trained more helpers together, but couldn't find anyone else interested in medical work. I didn't really know how the work would be carried on when I went home on furlough, so I trusted God would work it all out as he saw best.

Dallas Green and Uncle John came back from the Kenya coast with their vehicles: Uncle John, a new truck, and Dallas, a suburban (not good for hauling, but nice to have with children). They brought two school children back with them due to the missionary children's school closing because of increasing unrest in Kenya. Uncle John told us that even one of the missionary children, aged sixteen, was taking his turn with a gun on night watch. We hadn't been hearing too much, and prayed it might not affect us here, for we hoped for a little longer time to give the Gospel.

I had five women come to a new baby class I began. Yes, me, who never had any children, teaching the class. I used a book about infant care written for East African women. Of course, they would go home and do as they liked afterward, but hearing a thing always gives you food for thought. It gave me some contact and at the meetings I also tried to give some Bible lessons about women in the Bible and how God worked through them.

Medical work was busy. Onesimo did well, but I couldn't let him do what he didn't know anything about. I began teaching a new helper, Sulumoni, who I suppose was not quite grown up yet. One day, he locked the keys inside a cabinet, then came and got my extra set and didn't he lock those in as well. He told me that he just didn't think. Good thing that was the lock that had four keys, not just two. One day we had ninety-nine people and just couldn't seem to find another to make a hundred. I had many cases: a baby with jaundice, Uncle John's sore toes, a woman who had been kicked in the stomach by a weak-minded man, worms, an abnormal pregnancy. Once, I was called to the village for a sick person and asked Uncle John if he had time to go with me. He told

Olive and Acholi women

me, "The truck is there, go with it." His new truck drove so nice.

We went up to Katire Ayom for Kenny Green's birthday. I had to stir around in my boxes to come up with a present for a child that size and finally found crayons and some candy. Although there was no progress on permanent buildings on the station, there was work going on for the Lord just the same. They had good attendance at church, and the school had two teachers and about fifty boys. Surveying began for where to dig a well, and we thought Dr. Propst was coming out with a well digger. The government grant to stay there hinged on the water supply, and none had been found yet.

Dr. Constandine came by Opari, saw two patients, and asked me if I would do the school children's exams required by the government—a big task. He never asked me before, but I was right there, so why should he do it? April ended with 1830 visits.

All week I had that nagging feeling there was something I wasn't remembering to do. Then, when I sat down in Sunday school, I suddenly remembered and turned around to wish Aunt Mabel a happy Mother's Day. She wondered, "and whose mother am I?" I told her she had to be mine for the day because I had forgotten to tell my own mother.

"I must hide my face in shame, it is awful what I have done again this year in forgetting that day of all days, Mother's Day. I don't know why I do such things especially year after year. But really and truly I love you Mother dear. I hope I don't wait just for that day to tell you." (Excerpt from letter dated May 11.)

May was a busy month for the medical work with 2053 visits. I was called to the village of Kajagulu to see a patient who was unconscious and in convulsions. They brought her in the next morning, and I gave her some antibiotics and IV fluids. She had a reaction to that but by the following day was conscious, taking liquids, and talking—thankfully on her way to recovery. One of my endless jobs in the medical work was keeping my needles in good shape (sharpened and sterilized). Always busy. I had a maternity case come in and I stayed with her until 12:30 a.m. I came back at 3 a.m., 6 a.m., and she finally delivered at 8:15 a.m., when I was having my breakfast!

One day, I went in and took a patient's temperature, and when I went back later to give medicines her ear had stuff in it like ground grass of some sort. I knew what that meant—witchcraft. I was so upset for I didn't know how strong you could be about it here. I called the men out, and of course they said nothing was done. I told them I wasn't blind, and she wasn't that way before. Later, I had a talk with Elijah, the head teacher, who told me that when I was away in January he was called over to the medical work about the same thing and he had sent the folks home. I was glad to know that, so I knew next time I would be even stronger about it.

Uncle John traveled to Kapoeta to see what could be done about getting missionaries to the Taposa people. It was an area of much need. When you leave Torit driving out that way, you see a sign posted advising you to take enough gas along, for it wouldn't be gotten up there. When Uncle John went anywhere, we didn't know when he would be back, for he could get stuck for several weeks if it rained. Happily, that didn't happen this time and they even returned with buffalo meat for us.

During this time, we completed the school children's physicals. Martha came down and helped at Katire Ayom, and Dr. Doug and Martha helped at Opari. We finally got through all the physicals, examining specimens and writing the report for the government.

I wrote to my little brother George of the school boys playing football (soccer) until dark (about 6 p.m.) and often spraining legs or knees or injuring toes because they wore no shoes. I was always surprised they didn't have more cuts and bruises. I packed up a box of strange things for my little brother George: beads, a necklace made from a snake's spine, a basket, and an African knife. I also sent him a piece of string, made from small tree branches the size of a thumb. They peeled off the bark and used the white of the inside for string. If you leave it sit, it will turn brittle and break. When it is fresh, you can use it for anything and everything, from tying around a bleeding cut on a finger to building houses. I also sent some fried flying ants prepared in a vacuum pack and made a second set to check if they kept. When I opened those, they were ok and the cook's little son enjoyed them.

Letters and packages from home always gave me a boost even though my file overflowed with mail needing replies. Since we couldn't get American products in Sudan, my mother and friends sent special treats, but they didn't always come through intact. Once, a package containing buckwheat flour broke and spilled all over everything else in the box. After scooping it together and seeing so many bugs in it, I decided to feed it to the chickens!

June in the medical work was a busy month with difficult cases. Sulumoni, my helper, came down with chicken pox. I was called out two nights for medical cases. People were coming from all corners with all varieties of illnesses. Babies arrived with vomiting and diarrhea from malaria. A man and a wife had a fight—she came in right away, he delayed and his wound got infected and painful. A child had a snake bite which caused a huge ulcer on the upper part of his foot. It ended up healing nicely. Another boy, carried in strapped to the bed and delirious, slipped into a coma, and they carried him back home the next day.

We make plans, but the Lord sees ahead and knows best. Martha came to talk to me saying that if she was going to take my work while I was on furlough then she wished I would get going soon so no one would have to wait longer than four years for their furloughs. Everything depended on when I left. Martha would stay at Logotok until Kim had her baby and was up and about again, then come and take my place. Martha would go on furlough next, then the Reitsmas when she came back. So, I started making plans to that end and knew God would close the door if it wasn't right.

I would be home by Christmas, earlier than expected. I started thinking more about furlough and wondered what my impressions would be once I arrived in the USA. Dorothy had written and mentioned how things looked so wonderful and up to date. She told me that when you are in the field, you forget how things are in the States. She didn't remember what a kitchen was like until she was home again. I thought I might feel like a stranger in my home church in Hatfield. I knew my brother George had grown and would look different, and my other brother now had a wife. So many changes during the time I was away.

I looked into taking a midwife course back in New York. I knew it would be helpful as by now I only was called for difficult maternity cases (the ones that you really wanted to know what you were doing). Uncle John wondered why I thought I had need of it now, having been doing the work all this time. I prayed about it for a time but eventually decided not to take the course because of the expense and the six months of my furlough it would have consumed. I wasn't too disappointed as I was losing some interest in it even before I heard of the steep cost. I did hope I would have opportunity to learn more somewhere else in order to build my confidence in my work.

Preparing for furlough also meant preparing to leave *my* work for others to carry on. I didn't want to be so jealous for my work that no one else could have a say in it, but I had begun the work and watched it grow. I kept praying about all these little things that I might be guided aright.

I had the Fourth of July picnic at my house with the MacIntoshes who were passing through on their way home to furlough. Just when we wanted to eat, the rains came. Nevertheless, I opened my last two cans of doggies I was saving for just such an occasion, and the cook roasted them in the fire in the rain. Mrs. Mac took ill, I thought mostly caused by the exhaustion of packing, finishing their work, and handing it over all within a month. Never a dull moment at Opari.

Back when I was at Oicha, Miss Edna had told me how to care for a strangulated hernia, and after three and a half years a man was brought in with one. I hoped Dr. Constandine would come through to help on the case, but he didn't, so I kept on treating and was glad to know what to do. We had a small child come in with his feet, buttocks, and privates burned. The left foot was just a stump. His mother had died, and they were buying milk to keep him alive. The girl caring for him was just a child herself, and one night, he crawled into the fire. It was an awful mess and I didn't know what to do at first. So many times I sent up a prayer and the Lord gave strength and grace to care for these cases. In the end, I took him to the hospital in Torit along with three other patients.

The Buyses came along to take the patients to Torit and then travel on to Logotok. Into Uncle John's three–quarter ton truck went our lunch, extra food, suitcases, and our bed bags. It was the rainy season and we didn't know but what we might end up stranded somewhere. Extras joined those items: we hauled my washboiler to have soldered, the shovel for mud puddles, and chains for the same. Then we added in two African helpers, my four medical patients and their belongings, an extra child to carry the baby, plus another girl and we started off. One stop at an out school along the way to encourage the teacher and greet the people, another stop at Magwi to check for messages for Torit, and we finally arrived at Torit by noon. We stopped at the post office first, then dropped the patients off at the hospital. After a meeting with the District Commissioner, I finally located the doctor and gave him his messages. After that, stores, lunch on the porch of the rest home, and Uncle John took his forty winks. At last, we headed off for the last forty-five miles to Logotok. The first thirty were great. The last fifteen were the dread of every trip up there. You could travel an average of only fifteen miles an hour or less. We passed through at least twenty gulches, many so eroded you wondered if you could make it. The truck rocked from side to side until my neck was stiff from sitting in the middle of the front seat. Some gaps were deep, others narrow, and others very steep; some sandy, some a bed of rocks, and others mud.

Finally, we came to the end of the journey and drove into the station with its mud houses, bamboo fences, and beautiful hills in the background. We saw the first finished brick building and rejoiced at the beginning of a permanent station. After staying overnight, we started back the next day with Betty (who had been there for a visit), reversing our stops. Back in Torit, Uncle John got his forty winks, and I switched with Betty for my turn in the back of the truck. About twenty-five miles from Opari, we came upon four girls on their way back to school. Mr. Buyse stopped and said we would take their loads, but it was too full for them. Nevertheless, when we pulled out, they were on too, sitting on top of the baggage. As they were not big, I guess he thought it wouldn't hurt. The African always says there is room, and if you let them get on, they seem to find some corner to crowd into no matter how full you thought you were.

How we praised the Lord for the work He was doing here in Sudan,

Logotok

building a church for Himself made up of men, women, boys, and girls. We had a great door, but the adversaries were many. How wonderful to know that as we travel life's way, the Lord of Lords is with us to guide and keep. I was thankful to the Lord for keeping me free from the many sins of the world, but I didn't want to forget that neglect of His Word or prayer might be a greater sin.

Time flew by. The Greens came back from a trip to Oicha to consult with Dr. Becker for their baby Kay, who had not been gaining weight as they thought she should. I began a baby clinic to treat for malaria and had a much better response than I expected. I taught about malaria coming from mosquitoes and recited John 3:16. I told them how God loved us and sent His Son to die on the cross for our sins that we might believe and have eternal life. Now He helped people to find the medicine too. These people didn't want to be preached at, so I tried to give them the Word of God simply in very short and tactful ways. I thought maybe the work itself just might be a means of showing them the Lord and, through love, bring them to Christ.

I booked a passage on the Queen Elizabeth out of Southampton for December 9. I planned to travel home through Europe, so I also kept working through all the paperwork, trying to find out what I needed for visas for Germany and Holland. That was on top of the paperwork to deal with the government of Sudan.

My garden did well even with the chickens trying to eat the tender new leaves (which made the garden boy mad). I had so much extra food, I shared with the Greens. They were city folks and hadn't much success in their garden that year.

My chickens were native chickens, slightly smaller than American chickens and well able to hide when a hawk flew around. We already had the affair of the python and the chickens, then, in August, we had a visitor of another sort. It all began on a Wednesday night after I went to bed. I heard a commotion from the chickens, but I didn't get up. Then, I heard it a second time and went to investigate. I couldn't find anything but saw the bamboo apart and some of my chickens gone. I went back to bed, and at 3 a.m. I heard noise again and ran to the front window just in time to hear something run away. The next morning, my helpers told me it was a leopard.

We couldn't get hold of a trap that day, and he came back for another few visits the next night. This time, knowing what it was, I stayed inside. He got seven chickens the first night and five the second. Someone tried to build a trap line like they use in the forest—a wire like a lasso to catch his head. That night Martha (who was with me for the week) and I went to bed hoping he'd get caught, but instead we heard him get more chickens—another night of poor sleeping for us. The next morning, we noticed that wise leopard had pushed his head through the brushwork in a new place and got the chickens that way. That night they set two traps. Three nights passed without us hearing a thing.

John and Mabel Buyse

Altogether, I lost sixteen chickens, mostly my young ones and meat chickens, so I moved the laying chickens closer to the house and left a light on to keep that leopard away. When I wrote to my mother, I told her to not be alarmed because I knew not to go out at night when such things were around!

Uncle John and Aunt Mabel's anniversary rolled around again in April and we planned a big evening for their twenty-fifth. Letters traveled back and forth between stations for a month ahead of time. Martha and Barbara came down with the Greens and hid until it was time to eat. The Buyses were completely surprised. Uncle John looked up with a funny expression on his face and confessed, "I forgot," then quickly added, "but it's not till tomorrow and I may have thought about it in my dreams." At least he knew the date.

Betty decorated a beautiful three–tiered cake with a silver twenty-five on top. With only a few details, Dallas and Winnie put on a skit about the Buyses' wedding, and from the reactions of Uncle John and Aunt Mabel they hit the nail on the head. In the end, we heard the full story.

Uncle John's first wife had died in childbirth, and she and the baby were buried in the Congo in 1918. Aunt Mabel was a school teacher in the Congo Mission School when they met. They planned to marry and Aunt Mabel waited in Nairobi to meet up with Uncle John as he came back from furlough for the wedding. He gave her a vacation because apparently he was on a slow boat and Aunt Mabel had to wait three months. She didn't have the money to travel back to Congo and return to Kenya again. She just had to sit and wait! They were always fun when they started telling stories and could always see the humorous side of some of the worst things.

One Wednesday, medical work began easy and I thought we'd be finished early. But, at 10:30, here came people carrying in a man who had been gored by a buffalo that morning. There was no doctor and no way to get one. When I lifted the dirty cloth covering the wound on his abdomen, I saw it was all the way through. That meant set up for surgery. We started somewhere around noon and finished about 2 p.m. I put a gauze drain in and sutured, then stitched up his leg muscle and skin, and finally ended with a stitch in his lower lip. He healed well and I gave thanks to the Lord for sulfa drugs and penicillin. I can only say it was the Lord who gave me wisdom, and I like to remember that His telephone line is never busy; He always answers. The same day that man arrived, they also brought a woman with pneumonia and a child with malaria, so I finally sat down to lunch at 2:30. My helpers stayed by until the end and did very well.

In September, two school boys on their way home for vacation, were killed when the truck they were riding on collided with another truck. One of the boys was a relative of Onesimo, and he cried so hard in telling me about it. We prayed this would give an open door to talk more of spiritual things with him.

One Saturday, Uncle John came back from Juba with a fourteen–year–old missionary kid whose parents worked in Sudan. She would head to Rethy Academy when he went there to do the dental work for the school. While she was at our station, we planned to celebrate Aunt Mabel's birthday with a special supper before Uncle John left again. What did they do, but turn it around and make it for me as well. Aunt Mabel knew about it and I was the one surprised. I served my own cake! Uncle John and the girl left for Rethy early the next day.

Medical cases totaled 2387 for September, the highest yet. Once I had a man come in saying he had poison put on him. I made tiny cuts on his leg and put potassium permanganate in. Mumps afflicted the school boys as well as the chicken pox, and I continued my baby clinic.

I had to pembe (whitewash) my walls and get my house ready for Martha to move in, and I felt tired just thinking about it! I began packing on the side as I found time. Then the fruit basket upset. At the beginning of October, it was settled that the Greens would come down, and Winnie would take over my work instead of Martha.

Earlier, there had been talk, and I was waiting for Uncle John to come back with the official word; however, Dallas arrived first with some things, so that's when I knew for sure. That was a Tuesday. He came back Wednesday with the rest of their things, and on Friday, back with Winnie, Carol, Ken, and Kay. The days were hectic, and because of the mix up. I couldn't get enthused about packing. I wasn't even sure where I would stay until it was time for me to leave.

The Greens lived with Betty at first but stored their things, including their gas refrigerator, in my middle room and ate with me. The next week, Winnie began learning the medical work. Some changes would have to be made because of her needing time with her family. I worked with her for three days, then for the next three I worked on packing my things away. I packed a few tears in the boxes as well. My feelings mingled together—the sadness of leaving and yet the joy of going home to family. So it goes in life, the joys as well as the time not so much enjoyed. I felt like a slacker not going to the medical work. New patients came in and I didn't know them and it didn't seem right.

The following week, I moved myself, my bed, my sewing machine, and a few other things to the guest house until it was time to go. I took a malaria slide on myself as I was feeling so achy, tired and had the diarrhea. The Greens moved into the Egg and fixed it up awfully nice. It gave me some ideas for when I came back, although, who knew where I'd be when I returned after furlough. I might not even come back to the Egg. That week, I helped Winnie in the medical work. She had many people, and with Dallas away there was no one to watch the children. I found great difficulty in handing over *my* work. Yet it was the *Lord's* work.

During this time, Sid and Jennie Langford came back from furlough to Juba. They were transferring from the Congo work to be the new director for the Sudan field. Having dropped their children off at Rethy

Academy, they planned to live at Katire Ayom until they could build a house in Torit so as to be in the center of all the work. Jennie told us that on their way to Rethy, they had stopped by Aba, their previous assignment, and their four children were hilarious. They ran here and there, looking at this and that, checking a tree they had planted to make sure it was ok. "Won't we go back for Christmas vacation," they mourned. The Langfords had been on that station for fifteen years and it was hard for the children to move.

The Daniel Olsens were on their way out as well, but I would miss them. I was sorry, but that couldn't be helped. As things stood, they would start off at Opari.

In the midst of all my last–minute packing and arrangement to take my leave, the big news came from Logotok. At 10:30 p.m. on October 25, Jessie Rae Reitsma was born. I took a quick trip to Logotok to see her before I left. Jessie Rae was a sweet little baby, Kim did well, and I was happy for them. They had the foundation for their house built and 1,000 bricks being made each day for building the rest of the house. Martha continued her translation work toward having God's word in Latuka.

I finished all the last–minute details, and my passport came back with my re-entry permit to come back to Sudan within a year. Of course, it was dated October 3, which wouldn't have been enough time, so I would stop in Khartoum on my way through to try and get it extended. November 10 and 11, I closed out all my things, cleaned up my stove, helped in the medical work, gave farewell to the school boys, and sat with visiting village women (who brought me a gift of rice). I had a long talk with Onesimo and Moyi. They were undecided as to whether they wanted to continue on while I was gone and requested a paper of reference. On the twelfth of November, Uncle John and I left for Juba in the three–quarter ton truck and on November 14, at 10 p.m., I boarded the Nile Steamer for the first leg of my trip home.

Furlough

I sailed in the morning and soon left hills of any size and entered the flat country—nothing but land and sky and papyrus by the side of the river. Meals on board were excellent, and I satisfied my love of fish. Back to tea times as well, although I replaced the 6 a.m. tea with bananas. We stopped at Mongalla to take on a load of bananas, sugar cane, and mangoes, then we stopped at Adok and took on another missionary. We stopped at Malakal, and an additional missionary couple boarded. The weather became cooler, and on the twentieth we arrived at Melit and I saw my first camel in real life. From Melit, we finally arrived in Kosti too late for a revolving bridge and had to wait to pass until the next morning. I spent time on the boat sleeping (at night and in the day!), catching up on reading, and in conversation.

On the twenty-second, I rode the train to Khartoum, North Sudan and began taking civilization in my stride. Electricity! Everything was so modern! I was met by a man from the mission. Because of elections, whites were keeping a low profile, but I did meet an Acholi-speaking young man who was so homesick to speak his language. On the twenty-sixth, at midnight on Thanksgiving Day, I boarded the plane for Frankfurt, Germany. It stopped at Cairo—3:40 a.m., Rome—11a.m., Frankfurt—2p.m. When I booked my plans, I intended to visit Walter and Ethel Frank and their family in Frankfurt, but they had left early for home. (The climate in Germany and the coldness of all the houses began affecting their health.) Instead, I went straight on to Amsterdam, Holland to visit Anne Punt, my roommate from Bible School, now working with Bible Club Boat ministry in Holland. I was there just in time for the boat open house and had a lovely visit with Anne Punt and Annie Verboom. What a joy to be with them even though I couldn't understand the Dutch language.

December 2, I traveled on to London and had a nice visit with the Millers who had worked with Uncle John in Congo. I received my food ration card (necessary for eating there) and went on to visit Esther, from Oicha, who was now married to Cliff Holton and living in Wales. Finally on Wednesday, December 9, I boarded the Cunard Line RMS Queen Elizabeth for the last leg across the Atlantic. The ship was so huge, it was more like a city than a ship. I lost my breakfast, and thereafter I took Dramamine and was fine. Rough seas made rough walking with one's feet either getting to the floor too quickly or maybe taking a long step.

On December 15 we docked in New York. What a welcome. Mother was at the pier to meet me along with Uncle Howard, Forrest, Brother Henry, Brother and Sister W.A. Heffner (pastor of my home church),

Mrs. Feusner, my brother Raymond and his wife Evelyn, and the Beattys. Mother and I stayed at the AIM Brooklyn headquarters until I finished my physical examinations and paperwork, then on to home. The Lord blessed all the way.

For a missionary, furlough means lots of traveling, visiting, and deputation work and hopefully participating in special occasions. My parents and younger brother George lived in Germantown, Maryland. My sister Esther and her husband Stanley and daughter Esther Mae, my brother Raymond and his wife Evelyn, as well as my brother Edward lived in Pennsylvania. Both Esther and Evelyn were expecting babies during my time in the States. My home church was Bethany in Hatfield, PA.

After Christmas and New Year celebrations with family and a homecoming in my church, I began working on form letters, transferring my colored slides onto glass to show with the projector, and believe it or not, starting a list of what I needed to take back to Sudan. I was happy to be driving again, but when I took Daddy's car to the garage, well . . . I forgot to take off the brake. Did it get HOT!

In January, I went the rounds of doctors and changed my glasses prescription. I entered Grandview Hospital for a minor procedure which in those days meant a stay of three days. Raymond and Evelyn stopped by to visit me, and I took one look at Evelyn's face and knew. I told her to go right down to maternity. (She had been feeling pains, but as it was her first child didn't know if it was labor.) Because I was a nurse and had graduated from Grandview, they allowed me to be in the delivery room with her, and I was happy to go tell my brother he was the father of a daughter, Joann. Afterward, I returned to my hospital bed and slept well! Later on in April, I was also present when my sister Esther delivered baby Susan. I stayed with her for a time helping out. What a delight to be present for the birth of two nieces.

I arranged to work at Grandview Hospital as a float in maternity and the wards during part of April and May. The nurses were a joy to be with. I also worked with some of the doctors who had trained me, although it was difficult adjusting to doctors and their routines. Some of them were very interested and wanted to talk about my work in Sudan. With nursing, helping at home, and going out to meetings, I was tired. One night I fell asleep on my knees!

I spent some time with the Beattys and in May went to the pier with them when they sailed back to Sudan. I visited with Betty, also home on furlough, and her parents. News came from Sudan of success with well drilling: they found water at Katire Ayom! I met Jerry and Annie Rineer, who were heading to Sudan towards the end of the year. Martha Hughell and Edna Jackson, home from Oicha, and I fit in visits as well.

I enjoyed my deputation although it was tiring going from place to place. I traveled by train or car and to make things easier, bought a green '48 Ford Coupe for my time at home. That was a nice car.

Throughout the year, I went to missionary conferences in Lancaster and Allentown. I spoke at summer camps, including two weeks at Camp Gilead in Florida (the leader was a classmate in Bible school). On that trip I also visited the elderly of AIM living in Media. I was missionary speaker at Camp Lou Sun near Harrisburg and Camp Sankanac. I spent a week at Mizpah Grove, our denomination's camp meeting and spoke at many, many churches, Women's Missionary Societies and my Bible College in Philadelphia, as well as attending AIM prayer meetings.

It wasn't all speaking. I made time for nice, long visits with Mother and Daddy. We all took a trip to Canada to visit an aunt and ill uncle. My uncle passed away soon afterward and the Lord gave strength.

By mid-September 1954, my eyes turned toward Sudan, and I began preparing things for packing. Over the next few months, I filled and sealed jars with food and cleaned four drums for packing. My fingers got sore from pushing and stuffing things tight for travel! So important to keep foods and soap separate. One drum had my tools, soap, household things and the baby scale. One barrel didn't want to close (too full??). The Lord helped. By December, I began the shots I needed to return (Typhus, Typhoid fever, yellow fever) and I traveled to New York AIM headquarters for my return physical and office details. I had my visa and everything was working out well. I stayed up late finishing my last–minute washing, shipping papers and stenciling my barrels. Then, I celebrated Christmas and New Years and began my goodbyes.

HE GOETH BEFORE—The duties that would be my privilege as I went back were in his hands.

HE GOETH BEFORE—So I would not fear, but rather rejoice in His will allowing me to be His chosen in Sudan.

Term Two
1955 – 1959

1955

*And the Lord, He is the One who goes before you. He will
be with you, He will not leave you nor forsake you; do not
fear nor be dismayed. (Deuteronomy 31:8)*

What a joy to be HOME again in Africa. I didn't feel strange at all. It was just as it should be when you arrive back home.

I sailed from New York on January 10, and after four days and three ports, the freighter left the States. My fellow passengers (tourists and business people) and I adjusted to life at sea. We added color to the place as we stood in line with our orange life vests during the boat drills. Of course, I read, wrote letters, napped, and walked (eighteen times around the deck equaled one mile). I also learned to play shuffleboard. On three

Sundays, I led the services, and on the final one I read the story about the call of Moses and gave my testimony. Everyone said they enjoyed the meetings and took up an offering for my work.

After twenty days on the ocean and no rough weather to speak of, we arrived at the port in Capetown, South Africa beneath the beautiful sight of the Table Mountains with the "tablecloth" of cloud cover on top. Because I was the only passenger staying on the ship as it sailed up the east coast of Africa, I thought I would have time to catch up on my letters. What happened? There were so many things to see, I didn't get much done.

We traveled along the coast, stopping at five different ports for loading and unloading cargo. In each harbor, I went into town for sightseeing. Once when the crew asked me what I had done that day, they turned away in disgust when I replied that I had visited a hospital. I believe they thought I was crazy, but that's what interested me and I had enjoyed myself very much. We finally arrived in Mombasa, Kenya on February 25. With my seventeen pieces of luggage (including a new microscope and typewriter), I traveled inland by train, Lake Kioga steamer, bus, Lake Albert steamer, and the Nile River steamer. I ended up at Nimuli by March fifth.

The Beattys met me at Nimuli and it was off to Opari for the weekend. I was back again and the missionaries and Africans were there to welcome me home. It was so nice to see them all again. I kept pointing to this child, then that one—"Who are you? Who are you?" They had all grown so much. That Sunday, I read my greetings from my home church, my family, and my friends to the church at Opari—it took some time to feel at home in the Acholi language.

On Monday, the Buyses and I traveled to Juba so I could register back into Sudan and declare the supplies I had brought in with me. (Freight would be dealt with later when it arrived.) I left customs praising the Lord because I didn't have to pay for my new microscope. I had carried that microscope next to me in my hand baggage for the entire trip back to Africa.

Sudan was now independent from both Great Britain and Egypt. Northern Sudan was populated by the Arabs of Islamic faith and the southern part by tribal Africans with Christian or Animistic beliefs. The Buyses were in Juba to attend a meeting called by the new Minister of Education, a tall, stately man who was a devout Muslim from northern

Sudan. The governors of the provinces and their counselors were doing an investigation of the schools in order to present their findings to Parliament. Even though at that time I had no idea of how far the government hand would ultimately reach, I did wonder how long freedom of the Gospel would continue in the land.

Because the meeting was delayed for a week, I experienced an unasked for extension to my furlough. In this land, you think a few times before you travel 100 miles home and back again. So we sat and waited until the government was ready for the meeting.

Starting back in my new term meant a new assignment. The main medical work for the Acholi people was to be at Katire Ayom and I was to begin that work. I spent two days at Opari gathering my things from the Egg which was now used for storage. I also took medicines and equipment for the dispensary. Katire Ayom (with Bill and Dorothy Beatty, their three children, and Dan and Jean Olsen) became my home. Betty Wilson would join us when she returned from furlough. Dr. and Kim Reitsma and their children (due for furlough), Barbara Battye, and Martha Hughell remained stationed in Logotok. Sidney and Jennie Langford were in Torit. Dallas and Winnie Green with their children manned the Opari station with the Buyses.

As Uncle John drove me into Katire Ayom with my things, we passed a man on a bicycle bringing in a woman with a huge ulcer on her left arm. Even before I had a chance to unpack the truck, I had a patient waiting for me.

I never knew how the word got around so fast in a land without telephones, but it sure traveled. I averaged fifty-six patients a day in those first weeks. I had no time to get my own things out, nor could I easily find what I needed from the medical supplies that were already there. I struggled as I adjusted to the heat of the afternoons when I organized the supplies and made the medicines. I was so glad for all the rest time on my trip out.

Dorothy had carried on by doing what she could, but she was really assigned to look after the school and develop classes for the women. That hadn't left much time for medical tasks. Now we were able to do more for the Africans. Monwelli had returned the previous October and worked with Dorothy. When I first arrived, he was off on a hunt. I looked forward to the time when he would be back and I'd be better able to organize the work, but I still needed more help. I prayed that I would choose the ones of God's choice for the medical work.

I cared for the woman with the ulcer for several weeks until her wound was clean. On his last medical visit before furlough, Dr. Reitsma performed her skin graft in our operating room under a mat shelter. The woman had difficulty understanding why we made another wound on her leg in order to heal her arm. Happily, the graft was a success, and in the end she was a satisfied patient.

What a joy to use my new microscope. The Daily Vacation Bible School (DVBS) of my home church back in Hatfield had collected offerings to help pay for it. The first Sunday I worshiped in Katire Ayom was the end of their Bible School. I was happy to share that a DVBS in the United States had helped so I could have a microscope to help them. I didn't have my freight, but I did have my microscope.

Because I lived in a one room mud house with a cement floor and grass ceiling, I didn't unpack much. I ate with the Beattys one week and the Olsens the next. Medical work was carried out under a tree beside the house. To provide more shade, we put up poles with papyrus (grass) mats on top. A foundation had been dug out for the dispensary, but the bricks they had made were not strong, so some plans changed. We didn't want to build if it wouldn't be good.

Waiting to be seen

By the end of March, I was putting up a temporary place on the lot for my permanent home. I would live in there until more could be built, then it would become the cookhouse/storeroom/laundry. It was nothing elaborate, but it was my work and my home and I loved it.

It was discouraging to plan and never see those plans materialize, whether from lack of workmen, permits from the government, the right clay for brick, or time to haul materials. The men with cars and trucks worked as fast as they could—hauling bricks, lumber, sand, and stone. Most think of missionary pastors as preaching and giving out the Word, but there are many different ways to minister.

How time flew. The Lord gave many hearts to reach for Him through the dispensary work, and I wanted to be used of Him in the great task He had given me. I needed the prayers of others. I felt unworthy of the many responsibilities He had given me in the care of both Africans and fellow missionaries. Medical numbers were often up over 100. Some folks were very sick, some came with minor things, but all needed help. So many

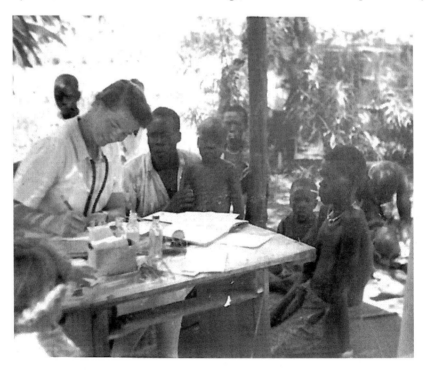

Madam Daktar Rawn

needed our Savior, and I wanted to be the vessel usable in His hands in the way He desired.

I had a variety of cases—from a strangulated hernia to a child with a white blood count of 25,100 (normal range is 4,500–11,000). The little one had been at home for five and a half weeks with an untreated leg infection. Several folks came in with injuries requiring sutures, and once I had a man who took his out the next day because it hurt! In June, a man turned up who had cut his toe quite badly while hoeing in his garden (so easy to do when one is barefoot in the garden). I sutured it so the cut bone could heal. I could go on and on telling of all the ways the Lord enabled me to help people.

Being a 'doctor', twenty-four hours on call, I never knew when a case would summon me; I just had to go. I had to take care of it. One Sunday in June, I saw nine patients who came for medicine. On Sunday we always tried to finish before Sunday school. At 9 a.m. I gave the Bible lesson which was the story of Ruth (*Lusi*, in Acholi), and Dan Olsen spoke in the morning service. As I got back to my room, I found a sick child had arrived needing help. Then the call came for lunch. After that, another child I had asked to return showed up. Finally at 1:30, I thought the afternoon was my own to read my Bible, study, get a short nap, and try to write some letters. But it was not to be. At 3 p.m., folks were at my door bringing in a new patient. After he was taken care of, I returned to my reading. At 4:15, I left my room for a cold drink and found two more patients, supposedly just gotten sick during the day. By that time, I had lost all the zeal I had to write letters.

Patient brought in on a bicycle. The father wears the dress of a government worker.

Surprise! Dallas Green came in for supper and brought the mail, so after that I could read instead of write. (Always pleasant to receive letters on a day you're not expecting them.) The next thing I knew, supper was announced. As we all sat at supper, I said, "Looks like a patient coming in on the back of that bicycle." Sure enough, about the time I finished eating, they called me. This woman had lost her baby and took quite a bit of care. By then, the folks had finished our usual Sunday night song and worship time. A typical day.

I needed the prayers of His people for wisdom in each and every day. That July, Matayo, one of Dan Olsen's helpers, began convulsing and had a terrific pain in his chest. People thought he was dying, but the Lord enabled us to care for him and he recovered. A maternity case arrived—completely worn out! They had walked her for three days and nights trying to make the baby come. Thankfully, after she got some rest, her delivery turned out to be very normal. A man with a broken elbow never returned after I suggested he go to the doctor in Torit. From time to time, folks just didn't listen and I had to let them take their chosen course of life.

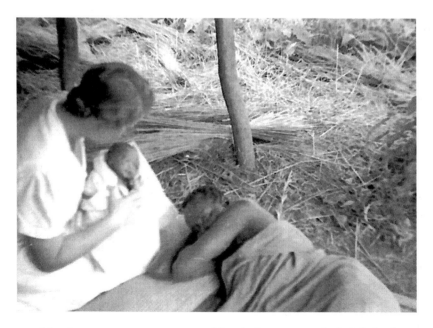

No place to stay so woman and her baby went to the brick shed

One Monday I awoke early with the cries from a nearby village. The cries were the cries of death. Oh, the wailing from those without hope! I remembered the child of the evening before who had seemed to be growing worse in spite of all the medicine. The Words of Jesus came to me from John 11:25, "I am the resurrection and the life. He who believes in Me, though he may die, he shall live." I thought upon them anew and prayed for those people, but the Lord seemed to say, "Not enough, get up and go over to them with these words." I obeyed and went to the village just after 6 a.m. Oh, the hopeless cry of those without Christ.

By August, Martha, who had the gift for learning new languages, began studying Arabic in Khartoum. Arabic had always been spoken in the north, but because of the Sudanese independence, it was becoming increasingly important in the south. The government set forth a timeline requiring that schools, including mission schools, teach Arabic to all the students.

On August 18, hostilities broke out between southern Sudan (African) and northern Sudan (Arab). The conflict came close to us when the postmaster, officials, and some merchants in Torit were killed. The following day, all mission women and children evacuated Sudan until we could see the extent of the fighting. For a month, we stayed in the school dormitories of our Rethy Station in the Congo and filled in wherever needed. I became a cook instead of a nurse. We were safe; however, many Sudanese died in that conflict.

On September 16, we began the journey back to Sudan. I traveled with the Olsens and Barbara Battye on another typical African trip. Driving through Uganda after a heavy rain the night before, we left our name written many places as we slipped around and nearly went off the road. We put the chains on for part of the trip even though that always ate up a lot of gas. It helped and we never did get stuck; however, at one point we heard a loud noise. After stopping to check it out, we found the exhaust pipe hanging down. An African happened by with some rope, and his rope along with some coat hangers fixed it right up. The man was such a great help and we were thankful.

I was glad to be home again after that trip. Barbara planned to stay with me until the Greens (now stationed at Logotok) came and they all could go on together. The Langfords and Beattys waited in Rethy until the children started school in order to avoid traveling home only to turn right around to take the children back. While they were waiting, an illness hit Dorothy which delayed their return even longer.

During the hostilities, the government in Sudan had confiscated our transmitters for security purposes (as they always do in times like those). We missed them for we had no connection with the folks in Torit or Logotok. I would have no way to get extra medicine for patients or to talk to Dr. Doug when he returned from furlough. I hoped we would get the radios back soon.

Home again! Sleeping in my own bed and back into my work. If I didn't think about the time I was away or look at the things still in storage, I'm afraid I wouldn't have thought about the conflict at all. Things were quiet and only now and again would someone mention something about being scared. But we were safe and happy to be back.

Betty had returned from furlough shortly before the troubles. We shared the small house until our bigger four-room homes could be built. It needed repairs and Dan Olsen worked hard to get everything fixed. He put up the chimney and finished the walls. The whitewash we had put on the walls before the evacuation wasn't good, probably because the walls weren't dry when it was applied. Our new gas refrigerator had been unpacked the day before we had to leave, and we praised the Lord that no damage had come to it or to anything else on the station—nothing had been destroyed. We unpacked and set up the house. Of course, in addition to arranging our home, I had to find all the items for the dispensary. Medical work had been closed while I was gone, except for the minor things the men could do. Monwelli's brothers stopped by to check if I had returned, so I knew he would be on the job soon. I was glad for a day or two to set up before patients returned saying they heard I was back.

About a week later on September 21, we had a busy day at the dispensary, then all my plans changed and 5 p.m. found me packing my suitcases again. Dallas Green came in asking for help for his wife who had gotten sick on their way back to Sudan. I left my work in the hands of Monwelli and traveled to Opari to find both Winnie and her baby sick. Praise the Lord, He strengthened both mother and baby. I returned to Katire Ayom five days later and picked up the next day right where I had left off.

In the midst of all this, I thought of home and I remembered that my older brother Edward had just turned thirty-seven, meaning I was getting up there in years as well. I didn't feel that old. But when I was back in the States, I found that I didn't fit in quite the same place as before. The younger folks had grown up and I was reminded of my age. My birthday was a busy day caring for fifty-five patients, having a big birthday dinner with the station folks, and finishing work on the house. The next day, Betty and I cooked in our own home and hung up our old curtains from the Egg (they fit just right). The refrigerator worked fine, and what a pleasure to have a place to keep foods from spoiling. Small, compact, and cozy—our home.

We thought everything was settling back to routine, then on the last day of September, Bill Beatty became ill. I cared for him along with all the work for the African patients, and at first it didn't seem like anything but to be a few days of sickness and all would be well again. Then he started having great pains and a progressing paralysis moving up his limbs. I didn't know what it was—polio? malaria? Feeling helpless and fearing it would reach his diaphragm and kill him, I sent word to Mr. Langford to come with his station wagon to carry my patient to a doctor. Just the day before, Dorothy had told me she was pregnant, and I prayed for the Lord to sustain her. At nearly midnight, Dorothy and I settled Bill on a mattress in the back, and with Jen Langford at the wheel, we began our 500–mile journey to Dr. Becker. Sid Langford followed in Bill's truck with the containers of gas. At the time we were not to know the trip would end up taking a full twelve hours longer than usual.

The first trouble began with heavy rains which made a shorter route impassable. Next, we found that the Nile River had risen so high that the car had difficulty driving onto the ferry. Passengers didn't stay in the car to go aboard, so we took off our shoes and waded into the Nile to board. Traveling was slow because roads were slippery, and at one place we found some sticks in the way indicating a bridge was out. As we turned to go back the thirty miles to get around it, we were told there was a short cut. Don't listen to words of a shortcut is my advice. We drove almost to the end, and what did we see there but something just like a swamp. We found ourselves stuck in the mud. Next, a fire ignited in the pickup. The car had to travel on alone while Sid stayed to fix the truck. Later that night, driving on an unfamiliar road, we feared we were lost. Jen drove most of the way. I tried to give her a break, but I was so tired myself that I didn't feel safe behind the wheel. We couldn't understand the reason for all the delays, but we did feel the presence of the Lord with us every minute of the trip. After thirty-five hours on the road, we finally saw the sign for Oicha and rejoiced. After all the tests were completed, Bill was diagnosed with a case of cerebral malaria. For the next ten days, he was in constant pain from neuritis; however, we were at the hospital with Dr. Becker in charge and we praised the Lord.

I returned to Sudan on November 16. The Beattys were not leaving Oicha as yet, but God had answered our prayers. Within those three weeks, Bill improved considerably. Although his nerves still had to reestablish themselves, he was able to walk well and didn't tire so easily. He could move his left hand and arm, but the right still needed to be helped or it just fell. With support, he could feed himself. The doctor was very encouraged that Bill would recover more function but couldn't say how soon that might happen. The pain was nothing to speak of anymore and nights were better. We hoped they could be back in Sudan by Christmas even if full use of his arm hadn't completely returned. It was hard to leave them there, but I knew the medical work had gone on long enough with only my helpers filling in. Betty's letters told of many hard things to deal with while I was gone.

I headed out to the Bogoro station for the first hop of the journey home then met up with the Olsens in Rethy for the remainder of the trip. Going back to Sudan, I trusted that if the Lord had taken me away from my work at Katire Ayom, I had no reason to be anxious. I could just leave it all in His hands. He gave me His wonderful peace.

With all the sickness in our midst, it seemed as though the missionaries were a special target of the enemy. We always had malaria, but it hadn't been striking us as much as it was during this time. Those back in Sudan had surely been tested in the days I was gone. One of the Greens' children had been sick the day we left with Bill. Winnie also became ill but recovered. Just when they were well enough to travel to Logotok, Barbara got sick with malaria. Once she recovered and they were back, malaria struck Dallas. Once he was up, Winnie got sick again. She was so ill that they took her out to see the doctor in Torit. They had arrived only to find the new Russian Swiss Doctor in Torit was away, so they had to travel on to Aba station to one of our mission doctors there. We heard she was improving, but they had to stay in Aba for a while.

Two of their children remained in Sudan with Barbara and Betty looking after them.

As I thought back on the events of the previous three months, I could only look up and say "He doeth all things well" and rest in His promise that one day we would know the reason for all this testing. My heart cried out to Him to use me anew each day as He saw best. The grace the Savior gave, I can tell you, was just wonderful.

So, November gave way to December. Our post office in Torit re-opened for the first time since the troubles in August. I thought the mail finally seemed to be caught up (unless someone I didn't know about had written). All our mail had been going to Juba and they didn't sort it out for us because it was too much. I had such a stack of *Gospel Herald* magazines. I didn't know how I would ever catch up.

My home church denomination was considering changing its name, and I sent my ballot back even though I knew it was too late. I wrote to Brother Seifert (the current pastor) that I was never really hindered in any way because of the name, but I would stand by whatever the conference felt was best. I prayed the Lord would lead as it was so important in those days of unrest and division. Out here on the foreign

Post Office in Torit

field, we saw how much we needed unity for the cause of Christ, especially because we were working with governments that upheld a different religion. Unless we were walking in one accord to win souls, we were here in vain. I felt the devil was trying in every way to distract our thoughts from the real thing so we would not have the strength for the Lord as we should.

The medical work moved forward and I took on more helpers. Since I had returned from the Oicha trip, my record number of patients in one day was ninety-three. We had some very sick ones. At this point, building was stalled and I only had one hut for patients. There was another hut I wanted to fix up to store medicines, but since I had so many needing a place to stay, I delayed that plan and used the hut for patients instead of medicine. I hoped to have some more buildings by mid-January and move the medical supplies out of my room. But out here, you never knew when something would hold you up, so me, I wasn't counting too hard! All the small trucks were wearing out and could only carry a little at a time, so Mr. Olsen hired a big truck just to haul all the stone, sand, poles, and bricks for the houses.

I thought again how this year had been a time when Sudan seemed to be a special target of the enemy. Surrounded by that difficult time of war, the people of South Sudan lived day to day, not knowing just what the future held for them. I prayed this would be a time of throwing themselves into His hands and not turning to the ways of the enemy for relief from the strain of the moment. I prayed it would be a time of building for the Church of Christ. I prayed for the Africans and for ourselves to know Him and the power of His might.

Gong home. Shell hanging in front is put over the baby for shade.

1956

*And when he brings out his own sheep, he goes before
them. (John 10:4a)*

Life settled into routine. Dry season passed and it hadn't been too bad. The temperatures had soared high in the nineties then broke into cooler weather which made everything easier to bear. The Africans said it was cold, but I enjoyed it. Finally the rains started and the flying ants arrived. Fry them up and they have a good nutty taste. Almost every year, someone came to the dispensary with diarrhea from eating too many.

Of course, we always had bugs around. The way bugs of all sizes dove in and out around my light and flew into my typewriter, I wondered that more were not stuck to my letters home. Once I was typing and felt something on my leg. I tried to chase it but didn't actually glance down. When I finally looked—it was a huge beetle bug at least three to four inches long. So it goes.

After a year at Katire Ayom, our medical work was still in the open air. Every step of the dispensary construction had been delayed. Yet I praised the Lord that we could daily give the word of God with freedom.

So far in the year I had four active TB cases, six leprosy patients, and a child with a fractured femur who was just starting to get around. I had only four maternity cases (by now only the difficult ones came in). Most of the folks sought treatment for malaria pneumonia, wounds, or, of course, the worms. Bill continued to improve but had not fully recovered the use of his arm.

Petero--learning to walk again with his stick

Ricky Beatty was born on March 28.

Once toward the end of May, a maternity case arrived. I didn't think it would take long, but the hours wore on and darkness came, followed by a heavy downpour. I took a quilt and fixed a place on the cement floor next to the woman to get some rest if not sleep. By morning things had not progressed, and I asked Mr. Olsen if he'd like a trip to Torit. We arranged that if nothing happened by 9 a.m., we'd take her in to the doctor. However, by 8 a.m., things started moving. When they first came in, I had suspected that the baby was dead and upon delivery that proved to be true. Thankfully, we had a living, though very tired, mother.

That May was not all sadness. Excitement and delight spread through the station when our records arrived from the Gospel Recordings. The previous year, some of their workers had recorded native speakers telling the gospel stories. Now we had the records in hand, and what a thrill to play them for the people and see their reactions. To hear a voice come out of a box is something, but when it is a voice of one's own language — that is really something! Everyone quickly gathered around to see and hear this new thing.

We did not have the Acholi recordings yet, but did have some in

Dispensary

Arabic and Madi, the language of the neighboring tribe. For all the years I had been in Africa, when those who did not understand Acholi came in for medicine, I had not been able to tell them about God. But now I played the records for them, and they could hear in their own language.

That first morning, I took the Victrola and the records down to the dispensary and played a few for the Bible and scripture lesson. Later, as we ended our day, the people were still around, talking about this box. One badly burned older fellow, who had been under treatment since Christmas time, stopped by to tell me that he was going back to his village as his arm was better. I talked to him about the Lord some more and then realized that he had understood the Madi records. I told him to wait just a little bit longer and I'd play some more for him. Another older Acholi man, who was also leaving at the same time, decided to stay and listen to the recordings again. I asked if he understood Madi and he said, "No, but I want to hear it anyway." I started the records and what a thrill to see those two men standing together with one translating from Madi into Acholi for the other. I didn't see the men again for they were from further away, but what a joy to know that they had really heard the Word of God and understood it.

Listening to the records

About mid-August, the Reitsma family was with the Beattys at Opari for the weekend. (By this time, the Greens were home on furlough, the Reitsmas were back at Logotok, and the Beattys were assigned to Opari.) Dr. Reitsma had to go out and visit several other stations, so Kim and the children, Susie, Jessie, and baby Charlie, waited at Opari for his return and then they would all head back together. Since we were only twenty miles away, the Olsens and I planned to spend part of Sunday with them.

First thing that morning, we had some rain that just took the dryness off the surface of the road, but Dan Olsen didn't think it would be a problem. Even without rain, the road to Opari was rough because of the many holes and elevations along the way, and the men who often traveled that way had landmarks to know where the bad places were. Because of the rain, one of the first bad spots gave us quite a little slide into the grass. Suddenly we were traveling sideways, then we straightened out again and continued on our way. We had a few more wet areas, but no real problem. After stopping for a service using the Victrola and records, the three of us arrived at Opari just in time for them to add a little water to the dinner. We shared the meal followed by an afternoon of visiting. Then we decided to stay for supper and a service as well.

About the time we should have left to get home in the light, an unexpected rain came from nowhere. And did it rain! Damage done. We found the road quite wet. Halfway home the rain began again. We stopped to put on the chains, and how thankful we were, for soon after that we stalled in the mud. We managed to move again without getting out and pushing. Mud sure is different than snow. For the snow you shovel until you hit the bottom, but with the mud you just don't find a good bottom very quickly. Sometimes we filled up the holes with big sticks.

The last six miles into Katire Ayom was a side road and not much had ever been done to it. The grass was high on either side and sometimes you just drove where you knew a road was supposed to be. Almost home and in one of the last bad spots (but not the one of the morning), we really did some sliding around. First, we went to the right and hit a stump in someone's garden and that sent us off to the left into the high grass heading for another even larger stump. Just missing that, we came back into the roadway again, and once on solid ground Dan Olsen got out to check the damage. A few extra dents, but not bad at all for the slipping and sliding. We praised the Lord and traveled safely the rest of the way home. At least we didn't get stuck and have to sleep on the road.

The very next week, I was called back to care for Kim. She was quite miserable and glad to see me when I arrived. On top of being ill herself, she was so concerned that maybe Dr. Doug was sick because he was four days later than expected. She didn't know where he might be. I found malaria in her slide, but the pains continued so that she couldn't get out of bed for any length of time. Finally, the rash came to diagnose dengue fever. She had just recovered from an illness before the baby came, so we were happy when she began improving again. As far as Dr. Doug, rainy season bad roads and several tough cases on the other stations had delayed his return.

Bill Beatty was the one to drive me back to Opari and that was a triumph for him. Doctor had used the truck and left his own little British car with the Beattys. The little car was easier to steer, and with the wheel on the right side and the gears on the left, Bill could shift with his good arm. He came out for me with two African teachers, but no one else to drive. Even though the reason for the trip was not a good one, for Bill—it was wonderful!

Because I had stayed with Kim for nine days, I came back to quite a pileup of work. My two helpers had carried on well while I was gone in spite of my neglecting to put out a few things in my hurry to leave. Once I was back, I worked to get caught up on all the tasks waiting for me. The month ended with 1,674 visits.

The need for medicine was always upon me. I had brought some back with me from the USA, but I quickly used up my supplies of sulfa, penicillin, and worm medicine. Khartoum had good prices, and I often bought from there to cut off the customs and freight costs of things ordered from the States.

Christmas approached, and I received the first of several boxes from the United States. Folks at my home church of Bethany in Hatfield had Christmas in September that year and packed up many things to send out in time for the holiday.

This past year had been a time of great testing and attack by the enemy. We looked to the Lord to guide our steps in the New Year.

1957

Be strong and of good courage. (Joshua 1:18b)

Martha Hughell, Mary Heyward, Jewell Olson, Olive

Dan and Jean Olsen, Olive, Betty Wilson

As the New Year began, I went on vacation and spent eight days of fellowship at our conference in Congo. Truly we sat at the Master's feet and enjoyed a blessed time together.

After my vacation, it seemed as if there might be quite a curtailment in the medical work due to new government restrictions. By this time, I had four huts for the folks who were either really sick or had traveled a distance. Now those in power declared I could not have anyone stay as an inpatient. I could no longer care for the truly ill. I didn't know what these restrictions might mean for the future of my work. I upheld the government of this new independence in prayer that the work of the Lord not be hindered. I prayed that, whatever the reason He allowed this, I would be ready to do His will.

Because I couldn't encourage larger numbers in the dispensary, I had more time for other things I had let slip. I applied myself to language study. Oh yes, I spoke the language, but not right. People were polite and tried to understand when I mixed things up in some terrible way. I could make my extra time profitable. As it turned out, my work was curbed for only a short period before the Lord overruled and we were able to go on as before.

By this time, we had more families working in Sudan. Donald and Ruth Fonseca were with the Beattys at Opari. Richard and Pauline Crossman worked on the wells, and Harold and Jane Amstutz took over for the Langfords in Torit.

That March, Betty had an extended illness and was out of the country. Since my medical work was curtailed at the time, I was available and

Reitsmas: Doug, Kim, Lily, Susan, Jessie, Charlie

helped Jean Olsen with the two weeks of Daily Vacation Bible School. We averaged about forty-three children each day. I hadn't been in such work before, but Jean knew what to do. She had the supplies and the ideas, so we had a good school.

The next week, Jean and I set off at 8 a.m. on our bicycles to visit some of the villages at the very end of the area with people. We crossed six river beds and rode about eleven miles in two and a half hours. The five workmen who carried the beds and food set up a nice little camp for us. We traveled out from there to hold meetings in three different villages a day, talking with people, telling the stories of Jesus, and singing songs with the accordion. We prayed the Lord would continue to cause the Word to work in their hearts through the power of the Holy Spirit. Such work was needed so badly. This was our first time out, and we saw some things that we would change for the next time (such as visiting fewer villages each day). Our workmen were good guides and took care of us on the path. I had been fearful that I'd be too tired and stiff with all the riding, but you know I asked the Lord for help and I marveled at how He answered.

Beattys: Ricky, Dorothy, Bill
Barbie, David, Barry

At the end of March, I was called back to Opari. Bill, Dorothy, Barbie, and David Beatty were all fighting malaria. Everyone recovered except Dorothy who came down with bacillary dysentery. After she regained her strength, I stayed long enough to celebrate Ricky's first birthday, even though I had some tough cases waiting back at Katire Ayom. Bill and Harold were off to a meeting in Juba, and Bill told me I could take his truck when I was ready to leave.

By the time Betty was well again, things had changed and I was back full time in the medical work but continued to assist with Sunday school and the girls Bible club. I felt grateful for Monwelli's help in the dispensary during this time.

I could go on and on to tell of all those times the Lord enabled us to help. Many had multiple problems. A sixteen–year–old boy was carried in unconscious with malarial meningitis. We had been to his hut when we were out on our trip to the villages. Praise the Lord, within twenty-four hours, he knew where he was and began improving. He was also very anemic and I found hookworm and bilharzia, so he had to drink medicine and get the twenty needles. On top of all that, he had a sprained wrist. Many times, the lack of sanitation out here caused the worms and a weakened condition, giving good ground for other diseases to develop.

The Beattys visited Katire Ayom one Friday early in May. Ricky was sort of hot and fussy, and Dorothy gave him medicine for malaria when they returned to Opari. He didn't seem sick on Sunday when we visited for the day, and he slept well that night. When he woke up on Monday, he refused his milk and his temperature soared to 102.6°. Dorothy gave him more medicine, but the high fever continued all day and by late afternoon he began vomiting. They decided that after supper they would bring him in to me. But, at 6 p.m., he went into convulsions and didn't gain consciousness. Then he began twitching on his right side. When he didn't come out of it, Dick Crossman (who was in Opari working on the well) and Don Fonseca came speeding out for me while Pauline, a nurse, stayed with the baby. We usually counted on an hour for the trip, but they made it in a half hour. I gathered medicines, and Jean and Betty fixed my suitcase. Another half hour back and we pulled into Opari by 8 p.m. When I entered the room and glanced around, my first sight was of all the African helpers on their knees praying. Oh, how I needed the Lord. The people had such confidence in me, and I had to trust minute by minute.

I was very concerned because Ricky didn't look good to me. As time went on, Dorothy confided, "I could have taken it if he had gone quickly, but now I find it harder and harder."

We got him into their big bed and I stayed with him. Dorothy got in bed with Barbara and then Bill went in with David for a little much needed sleep. Ricky just kept up the twitching and his high temperature continued. Near 2 a.m., his breathing began sounding awful. By 3 a.m. the twitching stopped and he closed his eyes and went into a sleep. I felt we needed more help, and, since we had only a receiving radio, I sent the men to Torit to the sending radio to call Dr. Doug. Bill wondered if they should take Ricky to Oicha, but I didn't want to move him. I suggested they get in on the Congo Broadcast and ask Oicha to stand by and get Dr. Becker to the radio. They headed to Torit and we prayed the Amstutzes would be there to give them access to the radio. They found Jane at home, and we could hear on our radio what Doctor said to the folks talking in Torit. So before the men came back with the sending radio, we knew the doctor's orders.

All day Tuesday, Ricky was restless and didn't seem to recognize anyone. He was agitated and continued with a high fever. By Wednesday we had a slight encouragement as he showed some signs of coming out of his fog, though he slept and had to be woken up for feeding. By Thursday he gave a slight smile and began to recognize people, and on Friday we saw a real change as he held his little car in his left hand. Saturday, he laughed and cooed and was much stronger, except for his right arm and leg. When I tried to get him to move, he shot me a look as if to say "You really mean I shall try?" His lack of movement was hard on Bill because of all he had gone through, but Ricky had no pain and Dr. Becker felt the movement would return.

The Lord surely prepared Bill and Dorothy ahead of time. Our Sunday evening lesson was on God's will, and Monday's *Daily Light* read, "Thou hath afflicted me but not unto death," and yet Dorothy confided that evening that she couldn't quite claim that death would not be in it.

We all finally relaxed a little on Saturday evening while David and Barbie went in the tub for their bath. Suddenly, David screamed and screamed! After they found the scorpion that bit him, we quickly treated David. Praise the Lord he soon stopped crying and we all had a good night's sleep.

I stayed at Opari until Bill and Dorothy seemed at ease in caring for Ricky. I rode back to Katire Ayom with Dr. Doug and tried to get settled back into the work again. Having left the medical helpers in such a hurry, I found a joy in seeing Monwelli strengthened by leaning on the

Lord for help. The next day, we had 117 in the morning and another two in the evening. I tried to get caught up on all the orders and paperwork, but it was hard.

Bill went to Rethy to bring Barry back from the school term. Ricky continued to improve. When Barry returned to school after vacation, the Beattys met up with Dr. Becker who gave them a good report concerning Ricky.

When the Olsens sold their truck in preparation for their furlough at the end of July, we had no transportation in Katire Ayom. For the time, we depended on the other stations. Gerry and Anny Rineer were back from language study in Khartoum and though assigned to Opari, they stopped in at Katire Ayom from time to time. Eventually they would move on to Logotok.

The government wanted independence in everything, and I didn't know how soon they would start pushing to take over the medical work again. The

Rineers: Gerry, Anny, Rusty, Ricky, Donnie

Lord had given us the time so far, and we prayed that while the door was open we might be able to claim much for our Lord for what He wanted to do in the hearts of the people. The government meant to be in charge, but since they didn't have the staff for the dispensaries, they wanted us. But I'm afraid they didn't want all of our ways. Our charging fees seemed to be a problem to them, but that's what enabled us to have medicine on hand to treat the people. Folks were finding, on the whole, that the government places ran out of medicine quickly.

The government wanted the schools in the hands of the Africans, but hadn't yet completely taken over there either. They didn't have enough teachers. Moyi's wife Yunia was working to pass her teacher's test and we were excited that a teacher who loved the Lord might go into the work of schooling.

Around the beginning of June, we caught rumor of a different kind of change. I found I might have to move. Bill and Dorothy brought the news when they came back from Congo, which had been hard hit for nurses. Many there were on furlough or ready to go on much needed furloughs. Since we had four nurses in Sudan, we could help. Bill talked to Harold Amstutz, who checked with the field council. I received word to transfer to Oicha for a few months since I had worked there when I first came to Africa. Of course, that would mean someone had to take over my work at Katire Ayom.

Change can be difficult. Doug didn't want Martha coming down because she was so essential for the language work up there. Then we thought perhaps the Beattys could come back to Katire Ayom with Dorothy overseeing the medical work and Pauline Crossman as the nurse on call for more difficult cases like maternity. The Beattys would have liked that, but they had a work going in Opari. By the end of June, matters settled down and it was decided that Pauline would come to Katire Ayom and look after the medical work until she and Dick left Sudan. She didn't have the language, but I felt it would be fine. It was the Lord's work, not mine. My heart strings pulled both ways—Katire Ayom and Oicha too.

In spite of all this shuffling of workers, Bill went up to Torit and then out to the Kapoeta area with Harold Amstutz to see the prospects for a new work up there. We certainly needed more workers in Africa if we were to fill all the places that seemed open to us.

Around this time, we had lots of baby news. At the end of June, I received the announcement of the arrival of my brother Ray and Evelyn's new baby girl to make a family of three children. In Sudan, Pauline Crossman was expecting. Kim Reitsma was due in mid-August. With the Rineers' and Beattys' children, we had a regular baby boom out here. There were so many children that we drew names for Christmas presents.

The Greens were home in the USA and not planning to come back because of all their sickness during the time they were in Africa. We then got word that Uncle John and Aunt Mabel would not be coming back either. The doctor in the USA didn't outright refuse Uncle John to come back but said if he did he would have to cut back. Knowing that wouldn't happen, they decided to retire. So from afar, they divided their belongings in Sudan. Betty, already caring for Nippy (the Buyses' cat), kept it. It didn't seem right to just get rid of it. She also planned to take the Olsens' cat when they left on furlough. Aunt Mabel gave me the organ as a gift, and various ones bought the rest of the furniture.

One Saturday night in July, I experienced a first. I went to get two bricks to use in the dispensary and never thought to look. Monwelli saw it on the brick and tried to warn me, but I had my thoughts elsewhere and I didn't hear him. Just as I began to realize what he said, I felt the sting. A scorpion! Needless to say, the bricks fell quickly. I held my finger tight and Monwelli cut it and put a tight tie around it. Then I squeezed the blood out and we put potassium permanganate on like we did for snake bites. I finished my medical duties with it throbbing, but not so bad that I couldn't stand it. The swelling didn't go up my arm and the pain turned to numbness; I was grateful it wasn't worse.

Creatures hid in many places. Betty had quite a few scorpions coming into her new brick home. We thought perhaps all the piles of rocks and bricks made good hiding places close to the house. She found four in one week and even one on the rug! Once, a few months earlier, we heard a bird on Betty's roof chirping strangely. When we went out to investigate, what did we find? A snake near the nest. Jean Olsen took care of it.

Before my trip to Oicha, I spent a great deal of time getting things in order—cleaning the storeroom, straightening my house, and writing down information to help

Jean Olsen shoots the snake on the roof

Pauline when she came. The Olsens left August 2 for furlough, and Pauline took over their house with Moyi helping her. Originally I thought we would have about ten days to get her into the work, but, as ever, the plans changed and she only arrived the evening before I left.

Because it was the end of the school term, I could ride with Bill through Uganda and to Rethy when he went to pick up his children. While we were there, a telegram came to tell us that another missionary, Cleo Mann, had gone home with the Lord due to cerebral malaria. I had taken care of his wife Marge eight years before when their son was born. Now the boy, at Rethy, had to be told about his father. I kept thinking about how two years earlier we nearly had to give the same message about Bill.

By mid-August I was in Oicha. I shadowed Vera Theissen one day before she left for furlough, and then I was on my own—supervising instead of doing. Dr.Becker wrote the orders and I saw that they were carried out. Supervising others proved to be a very different kind of work than doing the manual tasks myself.

I planned to stay with Jewell, but at first I lived in Vera's house, keeping a new missionary company. Dr. Wilcke, his wife, Wanda, and their children were joining the Oicha team. Their house would be next to Jewell's and was very nice with a hot water system and the first indoor toilet on the station, but at the time was still under construction. While Dr. Wilcke completed coursework in Kinshasa to qualify to practice in Congo, Wanda and the children came on ahead. Because she was a little concerned about staying alone in a new place, I lived in Vera's house with her and the children—three-year-old Karen who was adorable and five–month–old Keith. Wanda feared she might disturb me when she gave Keith his middle–of–the–night bottle. I told her not to worry because I would probably disturb her when folks called "hodi" at my window to summon me to the hospital in the middle of the night.

My time was filled to overflowing. On a typical day, I tried to get up at 5:30 in order to meet with the African women medical workers for prayer before we began the day. (Doctor met with the men.) We went on rounds at 7:45, then off to breakfast and prayer with the missionaries. By 9, I'd be back to patients. Dr. Becker operated on Tuesday, Thursday, and Friday afternoons and usually had at least four to five cases each of those days. There was always a long waiting list. On Friday nights, all the missionaries gathered for prayer meeting.

Oicha had wards for children, women, men, maternity. On Wednesday afternoons, I ran a mothers' clinic with as many as 103 at one session. We even had a dietician on staff. Some of the mental cases needed extra looking after so they didn't wander off or get into mischief. I never had to wonder about what to do next.

I wasn't sure when I could go back to Sudan. My visa was good until November 11, and we thought someone was coming out soon, but everything was uncertain. I continued on daily knowing the Lord would lead as was best.

I didn't have many letters from Sudan but did find out that Anny Rineer was expecting. Kim delivered her son Jonathan with only six hours of labor. The Fonsecas took Nippy the cat on probation. She slept in Aunt Mabel's chair and didn't seem to mind when the children came in. She even let Barbie and David pet her—that was a changed cat! I received a letter from the Olsens back in the States telling me they had adopted a baby girl named Karen. Jean had longed for a baby but never did get pregnant in spite of visiting several doctors. I was so happy for them.

Pauline Crossman also wrote to me with some disturbing news. Moyi wasn't showing up for evening work at times. I could only keep praying for guidance as to what to do about him in the future.

I heard good news from Dorothy while they were on vacation. Even though Ricky wasn't walking yet, Bill had made a new progress. One day he stood at the mirror shaving with his right hand and not supporting the elbow with his left arm as he usually did. She was thrilled.

Barbara Battye continued enjoying her time in Khartoum, studying the Arabic language. She was the one to learn new languages. I struggled at times with languages and thought it a wonderful thing that some people delight in language study.

My work continued at Oicha, and once our number was 1,700 for the day, not counting the hospital patients or the leprosy patients. So many flocked in, and we were continuously busy. By mid-November, my time there was nearing the end. I didn't know how I felt about leaving. I had become part of the work, yet I knew I wasn't staying. With Moyi gone and not knowing what was waiting for me when I went back, I felt discouraged. I thought time might be short for any of us in all places, and we needed to take every opportunity to spread the gospel. I longed to see more of the African Christians take an outright stand. Praise the Lord for those who were faithful.

Although anxious about what was before me, I had a good trip back to Sudan. I was glad the Lord was going ahead and I didn't need to fear. I heard on the radio that the Amstutzes would be at Opari with Betty, so I wondered if she had stayed there after Pauline Crossman left Katire Ayom at the end of October. Did the Africans carry on the work or close it? I was welcomed home at the Nile River Steamer by the Beattys, the Fonsecas, Betty, and the Amstutzes. The helpers had carried on the medical work. Another happy surprise awaited me when I found that more phonographs had arrived for our Gospel records (even though customs charged fifty percent).

I settled in back at Katire Ayom and had to get used to some things again. My home was infested with ants eating just about everything in the roof. I had some of the school boys helping me until I could see who would take Moyi's place. We now had a radio that picked up some broadcast stations, and I could listen to Billy Graham. I also learned that field council had assigned Dorothy and Bill to move back to Katire Ayom in February of the new year. Medical numbers were light and I visited Yunia (Moyi's wife) who was staying with her father, Andreya the Pastor. Apparently, Moyi had planned to talk to me about coming back but went to Uganda instead. She was expecting and had been having a cough with some other problems for quite some time; on examination, I found TB.

Shortly after I returned, the Reitsmas drove in and I met little Johnny for the first time. They had had a crisis at Logotok the previous week when Lily got away from the girl who looked after her. Kim heard her cough and wondered why she was in the house. When she went to look, she saw Lily put down the tin can that held kerosene. Doug had filled a lamp and there wasn't much left in the can, but she had swallowed some and was breathing badly. They washed her stomach right away and she vomited. By the time of their visit to Katire Ayom, you'd never have known anything had happened.

I had been spoiled by the regular mail day at Oicha and had to get used to irregularity again. Once I received a box from home I felt concern when I saw how thin mother looked in one of the pictures. I urged her to have a checkup. Sometimes it was difficult to be such a distance away from family and depend on mail with at least a two-week delay.

Bill was around when I opened one of my boxes. He thought it was the first term Epsom salts situation all over again, but no, this time it was the water softener broken and scattered throughout the box. Mother always sent a good supply of canned meats and toys. I also received three boxes from my home church, Bethany, but I left those to open on Christmas Day. While I worked on wrapping presents, I brought up the phonograph and enjoyed playing Christmas records. I didn't do that often as it took so much time to wind it up and change the records. I also made a tape so those at home could hear my voice. Just something different than a letter. Of course, lots of other voices were on the tape from the children wandering in and out.

I ended the year feeling the joy of being in His place of service day by day and seeing His hand working in the Salvation of souls and the mending of physical bodies. I prayed to meet each open door with a new sense of His Presence and Power.

1958

Blessed are all those who put their trust in Him.
(Psalms 2:12b)

January began with our missionary conference held in Arua, Uganda. The Sudan and Uganda fields had grown so much that we had our own conference instead of joining with Congo.

We headed out at 5:45 a.m. only to find the Reitsmas broken down at Opari. A quick dividing up of possessions and people and we continued on our way with one less car. We enjoyed very good sessions on the theme of "Lessons from the Early Church." During the conference, we received news from the Adi station of the death of four-and-a-half-year–old Raymond Steen. He hadn't been well all week, but it didn't seem like anything too bad. Suddenly, he became weak and within eight minutes, he was gone. We heard his parents were standing up well. Out here, burial took place so quickly that there really wasn't time to think about it.

Back home again, we continued with challenging cases, but the big challenges were not always in medical work. One of my days began at 5 a.m. when I was awakened to the sound of a wild cat making off with a chicken. I suddenly remembered I had forgotten to shut the door of the chicken house. We recovered one body, but that cat had gotten away with two others. I didn't want to eat the one we found, but my helpers didn't mind at all and enjoyed it very much. The cat came back at 7 p.m., and we had to hunt for the chickens it scared away. These wild cats were so brazen; it sure was one way to quickly lose chickens.

During that same day, folks came and told me the well was broken. I knew Bill would be sick about it when he heard because it had broken about this same time the year before. Some children had held their hands on the spout and then they couldn't get the water to come up. We had told folks to keep the children away from the well, but to no avail. Then in that same day I was called to the village to care for a very sick child.

Bill started coming by every day with loads of their belongings for the move and began setting up their house. One day Dorothy came along, and I prepared lunch because Willison, my new cook, was ill. I had a Christmas box lunch—everything supplied by gifts from home. I opened cans of chicken and fried it up (was it ever good!) and had mashed potatoes from boxes of instant. When I pulled out the fruit cake, Dorothy said, "Oh, you shouldn't."

Bill quickly responded, "So she says, but hurry because she really wants it."

All these things sent from home sure made cooking easy. One morning I had a pancake breakfast for seven of us using pancake mix sent from the USA. Then the Rineers came by, and I had a second sitting for five more. My mother liked sending things for others as well as myself. She sent diapers for Kim to use for the baby and dolls and toys for the children.

By the end of January, the well was repaired, the Beattys had moved into their house, and Betty was due back any day.

Yunia came in one Friday thinking she was having her baby, but it was false labor. The next Monday night, I had just finished taking care of a child and they came saying Yunia was finally getting somewhere, but no—not yet. She was so disappointed and tired of the false labor that she

117

seemed to be overcome with fear instead of trusting—even when I said the baby was fine and the heart good. Her mother was no help at all and thought the baby was dead and that Yunia would die as well, and she wanted to take her home. That talk went on and on. So I made a bed on the floor and stayed because I didn't know what would happen with the mother in such a state. By 5 a.m., we had a living baby boy. I had just sent the mother and sister to go make tea for Yunia and did they ever come flying back when they heard him cry. All the fear was gone and they were rejoicing. The next day, I took time to talk to them about their witness and why they had let fear come in their heart. Yunia immediately named the baby Martin Jima and didn't wait the normal four days. (I secretly thought it too bad Yunia didn't have a girl because she had told me she would name a girl after my mother.)

On February 16, I had a quick trip to Torit when I got word that Jane Amstutz needed help. Bill and Harold had gone to Malakal, and we knew she was alone and sick with malaria. She had been to the doctor in Torit who gave her medicine but hadn't told her it was a sulfa drug, which she couldn't take. She became so sick and didn't know what to do. She sent word to us and a telegram to Harold asking him to return as soon as possible. About an hour after we arrived, we heard the Missionary Aviation Fellowship (MAF) plane coming in with Harold and Bill. They had rushed back not knowing what might have happened. Poor Jane was upset at having caused so much trouble, but we took it that all things work together for good to those who love the Lord. Dorothy had driven me to Torit, so Bill decided to cut his trip with Harold short and travel back to Katire Ayom with us. He looked forward to a little extra time with the family.

I reported home in my letter of February 22 that Bill was improving and doing more things every day. Ricky was walking and doing fine. He fell a lot, but he would get right up and keep going. Jane was well again (according to her report on the radio). We praised the Lord for His keeping.

Three days later, we experienced, in a profound way, the presence and strength and guidance that the Lord gives to us in everything.

Monday was a usual day as far as I remember. I was working through my normal evening routine when Dorothy called and asked me to get a slide on Ricky as his temperature was 101°. I did that and got back to my letters. By 8:40 p.m., the call came that he was in convulsions. I ran and saw what was what, then came back for some medicine which I kept in my room. The convulsions worsened with his whole body twitching. I finally took Bill's car down to the dispensary to get some more things, and on the way back I called to Betty to let her know what was happening. By 10:30 p.m., he quieted down with his eyes opened but not recognizing anyone. His temperature climbed to 104.4° and by midnight he began convulsing again, worse than before. By 2 a.m. his temperature rose to 106.8° and I didn't know how he could go on living in such a state. At first, I was very upset, wishing I could do something more for him, but the Lord gave peace in caring for him. After vomiting at 2:30 a.m., he still didn't appear to recognize anyone, but he reached his hand out, seeming to seek something to hold. For the rest of the night, someone always held his little hand. He settled down until about 4:00 a.m. when his restlessness increased and his breathing became more labored. By 6 a.m., his breathing became quite difficult, and I could see he was nearing the end. Soon after this, Barbie woke up and came and held his hand for a little while.

At 6:40 a.m., February 25, Ricky went to be with Jesus. Bill had said good night to him a short time before he died, and I had added as a truth and as a comfort, "We'll see you in the morning."

While Dorothy and I stayed and began preparations for burial, Bill, Barbie, and Betty Wilson headed for Torit to send a message to Rethy to tell David and Barry. Bill also sent a telegram home and reported the death to the government, asking them for permission to

Richard Beatty

March 28, 1956 - February 25, 1958

bury Ricky in the cemetery we had started at Katire Ayom for the Africans.

Bill had planned to leave the night before to send out messages of Ricky's illness, but he was so nervously upset that he was too weak to travel at that time. Looking back, we saw that it was the Lord who kept him close; had he left earlier, he wouldn't have known of Ricky's death. The Amstutzes were out of town with the MAF people, and Mr. Marino, the Italian man in the government services, went down to the army plane to call the Kapoeta port to try to locate them. The Amstutzes were about to take off for another stop, but came right back instead. Bill and the others left Torit at 2 p.m. with Mr. Marino. The Amstutzes thought it was Bill's father who had died, meaning they would have to bring the message to Bill. But when they arrived in Torit at 3 p.m., they found out it was Ricky. By 5 p.m., they, along with the MAF pilot Betty Green and the engineer Mr. King met up with us at Katire Ayom.

While Bill, Betty, and Barbie were gone, Dorothy and I got on with the work to be done. When our African workers began arriving, they were shocked because Ricky had been okay the evening before and by the time they came back in the morning, he was with Jesus. The word got around quickly and everyone came and stood around the house with tears, but in silence, to sympathize. I caught folks as they came and asked that there be no wailing, and everyone was so good. The wives of our two evangelists and two other Christian women came and sat with Dorothy while I went to the cemetery to make arrangements with the workmen.

We began the task of preparing the body. Dorothy felt she would like to use a trunk rather than making another box, and we found one big enough. She got one of his blankets with a satin edge for the bottom cover and some blue dimity with pink ribbon fixed at the edges for the top. As Bill was leaving for Torit, Dorothy asked how to dress him, and Bill said that he didn't know, just whatever she thought. She decided to put pajamas on him and use a pillow and crib cover I had given him. She said he was sleeping and Barbie would understand better. At first, I wanted to rebel against the idea but kept quiet, and I was glad I did, because it turned out to be just the right thing for him.

Barbie had taken it quite hard because she couldn't understand what it was all about. He had been fine before she went to bed. She had asked question upon question on the trip to Torit with Bill and Betty. When she came in to see him after he was all fixed up in the casket, she looked up at Dorothy and said, "Mamie, he's smiling!" And that's exactly how he looked.

Harold and Andreya, the African pastor from Opari, took charge of the service. Mr. King and Mr. Marino were the pall bearers. Mr. Marino just loved that little fellow, and we felt he was seeking the truth about what we believe. Barbie didn't like the idea of leaving Ricky there in the grave, but she did get over it. We spent the rest of that evening looking through photos with Ricky in them.

In spite of having been up the whole night before, Dorothy and Bill didn't go to sleep right away but talked about Ricky and of things Dorothy never thought she'd be able to talk about so quickly. The Lord enabled them to trust everything to His will.

We were sorry Dr. Doug wasn't there to help, but even if someone had gone for him right away, he couldn't have arrived in time. He was due for the monthly visit the very next day. Many times in the past, he seemed to be around just when I had the most difficult cases. I didn't know why it worked out differently this time. The Lord knew all about that too.

Doug and the family had been sick again, and Kim had not been planning to bring the family down for the scheduled visit. But when they got word the morning of Ricky's home going, she decided to come anyway. She knew Dorothy would have been there for her if needed.

By mid-March, the Beattys were back from Rethy after a visit with David and Barry. They ended up staying longer than planned when David started with malaria, then Barbie got sick as well. The Beckers and Jewell were at Rethy for the monthly visit at the same time, so they all had a nice chance to talk together.

Mrs. Becker responded to the medical notes and a letter I had sent to them. She wrote:

> Your letter was so much appreciated and we do thank
> you so much for taking time to write to us in detail about
> Ricky. The darling little fellow is at home with the Lord,
> free from any handicaps which might have been his if he
> had tarried here. As the news came to us over the radio,
> we sorrowed with you each one. As we thought of

Beattys, Doctor said, "They have paid a great price for their missionary service." As I thought of that I remembered Bishop Taylor Smith's words, "The Lord will be no man's debtor. If he asks from you much, He will repay even more abundantly." I am sure He has much that is good in store for Beattys. It may be a consciousness of His presence, His preciousness, His peace such as they have not known before. These things are more precious than those we buy with silver and gold. Our hearts ached for you as we thought of the responsibility that was yours. But your letter tells us the Lord gave the grace sufficient which He has promised and I am sure you are feeling richer too for the experience. May the Lord abundantly bless you each one is our prayer.

Dorothy and Bill received many cards and letters, and Dorothy worked hard to answer each of them. Some of the things Barbie came out with caused me to write my mother asking what we talked about as young children when my sister died. Barbie wondered what Ricky was doing on his birthday and whether the angels made a cake for him. She didn't cry that much but mentioned him often. Dorothy and Bill thought of him often as well. Many times Dorothy caught herself thinking it was time for Ricky to do this or that, and just when she would be about to mention it, she'd remember.

Sickness continued to follow us in March and several of my helpers were ill. Dick Crossman, out digging a well for a government contract, somehow broke his leg and was flown by MAF to Nairobi, Kenya, near where his wife Pauline was staying.

For the whole of 1957 I had delivered only six babies. This year, I was already up to my fifth—a woman who had lost many babies and arrived in labor at least a month early. I hoped the premature baby would be old enough to keep alive without too much trouble. I went to get Ana, the African girl I planned to have help with maternity, and by the time I had her awake and we walked back, things were moving. I thought the baby was here, but no, not quite yet—it was breech. Happily, we were able to safely deliver the five–pound baby and trusted for the future.

The men continued trips back and forth among the stations. Field council considered moving Betty to the girls' school work in Kapoeta once a new couple, the Stranskes, settled there. Even though Hank Senff had a kiln of bricks made, building for that station had moved slowly. Apparently, the Taposa men were not the working type of people. They liked to sit under the trees and talk; however, the well there was operating with a windmill to keep them in water and irrigate the garden. Hank called it The Garden Spot of the World.

Our rainy season started, and we had the annual catching of the flying ants.

Drying the ant harvest—buckets to carry, baskets to winnow

Betty's move never did work out. At the beginning of April, she had to fly down to Nairobi, Kenya due to illness. We had exhausted every one of our tests and Dr. Doug advised her to go. I had hoped she would be back by Easter, a couple of weeks later, but she didn't return until the beginning of August. Dorothy continued the girls' school program in her absence.

We missed our April medical visit from Dr. Doug because Anny Rineer seemed likely to have her baby early. Her 10 lb. 4 oz. boy was born on May 3.

The Epps, from Congo, stopped by our station. The oldest boy, Peter, was in tenth grade, and before he went back to the States in August to continue his schooling, he wanted to hunt for buffalo. He did get one, and we enjoyed the meat. His younger brother Timmy and Barry Beatty were both in fourth grade at Rethy. Barry was at the dispensary when they first arrived and next thing I knew, he dashed outside calling, "Clumsy." I looked and there was Timmy Epp. What names they gave each other at school. David's nickname was "Jaundiced Pig." Dorothy hated it but I thought it was fun to see the boys so excited. Barry showed Tim around the dispensary. Then when he went for a needle for a blood slide, Tim woke up to what was happening and ran! Next, the bike riding started. Dorothy told me that after they left me, the first place they went was to the spot where Ricky was buried. David came back so thrilled to report that there was a pink flower growing on the grave.

In May, Barbara and Martha had a car accident in Juba; thankfully, no one was hurt. I had a bit of a vacation when I traveled with Barbara to get the car fixed. It all ended up taking longer than I expected, but it was a good trip. We stayed at Bogoro, and it took me back to nine years earlier when I first came to Africa and stayed at that station. How things had changed in terms of buildings and vehicles. After we got Barbara's car, I went all the way back to Logotok, then back down to Katire Ayom with Dr. Doug when he went for the monthly visit. After three weeks away, I was glad to be back into the work.

I noticed many changes in Logotok. I hadn't been there in four and a half years, and I now saw brick buildings everywhere. Doug had just finished wiring his house, and we had nice light for two evenings. Then something went wrong with the generator engine, and they couldn't use it. Such things happened all the time. The Rineers' little boy was so sweet. The medical work at Logotok was different as well. Of course, the married women had children to look after and the tribe was different too, so everyone to his own way.

At the end of June, I was right back at Logotok. Barbie had been sick with malaria again and did not seem to recover as usual. Bill was just getting over malaria and feeling weak with severe stomach pains. I thought that perhaps if Barbie hadn't been ill he may have felt better himself—but no one wanted to take any chances. So, the four of us set off for Dr. Doug. Bill and Barbie both improved, but in the end, the Beattys decided to head for furlough that summer instead of the next. Bill never seemed to be able to get on top of his illness, and with Barbie sick so often, Dr. Doug thought getting out of the malaria climate would help. So it went through all the channels, and the field office agreed. We had to figure out how to cover all the work before they left. But we trusted the Lord to work all things out—for He who goes before never does things wrong.

While we were at Logotok, Barbara Battye's parents arrived from the States to visit with her. We spent a lovely time together, and they sure had some stories to take home with them. They were to fly in from Khartoum to Juba on a Friday but didn't have their papers for the district. Barb had them in Juba. So, after wiring back and forth to straighten it out, they booked a seat on the Monday plane. By that time Mr. Battye was holding tight to his papers for fear the officials wouldn't let them out of the country—he even had a dream about it. Because of the heat, they slept on the porches in Khartoum. Mr. Battye kept getting up to go turn out the light only to realize it was the full moon shining! Mrs. Battye thought she saw two Arab men standing and watching them from the street and finally in the morning discovered it was the pillars on a house. During their time at Logotok, Barbara had her girls for school so her parents could see what it was like. One of the girls very calmly told her there was a snake in the roof right over her head, and it took a small battle before they managed to kill it. The Africans also killed a leopard that came onto the mission station. The Battyes had quite a good view of their daughter's life in Africa.

Back from Logotok, Dorothy got malaria almost right away. Then a few days later, Barbie had it again and a day or so after that, Bill came down for a slide. I also had it, but not as bad as the others. Everyone regained their health once again.

Betty returned to Katire Ayom on August 6, and the Beattys left for furlough the next day. The kids were so excited to fly by plane through Europe and then to home. Before they went, Bill brought his radio and charger down for me to use while they were gone, and I cranked it up just to be sure I knew what to do. Betty and I were the only two missionaries to carry on the work at Katire Ayom until someone else arrived. There could be so many small things to annoy, and I prayed we might have harmony in the work to praise and magnify His name. For the time being, I would look after the workmen and the things that needed to be done on the station, and Betty would look after the work of the church.

The dispensary hadn't been busy in August and I was glad. Because we had so much rain, the mosquitos were terrible and we had to keep swatting at them. Folks probably thought we were very happy in our work with all the clapping going on in trying to catch them. We marked the birth of triplets: Posey, the cat, had her babies on top of the mosquito net in the Beattys' house, and I never knew a cat to make so much fuss to show her kittens. She ran after me and cried and cried. Once we found the kittens—no more crying.

By mid-September, medical work picked up and we had at least 100 a day for several weeks. Monwelli had to do the cards one day when my other medical helper, Nicodemo, was off. The villagers started talking awful about Monwelli, saying he didn't put the cards in the right order. But when there are so many, they all want to be first and get home. He didn't talk back to them. He was a good and steady worker and I praised the Lord for him.

I enjoyed the radio. I couldn't listen long each night, for the battery ran down quickly. Also, I couldn't do bookwork and listen at the same time. I tuned in to Billy Graham and the news. Sometimes it was hard to hear, but at least I could know if something big happened in the world. Don shared his *Time* magazines as he finished them, so I could also read what was happening. These were surely difficult days. News came from the

Olive, Erasto, Monwelli, Nicodemo

BBC (British Broadcasting Company) for several days about the schools in Little Rock, and when the *Time* magazine came, I read the details.

I began to see more and more the way little things could come in and hinder the work of the Lord and the joy the Lord would give. For myself, I found I could so quickly become jealous of what another was doing or not doing, and I had to ask the Lord to help me. My work had enough to keep me busy, and I was responsible to Him for that—not what anyone else did. I was beginning to learn this a little, to appreciate the good in others and pray for them and let the Lord deal with anything else. We lived a close life out here and had to remember that the Lord gave to each as He saw best. If another seemed to have more, we could praise the Lord for that. The Lord supplied my needs in a wonderful way and I praised him. He saw that my needs were met and a lot of extra things too.

Pauline Crossman and the children came to stay with us at Katire Ayom while Dick went to finish a government commissioned well. As September ended, we had 2,456 visits to the dispensary compared to 1,536 in the month before. That sure made a difference in the amount of medicine we used.

November saw some changes with the helpers at my house. I had to ask Willison to leave for stealing. Onesimo, who had been with me two years earlier, was in the area again and came back to work. Patients came in to the dispensary at a busy pace (up to 100 a day), and I began getting new poles to fix up the dispensary huts.

At the end of November all my plans came to a halt and my heart was heavy when I heard the news that medical work must close. Harold received the word that only the Government Medical Services could dispense medicine in Sudan. I didn't know what would happen to the poor people who needed help. They seemed to take things in their stride and shrugged their shoulders and said, "What will we do? Get sick and die and nothing to do." The government wanted charge of the work but they didn't have medicine enough to go around. Someone said that in Juba you could get medicine if you had the money. The Lord knew all about it, and if it was to awaken His own to their responsibility to Him or what, I didn't know. We had always known our days here might be short, but I hadn't actually expected it to be this short.

We still hoped things might change, but for the time, with no medical duties, I caught up on letters and then began visiting villages. We were in

Doors closed; patients must leave

the dry season and I could walk right through the rivers—no water, only rocks. I went to larger villages further out and held services, often riding my bicycle instead of walking in order to save my knee which had been bothering me. In one nearby village, fifty children and thirty adults gathered around and I shared the Word. I saw sick people in the villages, but didn't feel I could give them any medicine.

One day I was down at Monwelli's hut because their one child was sick. I smelled the beer flour there and in Erasto's hut as well. The wives told me it was to get money to buy clothing, and my heart was heavy. Even the Christian husbands were not caring for their families as they should, yet where was any evidence of the women trusting the Lord? Were they doing it because their husbands were away, or was everyone in on making alcohol and hiding it from us all? I prayed for the people who wanted to have the way of the world in their lives and yet still say they were Christians. These were a needy people. I tried to help those who didn't have a lot, but I wondered how much I actually helped them.

By the end of December, several things were settled for our field. The

Olsens would come to Katire Ayom when they returned from furlough. Harold Amstutz told us the Reitsmas would leave Sudan. He was a doctor and wanted to do medical work. When the governor met with them in Khartoum, he would not agree to let any of us continue. The order was no mission medical work. Doug had until January 5 to leave the province so as to not cause embarrassment to the government. The Reitsmas left for Uganda until the Field Director could get something worked out for them. I would continue doing village work then go on my planned February vacation—to Rethy with the Rineers and maybe on to Oicha too.

After Christmas, I packed and locked up all the medical things. Nothing was easy. I had several different people come in for medicine and I had to say no. Sometimes they tried to come back more than once to see if I changed my mind. Once I found someone had tried to break into the place where I stored the medical things.

I didn't know what the future would be for me, and I kept turning things over in my mind. If people pressed the government, maybe I would be an embarrassment too. Then I'd have to leave. They said we were free to do religious work but no mission medical work. So much remained uncertain—not dangerous as far as I could tell—yet I was more alert to the fact that this was not my home. I was just traveling through to the Better Home Above, and I could not set my heart down here.

On one trip to pack up the dispensary, Olive, bicycle, and a tree came together. I had turned my head to look at someone, and when I looked back—too late. I went flying and ended up bruised and stiff, but no real harm to my body. I was sorry I couldn't say the same about the bike. Erasto worked on it a day or so and did manage to straighten out most of the bent parts.

As the year ended, I stood in prayer for the Lord's will. If He had a work for me in the villages, I would do as He led and be patient in seeing His hand in my life that souls be saved.

1959

And we know that all things work together for good to
those who love God, to those who are called according to
His purpose. (Romans 8:28)

With the help of Dick Crossman, I hauled the medicines and supplies to the storeroom behind my own room. We cleaned and repacked the dispensary storeroom with the tables, shelves, and boxes of old bottles. With all these things stowed in the windowless hut, the dispensary itself was empty, and I hoped everything would be safe. And so it went; medical work was completely closed.

I decided to put off the vacation I had planned for February. With Jean Olsen coming back I thought we could have Daily Vacation Bible School, and that would take some preparation. I also knew that once the rains started, crossing rivers to visit villages would be a challenge. I didn't want to take a full month away when the way was presently opened to get to the people. It seemed like the time was short.

One morning while I was eating breakfast, a man came to me and said his wife was having trouble delivering her baby. I went to the village and saw she needed help, so I went back to my storeroom, opened two drums and got some things out that had been previously sterilized. She delivered normally, but I knew the baby couldn't have lived if things had gone on too much longer. As it was, I had to work to get him to breathe. The older women wanted to say he was gone, but I told them, "You keep quiet and let me work." What joy when he finally gasped for air. I watched as his lips turned red and he began to breathe regularly. The poor mother was tired and stiff because apparently, they had beat her to try and make her have the baby. But in the end, we had a living baby and mother.

I trusted I hadn't done anything to spoil our giving forth of the Word of God. It would have been silly to take her on a two–hour ride in the back of a truck to a Torit hospital when in just over an hour I had helped her deliver. I prayed for wisdom because I could see that these sorts of decisions would arise again. I didn't want to go ahead of what would be called an emergency, or at least what the government would consider out of bounds for me.

The Olsens and Booths arrived in the middle of January by the steamer. For a time, the Booths stayed down at Katire Ayom until they were sure of the Riwoto permits, and we were back to six adults and two children on the station.

By the end of January, I came down with a bad case of the flu and visits to the villages ended. I recovered but was so weak I stayed in bed for over a week. Even a month later, I still needed to take it easy and limit my activity. With so much time to think, I prayed about whether I should seek an African to help with the village work. I had Monwelli in mind. I felt I had failed God when those who had been with me for so long were not going ahead faster in their Christian walk. But I trusted to go forward with the Lord and not weep over the past. I trusted Him to work in these hearts.

While on bedrest, I was called for a woman in labor who had been having pains for five or six days. I told them I couldn't go and guess what? They showed up on my doorstep. I couldn't find anything wrong, but I tried to change the position of the baby. Then, I told them they should go. They weren't thinking that way. All of a sudden, the baby came—right there in my bedroom! The dozen or so people finally departed for home with baby and mama (walking), and I had the best night's sleep since I had become ill. I suppose I was no worse for the wear and they were a happy group. The life of a nurse.

Dan Olsen set up a little light plant on the station, and I had an electric light in my bedroom every evening. Now it was also easier to charge batteries, so I listened to the radio each evening as well. One Saturday before the men were planning to be away on a trip, Dan fired up the big engine (the little one wasn't working). He wanted all the batteries charged up before he left, and I wasn't up to par in strength to start the big engine. By that evening, we yet again had cause to praise the Lord for His protecting hand upon us.

I turned on the radio about 7 p.m. to see if I could find my favorite station. Then I saw a flash of lightning and turned it right off again. I sat in my chair by the desk reading, my batteries still connected to the charger on the other side. Suddenly, there was an explosion and my light went out. Everything felt strange. I don't know how to describe it. I sat there, afraid to reach for my flashlight. I listened for the other folks and heard the engine still running. Someone screamed, and Dan yelled, "It's Jean!"

The Evangelist heard the cry and came running. I grabbed my flashlight and ran, and we saw Jean flat on the floor, face down. I quickly checked her pulse which was good, and she could talk although she felt funny. Apparently, the lightning hit the aerial coming down to their house at the back door just as she passed through. The current seemed to have hit her right elbow and threw her to the ground. We got her into bed, wrapped up in a blanket for her chills. Baby Karen had slept through it all. Jean almost made Dan go wake her up to be sure she was okay but decided to let her sleep instead. The next morning, in the daylight, we could see the singed hair around Jean's elbow, and it had turned all black and blue. When the women came to see Jean, they seemed surprised to see her alive.

The Booths lost their hearing for a bit from the explosion. Our electricity was completely knocked out, causing Betty's plug and charger to burn into the socket. My light bulb and the glass on the charger burst, and the cement floor was chipped in several places. No lasting damage. We gave the Lord all the praise.

At the beginning of March, Jean, baby Karen, Betty and I went to the Pajok area for a week of Daily Vacation Bible School. Jean and Karen slept in their tent, and Betty and I in the church there, which wasn't a finished building yet. The grass roof was only partly completed, so we either had sunshine or rain coming in. It wasn't bad; we just moved around until we found a dry spot. Not much privacy either, because the walls were just sticks with open places between. They did build a toilet for us. No roof, but a shelter without having to walk a mile away (no tall grass in the open plains). These were a friendly people and we averaged sixty-eight a day in our meetings. Some came asking for medicine and I had to say no. Andreya the Pastor was also there and baptized six people at the end of the week.

We found out that Doug and Kim were heading for the USA sometime around the middle of March. It was hard for a doctor to have no place for medical work, but we trusted all things would work together for His glory. I started thinking about my furlough but didn't really know what to plan.

By the end of March, the Booths settled into Riwoto, living in their tent. We heard they had picked out an area with three nice trees to fix up for their site. They changed their location when folks from the area told them that they couldn't use that site because those were worship trees and places to rest.

As Easter dawned that year, I looked at the sky and wondered what it looked like on that first Easter. What was it like on that morning to know the joy of the Lord that Christ was risen. We had a good crowd of folks at the service, and I trusted they would continue attending and not just that day for Easter.

I began preparing for my vacation. I sewed dresses and fixed up two that Jean had given me because they didn't fit her. I whitewashed the inside and outside of my house and cleaned up some things. Having moved my refrigerator to repair the wall, I decided to keep it in the new spot and change around the dining room as well. Jean was one to reposition furniture, and in just two months, she had rearranged her living room at least three different times. She told me that since she moved things to clean, why not change things up while you're at it. That was her way.

I started my vacation at Rethy. Then since I found a ride, I immediately traveled on to Oicha. How nice to be back again. It wasn't strange at all, and I felt right at home taking my noon meals with the Beckers. I walked around, looking at all the changes in the station. It had grown so much that I couldn't get around and see it all in one day. I traveled out with Margaret Clapper to see her work with the Pygmies. Observing her work gave me some ideas for lessons and objects to use when I returned to Sudan.

While I was there, some of the men took a climbing trip up the Ruwenzori Mountain. At that time, one was allowed to go up as far as the glacier. The climb took three days going up the mountain and two days coming back down. Jewell hoped to make the climb sometime before she left for furlough, but it wasn't really something I would have liked to do.

Catching a ride with some folks driving up to Rethy to take their children back to school, I finished my vacation there. We heard on the radio that Uncle John Buyse, who had been in failing health, went to be with the Lord, which was a great gain for him. Though we couldn't sorrow as those without hope—he'd just gone on ahead—we had lost a

133

faithful prayer warrior for our work.

I traveled back to Sudan with Harvey Stranske, and we had to stop in Gulu at the garage to get the tires fixed. While there, they first ruined the tube and didn't have a replacement, then eventually they found a cap to put on the tube to keep the air in. Once we were back on the road, I couldn't find my briefcase. Harvey couldn't remember seeing it, but we didn't have time to stop and go through everything again. When we arrived at Opari, we unloaded the back of the truck and still couldn't find the briefcase anywhere. At the garage, the truck hadn't been guarded, but the canvas was tied over the back. Apparently, someone was a thief. At least my passport, important papers, and money were in my purse. But I lost my Bible, Acholi New Testament, three boxes of developed color slides, my new check book, two notebooks, stamps, and letters to answer.

I immediately wrote to the police and prayed for the Lord's will to be done. If someone came to the Lord because of the Bible and New Testament, I couldn't complain. It wasn't until two months later that the police found the briefcase. Evidently, it was out in the rain at some point because the case and everything inside was ruined. I tried drying things out, but not much could be saved. I could just make out my list of addresses and a drug list, which spared me the work of redoing them, but all the other books and papers were done for.

After my vacation, I began jotting down thoughts in preparation to go into the bush to stay for a few days. The mission cleared me to go forward with the village work. I was getting some ideas and believed the Lord to be leading, but I was still uncertain. Since I was back, Benedeta, a girl who used to be in school with Betty, came and asked for work. I gave her some things to do around the house and thought maybe she would be someone to go out with me as a companion. Her parents gave permission, and I bought another bike for her to use. (It was Jean's old one that she had sold to an African and the same one Aunt Mabel had used years back.)

Thus, I began trips to villages further out. Jean, Karen, and I went out to the village of Baranaba and held eight different meetings. I led most of the lessons and Jean led singing. We also played the records several times. I went out on my own as well—sometimes with a wonderful welcome and sometimes discouraging. On occasion, only children came to the meetings. When I could cross the rivers, I went to more distant villages; if not, I visited those close by. Often I met folks I knew from my medical work. I saw one girl I had treated for burns several years earlier. Now she was a teen, and though we had thought she might end up blind, she wasn't. I praised the Lord for her sight.

While I was thrilled to see good results from contacts through my previous medical work, the more I was out amongst the villages, the heavier my burden grew for these people who had a form of godliness but no power. Then one morning I woke and read from 2 Timothy 2 and felt the Lord speak verses 24–26 just for me. "And a servant (me) of the Lord must not quarrel but be gentle to all, able to teach, patient, in humility correcting those who are in opposition, if God perhaps will grant them repentance, so that they may know the truth, and that they may come to their senses and escape the snare of the devil, having been taken captive by him to do his will." I prayed I might be truly spirit-led in everything I said and did.

I began making my travel plans for furlough. I wanted to pass through Europe and visit folks I knew there before sailing home. I learned, however, that there would be no extensions on a one–year re-entry to Sudan, so I reviewed my itinerary, trying to work it all out. By the time I left for furlough, I had abandoned the idea of sailing and flew all the way home. I also started thinking about what I might need for travel. I had my mother order some items from the Montgomery Ward catalogue and send them out to me. For a total of $12.48, I bought a skirt, two cotton blouses, a pair of slippers, and three pairs of ankle socks. Customs charges were terrible for things coming into Sudan, and when I received the package in October—I had to pay $6 in fees.

Mrs. Fonseca, Don's mother, came for a visit. She rescued my sewing machine. I hadn't known what was wrong with it, but after she worked on it and adjusted the tension, it sewed like a dream. It just needed a mama's touch!

About this time, my workers decided they wanted some of Uncle John's old dental gowns. I didn't think they would actually wear them, but they did. They fixed them up to open in the front, and I thought at least it was better than seeing the holes in the seat of their pants. I decided to give them the old medical gowns as well rather than have them rot in the barrel.

At the beginning of August, we all traveled to Arua for our conference.

Our vehicles caused the usual troubles—Barbara Battye's breaks wouldn't work some of the time, Dan Olsen's gas line gave a problem, Don Fonseca's truck didn't have the top on, and since it rained everyone traveling with him was late, cold, and wet. However, we had a blessed time at the conference. The Lord gave us heart-searching messages. Our speaker Rev. Robb was blind and spoke by reading braille. He had only been on the field about two years. I understood he had something to do with the mission before he went blind and then was put on the shelf. The Lord took him down and placed him in Africa. His message about being a vessel in the Master's hand was wonderful, and I trusted I would be able to live that out each day in my life.

The Beattys arrived back in Africa after their furlough, but they were 1,000 miles away, studying Arabic in Khartoum. Their children had flown back to school in Rethy, and the family was a bit lost with all three children away after a year of having been together all the time. I continued going out to villages, though at this time of year people were planting the last crops and beginning to harvest, so fewer stopped to listen. Any time I ventured too far off the main road the tall grass fell over onto the road making traveling difficult. Once, the people told us to go a different way because they had cleared the path in that direction. It was cut back for a little distance, but then we were right back in the tall grass again. We did find an easier river crossing that way which I suppose compensated for the grass.

About the end of September, I had to break the bad news to my mother, it was no use hiding the fact—we just had to face it together. Word came that the government would only grant me a re-entry visa for six months. The mission immediately appealed the decision. My mind started going around and around, trying to decide what to do about my furlough. If I left as planned, I'd arrive back just in time for tall grass season. If I waited until April, I could return in October, and by the time I settled in they'd be burning the grass and my work would be easier. I took it to the Lord in prayer. The very next day, I opened mail from Dorothy telling me that missionaries would be granted a one–year leave of absence if they had been in the country at least four years. Before they call, I will answer! I quickly sent a second letter to my mother. Independence was a great thing, but it brought many problems to face as well. The land needed much prayer.

Benedeta (Deta) proved to be a good companion on my safaris to the villages. She never could understand how I had so much to write in letters home. She wanted me to write in Acholi and get my mother mixed up. *En tye ka nen an koni ka en tye ka buto ping. Lok oloyo in?* (She's lying on her bed watching me. The words overcome you?) We went out for the last time right before Thanksgiving and had many hindrances. I finally found enough bicycles for my four helpers. Then one tire almost had a blowout on the way. When we arrived, Deta and I had a good dry season house to stay in, but not such a good shelter when the rain started. The roof lacked enough grass to keep the rain out and the sides were just sticks. When the wind started up in the middle of the night, folks came with some extra skins and coverings. The sack over Deta must have had bugs because she woke up in the middle of the night telling me that something was in her ears. I sprayed her and sorted out the wet things. Naturally, our morning got off to a slow start.

When I went out to these villages, I couldn't specify the kind of house I wanted. I had to take what was offered. A saying we had out here kept running through my head, "Don't need to fix the roof when the sun shines because it doesn't leak then!" I pushed on with the meetings and had a lot of children come out, but not so many adults. The Lord was good and I trusted Him for the glory in that week even with the hindrances.

After Thanksgiving, I began the monumental task of sorting through my medical things. What should I keep? What should I put in a cupboard for folks to have access to in case of need while I was away? It was a job. The Beattys' children stayed at Katire Ayom for their school break, and we took turns looking after them. I continued going out just for the day to villages close by, although it was discouraging to see alcohol so plentiful and causing so many problems in people's lives.

Sickness swept through the missionaries again. Betty was ill and I stayed two nights in her house. Martha was also ill. I had given advice over the radio, but with no improvement, she came down to see me. Don Fonseca brought his daughter Cindy in because she wasn't bouncing back from her illness. Poor kid. She didn't really want to see her Aunt Lolly because she thought there might be another needle coming.

I worried about getting my return visa in time. I wanted it in hand before I left the field. We tried to speak carefully so as to not give offense to the government or any cause for misinterpretation. I sent out the call for prayer and continued my planning. I arranged to leave Juba on January 25, and my itinerary called for flights from Juba to Khartoum, Athens, Rome, Zurich, Amsterdam, London, then finally arriving in New York on February 12. I also began working out speaking schedules, visits, and rest times for my furlough.

Deuteronomy 31:8 "And the Lord, He is the One who goes before you. He will be with you, He will not leave you nor forsake you; do not fear nor be dismayed." The Lord gave me this verse as I went back to Africa in 1955, and surely He had gone before. He was with me. He did not fail. He did not forsake. He helped me so in those times when fear was present, His presence dispelled all fear. Praise the Lord for His faithful unchanging love.

Furlough

Betty and I were both leaving for furlough about the same time. Her re-entry visa came through in the beginning of January. I received a letter from the governor stating that I could leave on my fixed date, and the question of my re-entry visa would be considered in due course. That sounded good, and I had it in writing, but I trusted I would have the actual paper before I boarded the plane. You just can't take chances in dealing with governments; I wanted the paper. I praised the Lord that I could go forward with my plans and tried to be patient in seeing his workings.

I continued packing and arranged with Anny Rineer to take the drugs, so that was another relief. We had ten children from the Sudan ready to return from vacation to school in Rethy. (Because it was a different country, Dan Olsen traveled to Juba to get the necessary papers for all the children.) A total of nineteen people stayed at Katire Ayom before heading out to Rethy for the school run. The houses were so full of beds that we ate and met together outside.

During my last lesson for the area groups, I had seventy-six children and eight adults at the station. Afterwards I gave out cookies and a bit of candy left over from Christmas. Everyone got a tract and a small paper notebook. I also paid one more visit to Yunia to supply her with the medicine she would need to care for her TB while I was gone.

By January 25, I was well on my way home. I met up with interesting people all throughout my travels. While I was in Juba, the Prince of Saudi Arabia lunched in the hotel. We ate in the same dining room (my back was to the party). I received my re-entry papers and other necessary documents in Juba, then on to Khartoum. Bill and Dorothy canceled their Thursday class to help me in town, and I needed them. When I went to get my ticket, I was told my smallpox vaccination was twenty days overdue. I had to dash out to get it when I really should have been at the airport. I found a Sudanese woman doctor who signed off, and then we rushed right back to the airport. We arrived there thinking I'd be late, but as it turned out, I still had to wait ten minutes to board the plane.

I flew from Cairo to Athens and then on to Corinth, where I met up with a friend of the Greek merchant in Juba. He found a protestant church for me and as I went to see the time of the service, I saw a sign in another window reading "Bible Society." Of course, I went in and there I found a woman named Athena. She invited me to her home and I was able to spend time there as well as tour around with her. (She was twenty years old and wore me out.) As I stood in my hotel room in Corinth, I laughed out loud and had to pinch myself. Me—little Miss Rawn—flying in planes and roaming the world.

Next, on to Rome where on a tour I noticed a family whom I thought might be missionaries. Later in the afternoon while we were all viewing steps brought from Jerusalem which were supposedly the ones Christ went up in Pilate's hall, she edged my way. Others were crawling up the steps on their knees, and she wondered if I was going to go up the steps. I answered her, "No, I'm serving the living Christ."

For some reason, a missionary can always spot another missionary. She asked my mission board and when I told her AIM, they jumped and said, "We are too!" When I told them my name, she asked, "Did you get your re-entry papers? We were praying for you in Brooklyn." As you can imagine, we hugged in excitement and chatted away (causing our fellow tourists to cast curious glances our direction). We had a grand tour and enjoyed dinner the next day before they flew on to Nairobi and I to Switzerland and the cooler weather in the shadow of the snow topped mountains.

At my next stop in Amsterdam, I visited with Anne Punt, my

roommate from Bible School, and I finally flew home and landed in New York on February 12—and so into the faster paced life of America.

I had a blessed year at home, seeing loved ones and rejoicing in the Lord together. I praised the Lord for the wonderful fellowship of my furlough and for the many times I could listen to preaching from His precious Word. I greeted a new little niece and became better acquainted with my nephew and other nieces. I gained a new sister-in-law, and what a joy to attend my youngest brother's wedding.

The Lord gave my parents and me the opportunity of visiting Mrs. Buyse in Florida. We rejoiced for the years we had had together in Sudan. We praised the Lord for those so faithful and shared the burden for those Sudanese who had fallen by the way in their Christian walk.

With fewer missionaries in those days, anyone home on furlough kept a busy schedule. I worked with some youth camps and Bible Schools in summer and also had the privilege of fellowship in many churches. I trusted it would help us all pray better, one for the other.

I received a letter from the Olsens with some clarification our medical situation in Sudan. The only objection was to an organized dispensary with set hours. If people came in one at a time, we could help them.

And so it went. My year of furlough drew to a close. I made my travel plans and said my goodbyes with confidence in this verse: "Lo, I am with you always." (Matthew 28:20)

Gathering supplies

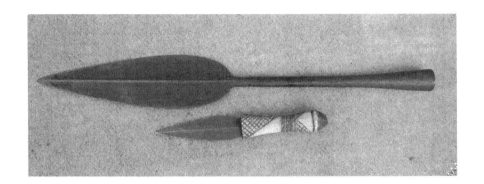

Term Three

1961-1964

1961

Lo, I am with you always. (Matthew 28:20)

Betty Wilson and I said our goodbyes to the friends seeing us off and boarded the jet plane for our flight back to Sudan via London. After a few hours in the London airport, we boarded another jet bound for Khartoum. The New York to London leg was not crowded, and I could stretch across three seats and have a nap of sorts. The London to Khartoum jet was too crowded for napping. After we landed at 3:45 a.m., we had no delay getting through immigration and customs. Once at the SIM (Sudan Interior Mission) headquarters, I slept until afternoon. Even with all that sleep, I felt slightly woozy from the twenty-four hours of plane travel. What a short time to travel so far. It took about three days until my sleeping was back in sync with the local time zone.

After a few days in Khartoum, we flew south to Juba by a smaller plane. I was at peace as I looked out the windows and searched for the Nile River winding its way below us. I praised the Lord for the confidence in Himself and could bow my head on boarding each plane knowing all was well with Him.

Harold and Jane Amstutz met us in Juba. We checked our papers, picked up supplies, and headed off to Katire Ayom. Khartoum to Juba by plane took four hours and fifteen minutes for 1000 miles. Juba to Katire Ayom by car took four hours and fifteen minutes for 120 miles. On the way, we stopped off at Opari for supper with the Fonsecas. Then it was on home to meet up with the Beattys and the Olsens then finally to sleep in my own bed.

I gradually worked my way back into station life. The Beattys and I enjoyed nice long talks. I told about my furlough, bragging up my nephew and nieces. The Beattys shared about their children's evacuation from Congo.

The UN had escorted all the children from the school in Rethy. By the last week in January, almost all the Congo missionaries had also evacuated by recommendation of the American Embassy. Oicha folks were out with the exception of Dr. and Mrs. Becker, Dr. Atkinson, and Mr. and Mrs. Uhlinger. They all chose to stay. The folks from the Congo who were ready for furlough went home. The others went to Tanganyika, Kenya, or Uganda. Even though at that moment the hotbed of rebel activity centered near Rethy and not Oicha, we felt some measure of comfort in hearing Doctor Becker's voice over the radio each day.

As the hostilities began to quiet in the Congo, missionaries slowly moved back. For at least two weeks, Dr. and Mrs. Becker, the Uhlingers, and Dr. Atkinson had carried on alone. Now four nurses as well as Margaret Clapper, Mrs. Atkinson, and the Atkinson children were back at Oicha. Doctor's voice sounded so different on the morning he reported that having these folks back was like Christmas—only better. He had carried so much responsibility while they were gone.

Oh, how Africa needed prayer. Changes were coming so fast. So many outside forces were pushing, all the while proclaiming that Africans should be left to themselves to rule.

Onesimo and Naptali came back as my helpers in the house. At first I fixed up just two rooms to live in because my old place was so poor. I intended to move into the Beattys' house when they moved back to Opari to cover for the Fonsecas' furlough. Bill and Dorothy had a larger house with a water system for the bath. I thought I might as well enjoy the convenience.

The Beattys kindly allowed me to set up my gas–powered refrigerator in their house before they left. It worked out well. I could keep my food in it and not worry about moving it later. Don Fonseca was going to sell me his small transistor radio when he left for furlough—such a pretty little radio. I slowly began going out to some of the closer villages and prayed to the Lord for guidance to give the Word simply and trust the Spirit to work.

I had been quite disappointed when I was unable to buy a new girls bike in Khartoum. I couldn't find one. There was no demand for such things as it wasn't considered "good" for Sudanese women to ride them. I had to use my old bike on trips to the villages. That was ok. It always got me to where I was going and back again.

The weather stayed fairly cool when I first arrived home. I actually put a sweater over my shoulders one evening, prompting Bill to start calling me "grandma."

I fell back into the routine. Then around the beginning of February, we experienced a thing that had never happened before in all the years I was in Africa. Bill was out to the "little house" and found a bug a bit like a bee flying around. He took off his slipper to hit it and the slipper went down! Yes, it's nice and it's necessary to have a good deep pit—but what a time. Dorothy and Bill went fishing for the slipper using a string with a stick on the end for a hook. I stood there holding the light and thought they'd never catch hold of it. Dorothy said we had to keep trying because it was such a nice slipper and Bill had never had such nice ones before. We nearly fell down laughing and had to keep wiping the tears from our eyes in order to have a clear view of our task. Finally when I had about given up all hope, the stick snagged the slipper and they so carefully lifted it up. Fortunately, it had fallen right side up which kept it clean on the whole. Dorothy did some scrubbing, and the sun did the rest. The slipper was useful once again. Bill claimed that though he knew his hand wasn't so good, the slipper had fallen down before he realized what happened.

The Fonsecas were ready to go home on furlough by mid-February, and the Beattys prepared for their move to Opari. As soon as the packing

Posey the cat and Bambi the oribi

started, Posey the cat hid out in my house. They also had a small oribi for a pet. While they were making their trips back and forth, she wandered away. I thought she was gone for sure. But to my surprise, she came back one night for her milk, and the Beattys eventually took her down to Opari.

Once the dust settled on the moving, I decided to set up my wood stove in the cook house (a separate building) and then make cookies. I began about 9 a.m. and by 1:30 p.m. the cookies were finished baking. Why so long? First, I knocked out the bricks for the chimney. That didn't take much time. We moved the stove in place then put the pipe on and ran it outside to the brick chimney. So far—so good. I thought the work was complete. No, one of the Africans said I needed to mud it in. So Naptali went for mud. Then Dan Olsen came around and told me it would hold better with some small stones mixed with the mud. Off I went with a tin can to collect stones. We all put our hands in to help fill in and mud the chimney. I finally started the fire, but soon all the smoke began billowing back into the house. I dashed in to fix the damper and my eyes teared up so I could hardly see what I was doing. Once the smoke cleared, we opened the back of the chimney again and cut off a piece of the pipe to make it fit the holes better. By this time, it was around 11:30 a.m., and I finally mixed the cookies and put Onesimo in charge of watching them. He didn't add the wood as I told him to, so the batch of cookies never finished baking until 1:30 p.m. I am happy to report that the cookies were quite good and worth the effort. I was glad to have the wood stove set up for my baking, but I planned to continue cooking on the kerosene stove in my room—too much running back and forth for the wood stove.

I enjoyed my little radio. *The Voice of America* came in, and I often listened as I wrote letters. I could keep up with news from various places in the United States, including Philadelphia, and from time to time I would stop typing and listen when something caught my ear. It was a troubled world, and a lack of unity was evident everywhere. Only the Lord Himself could bring peace to individuals who gave themselves to Him. Praise the Lord for the privilege of learning to know such a wonderful Savior.

At the end of February, fire broke out and raced through several buildings on the station. Naptali had noticed one of the old dispensary huts burning and called out for help. If he hadn't been there, the fire would have burned through all the tall grass around and destroyed even more buildings. As it was, three of the old dispensary buildings burned, but everything else was saved.

A few days later, I thought it looked like rain coming in. I was working in my house when I heard a terrific wind coming and decided I had better get the rain curtains down at the windows. The wind picked up and began kicking up all kinds of dust and dirt from the forest. I looked out the door, and all I could see was dust. I couldn't see the trees just a short distance away, and I had to keep blinking to get the dust out of my eyes. Then the downpour started and the rain began pouring into the house through a loose curtain.

When I went to fix it, I saw the nail dangling and the wood no longer wood. The ants had eaten away everything inside, and all that was left was a paper–thin shell. I fixed it temporarily by taking my thermometer off the wall and securing the curtain lower on that nail. By the time I finished, I was black with the dirt and wet with the rain that kept blowing in. Everything was just covered with grime. I had never seen a wind storm quite like that. The next day my helpers and I cleaned and cleaned. I did my best to fix up my damaged garden by mending the fence and propping up the beans and tomatoes. I picked up oranges and other fruit from the ground. By the time I finished, I was dirty all over again and glad for my bath. That was some excitement for the week.

One day Lucepu, our faithful head man at Katire Ayom, was attacked by a rhino on his way home from hunting. The man with him had tied up the abdominal wound, and they slowly walked for three hours back to the station. From the way the village acted when they got word of the attack, you would have thought Lucepu was dying. Of course, they didn't know how serious it was, and they usually got excited and scared right away. Once the news spread, a crowd gathered near my house. A good cleaning and a few sutures fixed Lucepu up, and I felt he would soon be well again. We had a song and a prayer of praise to the Lord.

I was putting my finishing touches on the Beattys' house and was almost ready to move in. The roof had been repaired. I had the cement floor patched and the walls whitewashed both inside and outside. The place was old, but because building anything new was on hold due to lack of government permits, it would do just fine. I was happy with the way all my furniture fit and it was nice to spread out and unpack a few more of my things.

Government oversight seemed to be increasing. School authorities came for inspection, and we were told that Betty could no longer have the school girls live on the station. They said the girls weren't getting enough food, but we didn't really know the true background motive. I once asked my mother to not send back my developed photos all in one lot because I was afraid the government would open the letter and cause trouble if they found so many photos of Africans. A few letters in each

Lucepu on his way to recovery

mail were opened by authorities, and we never really knew how they would take anything in writing. I was not planning to go to the annual conference either. We thought if we asked for permits for six to eight of us to leave the country, they might start wondering what was happening. Getting across any border required more red tape than ever before because of the unrest. One country didn't want the trouble of another to come to them.

Dorothy, Jean, and I had been getting together for language work. Jean had translated songs and some other things into Acholi, and we were going through it all to be sure the translation was understandable before printing. Every other week, Dorothy would come to Katire Ayom for a few days to work on it, and I was pulled in because I was there. By the beginning of April, Jean was ready to take the documents to Gulu, another Acholi area, to meet with others working on the language.

So it went. April continued and my time was full. I went out to villages, visiting with the women in their homes. From time to time people would ask for medical help, and since we had had the clarification from the authorities, I was happy to help as individual problems arose. I was called for one woman who drank some sort of insect stuff. Not too much, but enough to give her a good sore throat and those around her a scare. Apparently she and her husband had had a fight, so she drank it. They both had Christian names, but they were not reading the Word or attending church. They came back to me the next evening, and I spoke more with them about their need to return to the Lord and follow him.

Many times I recommended that folks go on for more help from one of the government dispensaries, but often they simply returned to their village. They told me that if you didn't have money, you wouldn't get good medicine anyway. I couldn't do much about that, but I just tried to be careful so I didn't do anything to spoil our opportunity to give forth the Word of Life in the land.

Hunger was also a big problem in the area. When the people were hungry, they often drank beer in place of food. Of course, it took away the thought of hunger and satisfied for a while. I prayed more folks would take a stand against the appearance of evil—something needed the world around.

Mid-May found me once again writing a belated "Happy Mother's

Day" message home. Around that time, both Martha Hughell and Barbara Battye were preparing to return from furlough. There had been trouble about the visas because of something the government had seen in their letters. Then we received word that Martha was denied her reentry to Sudan. We didn't understand, but we tried to trust the Lord anew for each step in the work. And the next step came.

At the end of May, Field Council determined that "Miss Rawn was to be temporarily assigned to Logotok to assist in the work of that station." The Rineers were heading home for furlough which would have left Barb alone as the only missionary on the station. When I first heard that Martha couldn't come back, I suspected they might try to keep that work opened because they had good African help there with the evangelists Tomaso and Metasula. I wasn't surprised when I was asked to go, but I had been rather hoping it would not come to be.

I have to admit that when I got news of the change I had to go back to my room and take the Word until I felt steady. I drew help and encouragement in reading back through the verses I had just written in a prayer letter:

"I love the Lord. I will walk before the Lord in the land of the living. " (Psalm 116:1a,
"I would have lost heart, unless I had believed that I would see the goodness of the Lord in the land of the living. Wait on the Lord; Be of good courage, and he will strengthen your heart; Wait, I say on the Lord!" (Psalm 27:13, 14)

Since it was a temporary assignment and I could live in Martha's house (which actually was quite nice), I wouldn't have to take furniture—only personal things. Even so, I had to get down to making lists and gathering all the things I would need. I would go up with Barbara when she returned to Sudan, and I wanted to be ready when she was ready. My garden was well underway, and I decided to plant the peanuts and cassava that I had already made a place for. My garden was dry, and I had to irrigate, but I hoped some things would come in before I moved to Logotok. I wanted to take food with me because they never had much success with the gardens up there.

I sure wondered what the Lord had in all of this. I trusted all would come to His glory. That was the only way I could look at it.

I prepared as well as I could. I canned fruit and looked through my stock of preserved items. I counted twenty-two quarts and eighty pints of vegetables and fruit. I also canned some buffalo meat that Dan had brought. I was not having much success with my chickens. A wild cat had gotten a few when we forgot to close up their house. The ones I had were not laying eggs well either. I started going through my medicines, deciding what to take along with me.

Before I moved to Logotok, I took one more trip down to the Beattys at Opari. There were changes on the station since I had last visited. The services were now in the Madi language, so I didn't understand much of our Sunday time together. I had fun staying in the Egg, my old home, which was now the guest house. Many of the other original buildings were in bad shape. The first house the Beattys had built back in 1951 had fallen down. The church had caved in as well so they were meeting under a tree. I walked around and noticed how tall my lime and mango trees had grown. They were so big now. Changes everywhere.

I stayed for a few days and went out with my bike to several villages in the area. I stopped in Monwelli's village. He wasn't home, but I did get to visit with his wife and children. After lunch we went on to another larger village and then to yet another. By the last village, I was walking instead of riding my bike, up the sides of hills and down through the river beds. I walked the last part of the main road to Opari and then jumped on my bike so I could ride in to the station. I just didn't want to hear Bill say I had to walk in.

By the middle of June, Barbara arrived and we were eager to get to Logotok. The Beattys came and loaded their truck with my things. I couldn't squeeze in my bicycle, bed, and washing things so they stayed behind. I could iron without washing!

My freight had arrived only the day before, and for the time it stayed in Torit. I could hardly wait to get it because I really needed more dresses. One of mine split right down the back while I was wearing it and that was the end of it.

Martha's house was great. The Amstutzes thought it was the nicest brick house built in Sudan. It had a living room, bedroom, study, bathroom, dining room, kitchen, and running water. No trouble with ants eating this house. I did find some in the kitchen, but I got the spray and quickly took care of them. A house sitting empty for ten months needs a lot of cleaning. I arranged and organized inside and began the garden outside. Most of the hundred and fifteen tomato seedlings which I had started in cans at Katire Ayom survived the move. I also planted thirty-nine hills of sweet potatoes. Barb said she never saw so many plants, but I gardened to preserve the food for later. After I cut down some overgrown bushes around the house, I felt settled in and joked that I was so comfortable I supposed it was about time to move again.

Then the language work began. I really had to apply myself because it was a terrific amount of memorization. After a few weeks, I began to hear and understand a word here or there, but most communication in those early days was by hand gestures.

We were not visiting any of the surrounding villages for services. Metasula said that we had better not. He knew it would hurt, and at first he didn't know how to tell us that the leader out there wasn't for us and hadn't been for a long time. We had to be Matthew 10:16: "Behold, I send you out as sheep in the midst of wolves. Therefore, be wise as serpents and harmless as doves." I dared not do anything like the visiting I had been doing in Katire Ayom because I feared I'd be out like Martha. I couldn't do my former work. I couldn't do my nursing work. As the Lord allowed this situation, I felt I had to be faithful in obeying—to simply sit still where I was and to make the sitting count for HIM.

My new home at Logotok

People came to our door and greeted us. We took walks and chatted with folks and helped women weed in their gardens, all very casual contacts. Folks came to Sunday services with the evangelist. We trusted the Lord to give opportunities for Himself.

At the end of July we took Barb's VW pickup for a trip to Torit. With the heavy rains, several of the bridges had collapsed or washed out, but we found our way around. At one place, people were walking through the water, so we thought it would be okay to drive through. Halfway across, we found the water getting deeper and deeper and deeper. It began splashing up as high as the windshield, but we got through without a problem. On the way home, we met Harvey Stranske (coming in from Riwoto) on the same long stretch of road. We drove through the water to him first. Compared with us, he was a careful man. We watched him measuring the depth of the water and only continuing on after taking off the fan belt to keep the engine from getting too wet. Helpers brought word back later that he had been almost through the long stretch when a bridge that was already under water gave way and he went down. Thankfully, a government truck came the other way and pulled his truck out.

We were not able to get away from the station after that first time.

My garden

Once or twice we tried but had to turn around due to the high waters. The rainy season that year was extra–long. I was grateful that Barb and I had a good relationship. She was fun. We worked well together, and things always felt like they were on an even keel.

I studied and tended my garden. With so much rain, the garden yielded well. I was glad, for it was harder to get supplies at Logotok. I picked huge tomatoes, cucumbers, lettuce, sweet potatoes, string beans, and corn. The paipais (papaya) were coming in as well as guava, pomegranates, and mulberries. Anything I could can and eat later was something I didn't have to buy. With the rains and the VW pickup not working well, we depended on others coming through the station to bring supplies with their bigger trucks. We asked that whenever folks came out to us from Torit, they bring salt, meat, flour and kerosene.

Once a native woman stopped by with some guinea fowl eggs. She had been weeding her peanut patch when all of a sudden, the bird flew up and away. She was surprised and scared but said that if she had seen it sooner she could have caught the hen just like that. I bartered with salt for the eggs and she was quite happy with her supply of salt for only having picked up some eggs. Salt was desired by the Latukos and we used it to trade for assorted items.

From time to time we heard of outbreaks of violence in various places. Just when things seemed better, the enemy got busy again. I tried to be careful in details I wrote home. Our letters were opened, and some mail from home never arrived. I wasn't sure what the government was concerned about. One worker at Rethy was in question because of something written in the mail. In spite of the troubles, even more of the Congo missionaries were heading back to their work. The radio gave us news of difficulties in the wider world as well. We heard information of the wall being built in West Berlin and of the Tunisian conflicts. Folks needed the Lord.

By the end of August, I was getting better and better at the language, and one day I realized that my house workers couldn't read. One had made a good counterfeit of it for a while. Too bad I had learned enough Latuka to catch on. I started helping them, and they were trying. I was beginning to be able to write up a lesson and have it checked by an African, then by Barb. It was hard to get the sentences correct because in Latuka the verb comes first, then the subject, and then the object. It was quite an accomplishment on the day I actually wrote one full sentence that Barb didn't change at all!

This was the year I turned forty years old. Barb prepared a special supper for me, even though no one else was around to help celebrate. Doug Reitsma and Martha Hughell were both turning forty this year as well, but they were not in Sudan anymore. I was the only one who lasted until forty at Logotok. At thirty I was at Opari, thirty-five at Katire Ayom, and forty at Logotok. I wondered where I would be at forty-five.

I still didn't have three of my barrels. I wasn't lacking in anything, but if I didn't get them soon, it would be almost a year since I had packed them. We were unable to get to Torit ourselves because of the rain and high water, but we continued to get mail and news as the men or messengers on bikes came through the station.

The Beattys had good news that they were expecting a surprise addition to their family. The baby was due about March. They didn't want to believe it was true at first and waited to tell folks at home in the States. I was happy for them.

Our Sudan missionaries who were not in country at that time needed prayer. Doug and Kim Reitsma requested, "Please pray that we'll be aware of His marching orders—if they change from stay put in the USA." There was no sign of reentry visas for the Fonsecas or the Rineers, and we were on our knees concerning these situations.

We found out that Martha would go to the station at Kuluva, Uganda and we began sorting through her things, deciding what she might want in her new placement. When she had left for furlough, she had packed as though going on vacation, not for moving, so we had a job. We planned to meet up in Gulu, Uganda with her things and prayed for her and all the changes in store for her. She would be in hospital work but still desired to get the New Testament translated into Latuka, if possible.

We made it to Torit but not all the way into Uganda. The roads were just too bad, and we also discovered that Barb didn't have an up-to-date visa for Uganda. Even traveling to Torit, we needed help several times to get unstuck. As it was, we came back with a good supply of kerosene and gasoline as well as my barrels. I found out that Congo and East Africa had flooding as well as Kenya. This was an unusually wet year in Africa.

I cleaned out the storeroom to hold Martha's things until we could get them to her, then I opened my barrels. I had to use a hacksaw on one to get through a stuck lock. Another of my barrels had been broken into, and several things were stolen. I had much to be thankful for because the mosquito net wasn't taken. They took my new flashlight and left the used one. They took jar tops, but I had enough others. My oil lamp, towels (but not the washcloths), half my candles, a dress, the wet stone and hatchet handle were all gone. They left two hammer handles, but not the hatchet handle which, of course, was the one that I needed. They really only disturbed the top, so I figured it could have been a lot worse. I thought they stole some funny items, but then again, maybe they thought those were funny things for me to have.

Barb and I went to Riwoto for Thanksgiving with the Stranskes. Because of the roads, the Beattys and Amstutzes were stuck in Juba for four weeks and couldn't join us. We had a lovely celebration even with so few. The return trip to Logotok took two hours for just thirty miles, and Barb gave me "E" for effort and a "B" for bumps. The rains continued so heavily that the children had to be flown from school to various pick-up points for vacation because no one could get through with the trucks.

By this time, I was teaching the girls two days a week. It took me quite some time to type the lessons and study them. I had to work hard to learn them well enough to present in the Latuka language. I kept praying for the teaching of the Word in the coming Christmas season.

I began preparing for Christmas in my house. I listened to Christmas songs on the radio and brought in some thorn branches for my Christmas tree. My helpers thought there was something wrong with me

My dining room with Fussy the cat and my Christmas tree

154

bringing home a thorn tree, but once I trimmed it they began to change their minds and think it pretty. I opened the organ and played, but my helpers told me, "Madam, Martha can play much better than you!" They could be so frank at times then just as easily deceive you. I never knew which way they would act.

Our Christmas services were well attended, and I had people from the village over for tea in the afternoon. Barb and I shared a Christmas dinner of roast chicken with all the trimmings. The Amstutzes stopped by with Christmas packages (with the usual high customs) from my parents and my home church. I closed the year at Logotok feeling well rested from doing only language work and housekeeping. I looked forward to how God would work in the New Year.

1962

Call to me, and I will answer you, and show you great and mighty things, which you do not know. (Jeremiah 33:3)

We were drying out, but traveling had not improved much. The radio reported that it might be weeks or months until things were back in shape. The ferry to Uganda was still unusable, and one needed a four wheel drive vehicle to get through the water-logged places. Roads were bad everywhere and the children flew in planes back to school.

Martha continued with her translation work at Kuluva and seemed happy. Barbara and I stopped teaching for a short time in order to go over Martha's translation of Ephesians and some of her other work. Metasula helped us and we completed our part of the work by the end of January.

One Friday afternoon, I was cooking and canning soup. Some children were playing and wrestling outside, and one was thrown down and broke his arm above the elbow. I went and splinted it up for his folks to get him to the hospital. In the morning they asked Barb if she would take them to the dispensary on the way to Torit. She didn't think she had enough gas to go, but she checked and decided she could make it. We agreed to take him in, and by the time we started out, two more patients came to ride along. (When word travels, it travels fast.) So, we drove an ambulance load of folks to the dispensary. Other than that trip, we stayed put on the station.

By the end of January, we had word that the Rineers and Fonsecas had received their permits to come back sometime before June. Metasula planned to go back to school soon, something he had wanted to do for quite some time. The Sudan Field Council met and decided that the Fonsecas would go to Opari and the Rineers would serve at Logotok. The Beattys would move to Riwoto to take the place of the Stranskes who were due for furlough in the summer. The Olsens were also due for furlough. The Booths were at home, and their reentry was in doubt.

So Dorothy had to pack up before the baby came, and they would move when the Fonsecas arrived back. The language at Riwoto was new and difficult, and they wanted a little overlap with the Stranskes. I had a note from Dorothy that said the Lord gave His grace for another move and they would go as He led.

Of course, all of this moving led to my question of what the future held for me. What would happen when the Olsens left Katire Ayom at the end of August? Would they close that station? I didn't know if I should move more of my things to Logotok or just wait. Barb hoped I wouldn't be transferred because we got along well and both enjoyed our conversations. She wanted company other than a couple, and I was settled and getting on with the language. The thoughts of moving again kept me awake one or two nights. Step by step.

At the beginning of February, Barb came down with malaria, and she wasn't able to shake it for quite some time. Even when the malaria seemed to be gone, she didn't regain her strength. Her eyes bothered her a lot and she had headaches. I asked her to stop her classes for the girls for a while, which she did, except for the Tuesday class for baptism. She didn't want to give up that one. I took over her Sunday school class and worked with her girls who came for sewing/Bible classes.

I still listened to my little radio and heard about John Glenn going into space as it happened. It was really something the way *Voice of America* could bring things to us in Africa just as they were happening at home. But then, if you could travel five miles a second through space and be over Africa in half an hour, we were not so far apart after all! Though I didn't remember much about it, I thought of Lindberg crossing the Atlantic by plane and now man flew into space—and it all happened in my lifetime. So many things were changing. I couldn't understand everything about this space travel, but I did know I'd travel into space when my Savior Jesus Christ would come and call me home—a safe trip and much cheaper. I wrote in my newsletter at the time, "Let us all be ready for that wonderful trip to be forever with our Savior. Remember we'll only need a one way ticket too. Yes, it is a joyful wait as we look for our Savior. Let us keep looking up and be faithful to Him for the time doesn't seem far away. "

At the end of February, the Beattys packed all their things at Opari then traveled to Uganda for the birth of their baby. Their permits had arrived just in time. Robert Edwin Beatty was born on March 6 at the Kuluva station and everyone was fine.

Barb and I hoped to surprise the Beattys there. Barb hadn't been recovering from the malaria, and we headed down so she could see the doctor as well as take some things to Martha. The Amstutzes took the trip with us, so the entire Sudan team except for the Olsens and Betty were out of the country. Barb and I rode with Jane in their vehicle, and Harold drove Barb's VW pickup so we'd have it when we were ready to return.

Bobby Beatty was so sweet. His brother Barry wrote a letter declaring, "I said it would be a boy! Can't wait to see him." Little Bobby was small but growing well. Dorothy told me that at times, both she and Bill would forget themselves and call him Ricky.

The doctor found malaria still hidden away in Barb, so she took more treatment. Because we needed more time, we wired to Juba and requested an extension for our two-week visa for Uganda. We didn't want to risk staying without permission because we feared they might refuse us entry at Nimuli. Things moved so slowly in this land. While at Kuluva, I also underwent a medical checkup and found I had somehow picked up hookworm. I guess it wasn't surprising as the Africans working for us had no treatments anymore. New drugs made the cure an easy one—just take the medicine and eat as usual, no starvation as in the old days. I was thankful.

Barb slowly recovered but still had headaches and fatigue. She worked with Martha on the translations and wanted to get some finished to take along back with us; however, it seemed every time she worked she had a physical setback. She didn't feel well, yet she was tired of lying around. We could only trust the Lord to show us the way and go step by step. He had always revealed the path even if not so far in advance.

The beginning of April found us heading back to Sudan in stages. Rising waters prompted us to leave Kuluva before traveling became too difficult. At a stop in Gulu to rest and repair the VW, we met up with the Stranskes, who were returning from a medical visit, and the Beattys, who were picking up their children for their school break. It was fun to see the children get off the plane and run to see the baby for the first time. The pilot came over and told us he had heard so much about the new baby that he wanted to see him too. The Beattys planned to stay at Opari until the children went back to school again, rather than make the move to Riwoto with so many children. Martha and I decided to stop at Katire Ayom for two weeks then, Lord willing, would head on to Logotok.

Both Barb and I picked up bacillary dysentery somewhere along the trip back and spent some time at Katire Ayom recovering. My days were filled with reading, visiting folks, and getting my Acholi and Lotuka mixed up. I questioned Harold and Bill as to whether I should take more things back to Logotok or not. Field Council acted as though they didn't want to move me, though I couldn't see them leaving Betty alone on the station when the Olsens left for furlough. The men told me that if I could use something, I should take it. Not really knowing what to do, I loaded my sewing machine, pressure cooker, and old curtains in the truck and organized the remainder of my things in the storeroom. We would be back down in the beginning of June for our Sudan conference, and if there were no changes by then, I would get more of my things. Once again, step by step.

We thought the Fonsecas and Rineers would be back by the conference. Because exit visas were so difficult to get, Harold Amstutz recommended they try to come in through Kenya and pick up their trucks from the boat before coming into Sudan. That seemed like a good idea, but we didn't know if they had shipped them in time.

We arrived back at Logotok for Easter (April 22) and found our evangelist was not there but was sick in Torit. Barb and I took the Easter services. We had Thursday prayer meeting, Good Friday service, and Easter service. I took the singing, Iromo read scripture, and Barbara gave the main message. After the scripture, I stammered through a flannel graph lesson of the women finding the empty tomb and afterward Barb asked me where I found fifty chapters in Mark—I had said fifty instead of fifteen. I also said "angel" in Acholi, but caught myself and changed it. In spite of my language difficulties, they were good services.

I was happy to be back home in Logotok. My house was in good shape, just a few extra residents. The tiny ants got a taste of being in the house and I had a time getting rid of them. When I arrived home, I found a small snake curled up under the sink, two scorpions in the sink and one lizard. The spiders had a heyday while I was away. I cleaned, started up the fridge, and used the hacksaw on a door lock because my helper lost the key. I settled back in, but I hesitated to do too much extra in case I had to move again.

I finally did it. This was the year. My mother received her Mother's Day greeting on time!

We had about thirty little folks coming out to children's meeting. One week, it had just stopped raining, and I gathered everyone in the living room. I had taken up the mats so they wouldn't get dirty from all the feet, and it was good I did because one little girl wet the floor. Many of the older children carried little tots on their backs. At times the one carrying seemed to be small enough to need some watching themselves, yet they had the care of another. They started out so young but seemed to manage.

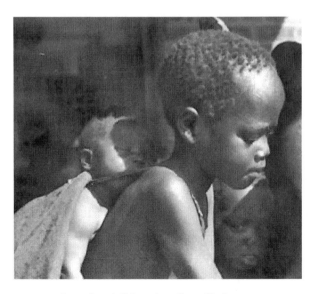

Latuko child caring for a little one

159

My young helpers Osenger and Muras continued working on their reading. Osenger finished learning all his letters. It took him about seven months because he played so much, but I was glad I stuck with him. Muras was beginning to understand what he was reading. I felt the year was not in vain if two more could read God's word. My helpers were so young; sometimes they needed extra guidance. They were just boys, but I knew if they didn't learn now, what kind of fellows would they turn out to be? I had no children of my own, but I sure felt like I did. I needed to ask the Lord for wisdom and knowledge to deal with them.

The beginning of June arrived, and we gathered at Katire Ayom for our conference. What a blessed time. Mr. Sidney Langford, the former field director of Sudan, returned to speak at the conference. It was good to have him among us again. Our theme for the four days was from Psalm 118:24. "This is the day the Lord has made; We will rejoice and be glad in it." We rejoiced that the Fonsecas and Rineers returned from furlough just in time to attend the whole conference.

The Field Council also met in Torit about this time. I was called in to answer a few questions about our situation. Harold asked me my thoughts on where I would be assigned. I told him that I didn't really know. In truth, I felt my home to be at Katire Ayom as far as the people. I was still not quite at ease in Logotok, but I wasn't unhappy either. When I felt discouraged from time to time, the Lord was always there. After due consideration, Field Council determined that I should be assigned back to Katire Ayom and begin there at the end of July. The Beattys would take me and my belongings down when they went to get the children from school.

So, the Fonsecas would oversee both Opari, where they lived, and Katire Ayom, where Betty and I would carry on the work. I could live in the Olsens' house as they would be on furlough — and what a pretty place with all the fixtures and even an inside toilet. I wasn't really sure of all my feelings at the time. The talk during the year was that I wouldn't be moved, but underneath, I had never really been sure of it. I didn't know what kind of work I'd be doing. That was the hard part. I hoped to do some visiting again, but I didn't really know. The reasoning behind the move was to avoid having the nursing personnel (Anny Rineer and me) both at the same place.

I tried to make use of the remainder of my time at Logotok. We helped the Rineers until they unpacked and settled in. It was different to cook for eight instead of one. They were happy to be back. The children had grown so much. I never did see Becky the youngest before, and Rusty the next youngest sure was a clown. The two older boys were in school. They would have a long time at home because they had finished the school year in the USA before coming out. Now they could wait until September before entering school. The Rineers hoped the way would open to get them back into school at Rethy.

Dorothy wrote to me of her precious experience when she went out to visit the cemetery at Katire Ayom. She walked there, thinking of the women and others who had been ministered to and believed, but were not in church that morning. The cemetery was full of weeds with no sign of any of the flowers they had planted. She pulled the weeds from around Ricky's stone and found a tiny living portulaca under all the grass. The further she went, the more she found—some sturdy plants, others just one little piece. The Lord spoke to her heart and showed her that a seed planted is still alive and growing, though perhaps not visible to us. Some hardy, some tiny, but alive, and when He, the Lord of the Harvest, comes to separate the wheat from the tare, we'll see the fruit and rejoice with Him.

I continued on until my time to leave Logotok. The folks there would get my garden. I didn't know what the Olsens may have put in at Katire Ayom, but I hoped there would be some tomatoes because I would have liked to can some more. I figured I could take along some seedlings that I had started. I turned my attention to packing my drums. Jerry couldn't move all my things at once, so I had to sort the most important items from the things I could do without for a time.

Barb and I finished the translations that had to be checked one more time. They were almost ready to give out, and I helped type the stencils for the duplicator machine. This meant typing slowly and carefully because of the difficulty in correcting mistakes on the special paper. I actually spelled better in another language than my own. We were also working on Corinthians, going over it for the first time with a Latuko man before it was sent back to Barbara again.

We were not having as many out to services or children's meetings because the village gardens were planted and growing. The children left for the fields at the crack of dawn and stayed until sundown, scaring the birds away from the grain fields. The birds came for the seed and again when the fields ripened. The children returned at dusk with their voices hoarse from shouting at the birds and, of course, between fields to one another. They had to work, but they had their fun in it too. They made mud balls and threw them back and forth. Guarding the fields was just part of a child's life out here and everyone had to do it. They were there if it was rainy or sunny, and some built shelters with grass roofs.

We heard on the radio of the American Supreme Court upholding the decision that it was unconstitutional to have prayers in school. I wondered what our nation was coming to. The things that I heard were going on in the White House and government places made me remember to pray that much more. I prayed that perhaps those in government might yet turn to the Lord and seek His face. I almost felt like I'd like to write to President Kennedy and tell him I was praying for him.

After the Stranskes left for furlough, their house became the Beattys' home. The larger place would hold all the children when they came home for vacation. According to Dorothy, Bobby was growing and so pleasant. He was holding his rattle and sleeping well. The Rineers went to get their shipments in Juba. It was nice that they could go while I was still at Logotok with Barb. More and more, the men didn't want us to stay alone on the stations. When the Rineers took their children back to school, we had a plan that Barb could come along and stay with me. I did my final cleaning out and at the beginning of August was back at Katire Ayom.

The weeks flew by as I settled into the Olsens' house, unpacked my barrels, and set up the house. I made bread and cooked enough food so that I could reheat instead of cooking new each day. I had so much to do. With boiling my water, cooking, canning, and one whole day of baking, I went through between three and four cups of kerosene a day. My little stove had only two burners, so I had to think ahead and get the stove things finished before I turned on the oven, but I managed well. I was thankful that Onesimo came back to work with me. Don and Ruth Fonseca stopped in to get a slide taken and I found malaria in both. They were expecting another child and were very happy about it. Ruth and the children stayed with me about three weeks until she recovered from both malaria and the nausea from pregnancy.

We, the missionaries, remained aware that we were foreigners in the land. More and more decisions made in Khartoum affected us and our stay in the country as well as those who wanted to come in. I didn't really understand all that was happening, but I knew lawyers were investigating on behalf of the missions here. I always kept in mind that we were being watched. We had our homes to live in but no longer anything the government considered a station. There was also a rule that no one under eighteen could be baptized into the Christian Faith unless he or she declared it before the administrator. The Lord had brought us here and would give a testimony just as long as it could bring praise to his name. I prayed wisdom might be had by all.

During September, I kept busy in my assignment as Mission Nurse. Ruth was back at Opari for a week and then returned again to stay with me. It seemed like the malaria hadn't been hit right by the medicine, and she had to take treatment again. Don was heading to field council soon, so I suggested Ruth stay with me to regain her strength. If she didn't recover, they would have to try and get a pass to go out to the doctor. The Beattys came through on their way to take the children back to school, and Bill was sick with the fever and vomiting of malaria. By the next morning his temp was down, so they left at about 10 a.m. to meet the plane. Dorothy and Bobby returned to stay at Katire Ayom during field council meeting. Then Barb stayed with us as well because the Rineers were away and they didn't want her alone at Logotok. It was a busy month, and I was glad I had settled in well before all the company came.

I praised the Lord for His protection upon us each day. One evening after the Fonseca children had had their bath and put their PJs on, Cindy escaped into the living room before I got her into bed. I called her and she ran back down the hallway—and stepped on a tiny snake that no one had noticed until it was too late. I suppose it got in through the break in the door meant for the cat. Thankfully Cindy wasn't injured. The incident helped the children see that we meant it when we told them to not run around in the evenings without shoes.

Our Acholi hymn book came back from the printers and we began the first check for mistakes. There were quite a few. I also began typing in the Psalms where Jean had stopped. It sure was hard, but I felt it was something I could do, and I wanted to get the Word out while we still had time. I also started up classes for children and the women.

163

It was very quiet after all the visitors went home. Onesimo seemed to enjoy all the work in the house while we had so many folks around. Now we had to turn our attention to the outside of the house. I was glad to catch up on letters and other things I had neglected.

October passed and my classes were well attended. We worked in the gardens and canned. I went out from time to time and helped weed with folks in their gardens. I felt it might be helpful to connect with others in this way. The Word of God is for all, and no one is better than another.

We heard from the Reitsmas that their five children were all in school and their sixth was due in April. I enjoyed all the letters and pictures folks sent from home. It was nice to keep up with the nieces and nephews. I found out by radio that Mrs. E. Roosevelt left the hospital (hadn't heard she was sick), and heard the commentary on the Cuban crisis and prayed again for the hurting world. How time flew.

We gathered in Torit early in November for our Thanksgiving celebration. The Fonsecas had ordered a turkey in Gulu, and the store keeper got a frozen one from Kampala. Believe it or not, it originally came from Virginia in the USA! Surprising how things got around. Mr. Marino, who worked for the government, was back and came to our feast as well. While there, we found out that the Booths would not return and some other missions had workers who were given six weeks to leave. School workers, builders, clerical workers, and language workers had been hit hard. Of course, we were concerned about Betty. Her notice would most likely come sometime, but even when it's expected, it hits home. If we lost any more missionaries, it would be almost certain that some of the work would have to close. So we kept praying for each other that we might walk day by day and not take on the morrow but leave it in His hands.

Towards the end of November, I began preparing for Christmas. I wanted gifts ready for the folks as they returned with the children from school because there wouldn't be much chance to see them again before Christmas. We had about ten children on the field at the time. Because it was so warm, it was hard to think that Christmas was coming. Betty and I went to Opari when the children came in. As we were traveling home again, a buffalo came out of the grass in front of our vehicle. Betty was driving, and the native man with us thought it was quite something to see on the road. It didn't go too far into the grass before it stopped again and looked back our way. Of course we didn't stay and visit with it. Poor Don Fonseca had wanted to go hunting so badly, but the grass was too high — and we were the ones to find a buffalo on the road.

One day at 6 a.m., I had a call at the door for the wife of one of the teachers who was having trouble delivering her baby. I was too late to save the baby. This was her fourth, though her first two were born dead. She had her third in the hospital in Juba and they must have helped her with the forceps because that little girl was alive. I would have tried to get her help had I known her history before it was too late. The baby came within an hour after they called me and a trip to Torit took almost three by truck, so there was nothing to be done at that point.

By the end of December, the notice came that Betty had four weeks until she had to be out of Sudan. (Government would later extend that to six weeks.) Things would be quite upset again as everyone moved around. Who knew what would happen next, or who would be next to go. The Stranskes also received notice that they would not get permits to return at the end of their furlough. I thought that might be the end of the Riwoto station. Hank Senff was retiring and the Beattys were due for

Sandy and Cindy Fonseca wearing gourds for hats in front of the Fonseca home.

furlough in summer. We worked out a plan. Once Betty left, Barb would stay down at Katire Ayom with me. When the Fonsecas went out for the baby in February, there would still be workers in each area. So we went day by day.

Betty and I closed the year by spending some time at Opari. Several visitors came through the station while we were there. Mr. Marino stopped by as well as Americans from Juba. The one couple had a ten-year-old girl, and she and the Fonseca girls had quite a fun time together. With so many people in and out, the girls woke up one morning and wondered where we might be going that day. And all the grownups ended the year wondering where they might settle in the New Year.

1963

That Christ may dwell in your hearts through faith . . .
(Ephesians 3:17a)

I enjoyed my work with the children at Katire Ayom. We met two mornings a week with up to fifty little folks coming in to learn about the Word of Life. How they loved to sing choruses, and we always began with *Rolled Away*. Even the tiny little ones tried to do the motions. What a joy to see them continue singing in their homes too. Some of the

Beating grain from the stalk

children returned in the afternoon for memory work, and one of our fellows finished memorizing the one hundred and fifty verses for his gift of a New Testament. Evangelist Nikolau was thrilled.

Of course, children are children and they had to be told some things, but they came and learned their verses, and we prayed they would learn to know Christ as Savior of their lives. I also met with the women on

Sunday after church. Because all of Sudan now took off on the Muslim Friday instead of our Sunday, the church service had to end by ten o'clock when schools went into session. We were thankful that the present government allowed classes to begin later on Sundays, which gave the Christians opportunity to attend worship.

Winnowing cassava

The Beattys stopped by for a visit late in January. We had a lovely time of singing and praying together. After our meeting, the children had just begun nodding off when I pulled out the blood pressure apparatus to check Bill's pressure. Suddenly they were wide awake and wanted theirs checked as well—that is once they found out no needles were involved!

Betty found a new assignment with the women's economic program in Linga, Congo. It sure hurt to see the breakup of the work after all the years we had been together. She sorted, packed, and planned where to sell any unwanted items. Actually, we still had furniture and many other things belonging to those who had left Sudan and had not returned. If we all had to leave, there would surely be a lot of stuff to haul out.

For a time, we had a ray of hope when Harold Amstutz told us that the Booths and the Stranskes might get their return permits after all. In the end, neither couple was allowed back into Sudan, though the Booths did return to Uganda. We continued to look to the Lord and trust Him for each day.

167

Betty moved, and Barb Battye came to Katire Ayom. Barb planned to stay at my house until she could fix up Betty's house and move in. Betty's house was nice, but it still needed the installation of running water in the kitchen and some other work completed. My house (originally the Olsens' home) was large, and we discovered some advantages to sharing the living space in that we could save on our use of kerosene and the water supply. We decided that it made more sense for us to carry on in the one place, rather than set up two households. The house had plenty of room should we need time to ourselves. Even though we had some different ways of doing things, we had a mind to make it succeed.

Barb continued her Latuka translation work. She also studied Acholi, and the village folks were delighted to find her trying to speak with them.

The Fonsecas arranged to go to Kuluva, Uganda for the arrival of their baby. Ruth and the children stayed with us for a short time while Don went to Torit for their papers. It was a bit early, but when you have to travel far, you can't wait until the last minute.

One day while Ruth was still with us, I was called out for Kot, one of my house helpers. He had gone for bamboo on his day off. While he was cutting it, his knife slipped and went into his leg. I fixed up the wound; however, infection set in, and he couldn't walk on it for an entire week.

Our house at Katire Ayom

Who knows what was on the knife. Out here, infections developed so easily.

Around the beginning of March, we received notice that the Olsens were to leave in six weeks. Of course, they were on furlough in the States, so that meant they couldn't come back. It looked like Barb and I would be together for a lot longer than we first thought—unless our walking papers came as well. This made three months in a row that the government had sent someone out. We didn't know what would happen next. We heard that even an African Pastor from Congo was told to leave the Logotok area.

Barb and I traveled back up to Logotok so she could pick up additional belongings. Once there, she found that the rats had gotten into her things, so she worked to pack and close up her house more thoroughly. We all made lists of our possessions, so if any of us had to leave quickly we would be ready to get the export papers.

We still hoped things would settle down and even that we might get additional workers into the country. The Amstutzes returned to Juba for meetings, and we awaited word of their dealings there. Only four mission men were left in Sudan, and the Beattys were due to go on furlough in summer. We felt God was strengthening His Church, but we didn't really see a way forward. We could only try to be faithful for this one present moment while we were still in the country. Step by step.

We enjoyed visiting with the Rineers at Logotok. I found out that Anny was expecting a new addition. Barb had already known the news and was relieved to be able to talk without the fear of slipping up. The Fonsecas welcomed baby Diana Marie into their family on March 17.

At the end of March, Barb and I traveled back to Katire Ayom driving the two VW pickup trucks. We had to get ready for the whole Sudan field to meet at our station to discuss some of our future plans. I was last in line, driving the truck with less of a load and more of the passengers. We usually loaded the people in the final vehicle, so if something went wrong at least the one at the end wasn't without help.

Barb and I worked hard to get things ready for the meeting. We baked rolls and cinnamon buns, boiled water, and prepared a whole leg of beef for the gathering. I didn't have enough room in my gas refrigerator for all our supplies, so we hauled up the fridge from Betty's house. We only scratched it a bit trying to get it out of Betty's house and decided to settle it on the back porch of our house instead of risking more damage moving it inside. I had a time to get the gas refrigerator to light, but I finally managed to fire it up after I changed the wick.

Everyone on the Sudan team was blessed in our time of fellowship and prayer around the Word. We knew the Lord was leading and would continue to keep His promises and guide us each step in every day. We couldn't get our hearts set on things in the world, for they would pass away. We praised the Lord that we had a bright hope. Any difficulties here on earth made us look up that much more.

Onesimo's wife Martha was expecting a baby about this time. She had gone to visit at her mother's house and wanted to be home before giving birth—but she didn't make it! Labor pains started in the middle of the night and she thought for sure she could get back home before the baby came. The man trying to take her there on his bike had to stop about five miles from her home and run to a nearby village to get someone to help. They returned just in time to deliver the baby. Martha laughed as she told us that she didn't know if she would have the baby all by herself or not, but she sure couldn't walk anywhere to get help. Just think of riding on a bike that close to delivery! We rejoiced that baby and mom were fine.

A few days later, Barb and I did a medical run to Torit, transporting a very ill patient. Malaria had gotten a hold on him and he went unconscious. Praise the Lord, he recovered. At the time, Barb wasn't feeling well herself, so I drove for the two-hour, middle-of-the-night trip.

In Torit, we met Pastor Simeona, who was wonderful in going over to the hospital, staying with the man and his family, and pointing them to the Lord. We couldn't speak his language, but that made no difference in the things of the Lord. He prayed in Bangala yet we felt the fellowship of prayer as God's children. The Amstutzes were not in town but had sent a telegram telling both Pastor Simeona and Metasula that, though both pastors had been in danger of being sent out of the country, they would be allowed to stay and do the Lord's work. Pastor Simeona came to show us the telegram, joyfully repeating over and over, "God is! God is!"

The Amstutzes also reported that the Beattys, due for furlough soon, would get their return visa. They had been in the country long enough to have permission to return. We were encouraged, but we continued to pray about how to use the time we might have left.

Barb and I headed back home through Opari. The Fonsecas were returning with the baby, and no one was there to get things ready for them. We wanted to make sure they could settle in and have enough food on hand.

I began preparation for my vacation. I planned to go with the Beattys when they took their children back to school. Barb would return to Logotok for the time I was away, so she would not be alone at Katire Ayom.

The week before we were to leave, Nikolau brought our papers. When we looked them over, we discovered that the date was wrong and the police papers were missing. Without proper papers, we couldn't travel to another country. Bill, I, and several Africans took a quick trip to Torit. We did the fifty-five miles in three hours and straightened out our paperwork. Coming back home took five hours. One bridge had water over it, so we drove fast to try and cross quickly before the water rose even more. When a big truck became stuck ahead of us, our men helped them get going, and then their men helped us. Home again, we praised the Lord for another safe trip.

We headed out for our vacation in Kampala, Uganda and arrived just in time for the Beatty children to catch the train that would take them to their school. (They quickly changed into their school uniforms in the truck.)

Kampala was an interesting and up-to-date city. Many dressed in a more modern style of clothing than those I wore (not hard to do). Heavy traffic filled the streets, and I even saw African women driving. I spent my time shopping and visiting the dentist. Dorothy needed extensive dental work, and we all took the opportunity for a checkup. I also got to tour the Mengo Hospital. It was such a nice facility, so large and modern.

The highlight of my trip happened on May 3. I spoke with my Mother and Daddy on the phone! What a thrill to hear their voices, though of course we had just started to warm up and the time was gone. The call was by radio service on the international call system. I paid $10.00 for three minutes and counted it well worth the price. That phone call took a lot of energy to work out. First, I sent a letter making arrangements with my parents for the day and time. (I had to be sure they would both be home.) Then on the designated day, I phoned the operator to set the call in motion, hung up, and waited. Meanwhile through a series of operators, he connected with my parents. After quite some time, the operator called me back, and finally my parents and I were connected, and our three–minute phone call began. That's how it was done in those days. I suppose I was a bit surprised that it all worked out.

The Amstutzes used the system quite often. They had recommended we think about what we wanted to say ahead of time. One wouldn't like to lose time trying to think of what to say, or worse yet—talk about ordinary things that didn't really mean anything. In spite of taking that advice and thinking beforehand about what I wanted to say, I hung up and immediately filled three air letters containing all I had forgotten to say on the phone.

Before we left Kampala, I had an opportunity to talk to Dr. Peter Williams, the doctor in Uganda. He helped me get the medicines I needed and gave me advice for an allergy problem Don Fonseca had been experiencing.

I enjoyed my vacation very much. Heading back home through Gulu, Uganda, we noticed that the railway had come to town. Gulu was now connected to Nairobi and the Coast. Central Africa was changing.

Mid-May, we all gathered at Katire Ayom again. We had many things to decide. This was also the time the men went to Field Council in Torit. We needed grace for all things.

Even though all had been quiet, the southern Sudanese were not happy with their lot, and many crossed the border trying to change things. The governor did tell Harold Amstutz that if there was more border trouble, they'd be available to give us an escort out. We didn't know what might happen. So we went on, not fearing, but trusting. What would we do about all our worldly possessions should there be a quick exit? We needed to keep our eyes on the Lord, and He would take care of the other things.

The Rineers had three boys and one girl, the oldest two at school in Rethy. The Fonsecas planned to send Cindy to Rethy the next year for second grade. Don had taught her first grade year and would teach Sandy at home as well. It was better that the children were nearer to seven years old before they went away to school for three months at a time. Baby Diana was growing nicely and such a good baby. The Beattys would leave in July to pick up the children from school in Kenya and go home for furlough from there.

The Central Field Council met in Torit and made their decisions. Barbara would stay at Katire Ayom with me in order to keep that station opened. Another African worker would go to Riwoto with Abednego (Pastor Andreya's son) to continue that work after the Beattys left. The Rineers would stay at Logotok and the Fonsecas at Opari.

Barb and I fed fourteen people for our time together at Katire Ayom. Things went along well until the last night when we had the "big accident." Actually, I suppose it was more a series of little accidents that led up to the big one.

It all started when Dorothy took a pie out of the oven and set it on a plastic bag. Of course it stuck. Then Anny took spaghetti sauce out of the fridge. You guessed it. It slipped from her hand and splashed all over everything. We set to work, cleaning it up. All the children were playing indoors because of the rain, and while Ruth was setting the table, little Becky Rineer ran Bobby's stroller into the cupboard door. The top shelf where I stored my glasses came loose and what a crash! We had just enough glasses left to set the table once. I wasn't too upset—I told everyone, "Better broken glasses than broken bones."

We cleaned up the glass and went on with supper—that is until Anny leaned against the tap and got herself wet. The rain wasn't pouring outside, but things inside were. So it went.

It would take a little while to get back to normal after everyone departed. The next afternoon I stretched out on my bed, prayer list in hand, and promptly fell asleep.

At the end of June, I took a trip to Opari to check up on Ruth. She hadn't been feeling well and eventually went on to the doctor in Kampala. While I was in Opari, I had visits from Yunia and Tabita, Pastor Andreya's daughter and daughter-in-law. Yunia was a fine Christian and had lived alone with her five children since Moyi (my former cook) had left her back in '57. All her children were growing well, and she desired to teach them in the way of the Lord. I also visited Erasto and Lucia. It was great to see their children again.

Back at Katire Ayom, the wife of one of the teachers invited Barb and me to the coming out feast for her new baby. That was the first time I was specially invited. We were eating lunch at our house when they called us, so we went and had a second meal. The meal included their mush, beans with peanut butter, and some meat and gravy. It was tasty, and while everyone else ate with fingers, they were kind enough to give us spoons. We were sitting at the table with the new mother and another wife. When they mentioned that girls who haven't had babies didn't eat at this feast, Barb remarked, "But I haven't either!" I guess we were the exception. Usually the men were not in on this celebration, but some fathers were beginning to take more of an interest in the naming of the child. In this case, the father came by and told everyone the baby's name would be Martin.

My work with the village children went on. They came in for their memory work. Barb and I also memorized the scripture. About this time we finished learning the book of Ephesians. Barb and I began planning a trip to visit Martha sometime in November.

Mid-July, the Rineers stopped in on their way to pick up their children from school and dropped off Barb's dog Isyo. They planned to stay out for the month until their baby's due date because the roads were too bumpy for Anny to travel back and forth. Isyo had been in the care of the Rineers since Barb had moved to Katire Ayom, but they couldn't leave him there alone for the length of time they would be gone. The dog was afraid of people, and the children took their time to get their nerve to go near him. He found his favorite spot at my feet as I wrote letters. I didn't know why he should have picked me because I didn't really like dogs.

We went to Opari for one last visit with the Beattys before they went home for furlough. Dorothy spoke with the women and girls for the last time. Then as they went outside to go we saw Bambi, the Beattys' pet oribi, walking along below the house. I called him closer for the women to see him. They went wild about it and wished they could get him for food. Bambi always managed to stay out of the way of spears. He put on quite a show for the women. I went slowly, closer and closer to him calling his name and got to within two or three feet when he reared back and jumped around coming close to buck at me. I ran for my camera, but I couldn't get as close to him again. He was afraid of the click of the camera.

Around the end of August, two men came to have their picture taken with a big python about twelve feet long. It had a very pretty skin, and I would have liked to buy it to have something different for furlough. I gave the men some salt to try and preserve the skin, but it spoiled.

174

Men with a python

In August, we had a great sorrow in the area. One of the younger men in a nearby village died quite suddenly. He had begun to feel sick when he was out in his garden in the morning, and by night he was dead. I went out to sit with the wife to comfort her. The man's sister was married to Onesimo's brother, so he helped with digging the grave and such things. Sorrow all over in the loss of life.

Voice of America over the radio kept us in touch with news. I heard of the death of President Kennedy's baby. News of the civil rights march in Washington with Marian Anderson singing at the Lincoln Memorial came through almost as it happened. Sometimes it seemed too bad that we couldn't get television over the Telstar satellite, but I suppose I didn't really desire to have it.

How quickly the children grew. In September, the Fonsecas took Cindy off to Rethy for school for her first term. She was eager to go, but of course making the break from her parents wasn't easy.

Harold Rineer was born on September 2, weighing in at ten pounds.

One night, I woke up at about 10:30 p.m. to the banging of pans and shouting. The village folks were trying to chase away the elephants. Everyone was thankful that the animals hadn't damaged the gardens near us, although they trampled through some of the gardens near the river. Lucepu speared one of them. The next morning, Onesimo came by with his spears and told me he wouldn't be in at his usual time because they were going to hunt. An elephant herd could trample through an entire grain field, making all that hard work come to nothing.

The Amstutzes drove in with Abednego and some of his family members. Abednego's baby had died in Torit, and he was heading to Opari to bury the child where his father Pastor Andreya lived. (Abednego and Nikolau were both Pastor Andreya's sons.) As they traveled through, I grasped Abednego's hand and gave him words of comfort from the Lord. He was one of the few strong Christians in the area who could see comfort in the midst of heartache.

The Rineers stopped at Opari on their return with the baby. Barb and I joined the crowd, visiting from Sunday until Tuesday. Then Wednesday found us on the road back to Opari again. We had been hearing sporadic reports of mutineers in the area. With an increase of these reports it seemed best that Barb and I not be at Katire Ayom by ourselves. We took our work and camped out at Opari for a few weeks. I was glad the garden season was at the end. We hoped all would be well soon so we could return.

I passed the time typing out the Psalms and taking care of the ill. Don, Ruth and Barb all needed blood work. I gave baby Diana her vaccination, which made her cranky. We had one happy family.

I went down to the remaining cement slab at the old dispensary site and found a tree growing up in the middle of it. Four of the classrooms that had been built by Uncle John were still in use. Of course, they had been repaired, but they were the same buildings. Pastor Andreya still lived in the Buyses house.

The days marched on. I finished typing the Psalms and completed a quilt that I had been working on for quite some time. We waited for word

Nikolau and Abednego at a happier time

from Harold Amstutz for our next step. After about two weeks, we were told to pack up the trucks to go to Torit and then on to Logotok so all the missionaries would be at one place in Sudan. From this time on we were directed to travel in a convoy. A UN couple had been injured by gunfire due to mistaken identity while driving and the wife's left arm had to be amputated. Jane Amstutz provided meals and bed care to the woman for the four days she was in the hospital in Torit before being transferred to the Juba hospital. We had five vehicles in a line in our convoy on the way to Torit—oh the dust! The parents of the school children carried an extra burden in these times with concerns for the coming school vacation

Barb's truck broke down on the way to Torit. Don tried to tow us, but the cable kept falling off. They reconnected it, not knowing it was the wrong place. That damaged something in the steering, and we went into the bank before Don realized he should stop. Praise the Lord we didn't flip over. After that the gears wouldn't shift. Eventually the section of Don's Land Rover where the cable was attached fell off as well. We connected to a different truck and managed to get all the way to Harold's yard in Torit six hours after we had set out. That was a long day for a sixty–mile trip that should have taken three to four hours.

With one less truck, we cut down on our loads and headed to Logotok. Maybe things would clear up quickly, but it didn't look encouraging.

I told Mother to not worry. Mail was not moving regularly and she hadn't had word from me for four weeks. So we went step by step and day by day. It took prayer to be satisfied with everything uprooted. God knew and cared. We trusted a loving Lord.

Six adults and five children settled in together at Logotok with very little word from the outside. Our radio didn't broadcast local news. Then mid-November, we received a telegram from Mr. Marino, the Italian worker in Torit. The Amstutzes had been injured by gunfire on their way to Juba.

Harold and Jane had been traveling in a convoy and were about six miles out of Torit when they were hit by men hiding in the bush. Their car was a Land Rover pickup like so many of the officials. It seemed like the mutineers were after heads, trying to get what they wanted in the ruling of their part of Sudan. At least three bullets hit the pickup. The first went into the jerry can on the front of the car. The second hit the gas tank under the seat. The last came through the door where Harold was sitting. After the first bullet, he leaned toward the center of the truck, and that saved him. The third bullet came through the door, under his arm, and out the front windshield. Shrapnel from the door hit his right arm above the elbow. They went on to Juba, but they had to be towed because all the gas had leaked out of the truck. He was treated in Juba and his arm healed, but his nerves were shot. When he heard a sudden noise, he jumped and went weak.

Barb and I had planned to stay in Torit when the others went out to get their children from school. After the shooting, the Amstutzes recommended we all go out together by the back route when the time came to get the children. We would not be able to get back to Katire Ayom before we left the country.

The evening of Friday, November 22, both Barb and I turned in early. Lights went out at 9 p.m., and I decided to go to sleep without putting on the radio as was my habit. As I was praying, I looked out the window and saw Don walking rapidly up the path towards the house. He told us he had been listening to the Armed Forces Broadcast and that they broke in at 9 p.m. with the news that President Kennedy had been shot. We quickly turned on our radio, and it wasn't that long until word came that he was dead. We listened in shock until at least 10:30 p.m., hearing the news just as fast as those in America. I felt that the world had been hit hard. For the whole next day, no matter what station, no matter what language, we heard "President Kennedy" in one report after the other.

The Armed Forces Radio broadcast the news as CBS gave it, and we could hear the emotion in the voices. I wondered what that must have been like to see the report on TV. We heard there were no programs of entertainment or advertisements on TV the next day. Not too much was said about the Kennedy family or of Mrs. Kennedy, but I knew it was a terrific shock for all of them.

The women of the Logotok area had many questions. They asked Barb, "Did the people of the grass kill him? Do they have tall grass in America too? Why was he killed?"

Before Barb could answer, another woman said, "Because he wanted to be the leader." Since two people had been shot in cars on the road out here they understood a bit of President Kennedy being shot while riding in a car.

Everything in the social line concerning the Americans stopped in respect of President Kennedy. We heard that some of the African nations had a time of mourning as well. We missed being home at this time, and I filled my letters with questions.

By Tuesday, November 26, we were all out of Sudan and in the Gulu hotel in Uganda, waiting for further word. The Amstutzes (still in Juba) told us to come out for the children and then wait to hear from them for the next step. We trusted we could be back within the two weeks our permits gave us.

The day before, we had packed and left as planned from Logotok. We arrived at the police post eighteen miles out only to find the police truck that was to go with us had a broken fan belt and couldn't travel. They had sent for help to Torit by a man on a bicycle (a thirty-mile trip) but he never returned. Another convoy coming from the Kapoeta area heading toward Torit passed us and promised to tell the police so someone would come back for us. We waited and waited and finally ate our lunch. About 2 p.m. we headed for Torit on our own and bunked down at the Amstutzes' house.

The next day we picked up our escort (only twenty-five hours late) and went on our way out the back route to avoid the mutineers in the Opari area. Though Jerry Rineer and Barb had been to that area for some work years back, it was new country for me. At Ikotos, another police post, we were greeted and served Pepsi-Cola in the home of the Inspector (a Dinka man from further north in Sudan who knew some of the missionaries up there). From there we headed toward the border of Uganda. Because of recent rain, the road was quite bad, covered with mud holes. At one place, our two trucks drove through fine, but the escort became stuck. Mr. Rineer went back and pulled him out with the winch, amazing all with the working of that. We slipped and slid and finally arrived at Madi Ope on the Uganda side. There our convoy left us and returned to Sudan. The first 100 miles to Madi Ope took us six hours; the last 100 to Gulu took two and a half hours. The Uganda roads were of graded hard dirt with bridges to go over the rivers and gullies instead of driving down and up again as in Sudan.

Because Barb's truck was broken, we traveled out with the Fonsecas. Don Fonseca's Land Rover was so much like the one belonging to the head official in Torit that we drove in the middle of the convoy because they were fearful of the men in the bush. We were relieved when we were out and safe. On Wednesday, the Fonsecas headed for Goli, and Barb, the Rineers, and I headed to Kuluva.

About five miles out of Kuluva as we drove over a bridge, some children threw a long stick that passed over the windshield of the truck. One second later and it would have come in the window and hit Mr. Rineer as he was driving over the bridge. We thought we were away from the danger, but one could never tell. We praised the Lord for His protection all along the way. The Lord is so good.

We waited for word from Mr. Amstutz as to the next step. Would we return in the two-week time, or was there something else that would change our plans? We went forward step by step as the Lord opened the way.

Barb and I stayed with Martha Hughell whose house I had lived in for the thirteen months I was at Logotok. The Fonsecas also lived in that house for the five weeks they had had up there before we left Sudan. Martha's new home in Kuluva was lovely.

As single women, Barb and I hadn't minded the uncertainty in the same way as the couples. At Logotok there was no danger at the present, but of course they wouldn't leave us there alone as they might have in years past. So we had our vacation, only a little earlier than expected.

We praised the Lord for His leading and undertaking in all things. Truly the Lord is good, and we can trust Him for all things. Even when we don't see ahead and know just what the future holds, yet we know Him who holds the future.

We had no news from Katire Ayom or Opari. Mutineers were between the areas of Torit and Magwi, so no one traveled to Torit. The mutineers didn't have many supplies, and a big reason for us to be away was to avoid getting caught in the middle. We couldn't help them because we'd be going against the government that allowed the missions be there. If we didn't help the mutineers, they would give trouble. They had beheaded a schoolmaster at the girls' school because he gave information to the government (so we heard through the grapevine). We prayed for the Christians left behind and the work He had yet to do in Sudan, whether we were a part of it or not.

A week passed, and we were still waiting for word from Harold. The school children were back with their parents, and Christmas was coming.

I would have liked to get to Oicha. The Beckers were already back from their furlough (they only stayed out two months.) My visa was not in order, and I had to wait until that was straightened out before I dared travel. I wished I could visit with the Beckers and talk to a "mother" again. I sure couldn't get to my own mother, and I hadn't had one to confide in for so long. The Lord knew all.

By December 6, some things were settled. The Amstutzes were out of Sudan. Harold was fine; the metal in his arm didn't bother him even though he could feel it. He and Jane took our passports to Kampala for their update. For the present I would head to Oicha, Congo. Harold had talked with Dr. Becker, who told him there was always a welcome for me at Oicha. Barb would stay with Martha and concentrate on the language. The Rineers and Fonsecas would go to Kuluva.

Our time out of Sudan was uncertain. Barb was shocked that it might go into months, but I'm afraid I didn't have any hope built up one way or the other.

On December 15, I traveled through the Bogora station, then to Oicha with Zola Smith. I understood some of the things spoken to me in Kingwana. But, when I wanted to speak—I first thought of Acholi, then Latuka, and finally, maybe I could say what I wanted to say. I figured if I stayed around long enough I'd remember more.

I settled into the study/sewing room of Jewell's house. It was great to see all the people again. I had wonderful visits with Mrs. Becker. Miss Edna was still busy. She was at least seventy-three years old and walked with a crutch, but she looked good.

I listened to the East African news, hoping to hear something of my country, but things were kept very silent up there, so I didn't know when I might know anything.

We were starting to get more papers and magazines that told of Kennedy's funeral. I supposed there would be much we'd never know about that awful affair.

I began making the drugs in the pharmacy with Mrs. Becker and went on rounds with Dr. Becker. I was rusty. There was so much that I had to remember about medicine, dosage, and the French medical terms used at Oicha.

Church was filled on Christmas with about 700 people. There were sixty baptized the day before and twenty-four taken into the church. We were in church from nine until noon, and I was glad for our break at 11 am, for the backless board bench was going through me.

The year ended with the Sudan team spread out on various stations. Harold and Jerry planned to go back sometime towards the end of January. After six weeks with no letters from Mother, I started getting more regular mail. So it went. We prayed, particularly for those Christians in Sudan, and we trusted.

1964

I will never leave you nor forsake you. (Hebrews 13:5b)

I was back in "white," living with Jewell and helping around the hospital and pharmacy after a very long stretch out of full–time medical work. Our Sudan situation remained up in the air, and I sent for an extension of my passport in order to stay in Congo. Most of my news about Sudan came through Barb. She told me that Harold Amstutz received promise of reentry papers from the Sudan Embassy in Kampala for whenever he was ready to go in. He remained jumpy from the shooting, so things were uncertain. I prayed for the church leaders and people in Sudan.

Oicha was a busy place with something going on all the time. I took my turn on night call and had the rusty places shined up the hard way—by doing. I eventually grew used to the pace, but I continued my afternoon rest time as had been my habit in Sudan. Folks here thought the weather was hot, but it didn't seem so to me. From time to time we could see as far as the snow topping the Ruwenzori Mountain.

The work in Congo needed more doctors. Dr. Brown's wife was ill, and they had to go on furlough early. Dr. Kleinschmitt was in such failing health that he would pass away that April. Of course, Dr. Becker was still going strong, but he had just turned seventy years old. Mrs. Becker now wore a brace on her leg and moved more slowly than before. When Dr. Becker was out visiting other dispensaries, I would stay in the Beckers' house so she would not be alone.

Some of my December mail finally caught up to me by mid-January. I had a special surprise at the beginning of February when a tape that had been made by my family at Thanksgiving arrived along with sixty-eight other letters. I spent three and a half hours just opening mail. Regardless of the fact that nearly all my letters had been opened and sealed again by government—I still got two bills. One letter that had been enclosed with a card was put back in a different envelope. At first, I couldn't figure it out, but finally realized what must have happened. I wondered if they enjoyed reading all the news.

Even mail sent directly to me in Congo came in slowly. I supposed that the happenings in southern Congo might hinder the handling of all things in time. Though our district was not affected by the rebels, we needed to remember that Satan was busy. So many areas were troubled throughout the world. We never could tell where or when something might begin. No place was safe in the world, but in Christ we were safe. Praise the Lord for that.

Having worked at Oicha at least once each term, I could fill in wherever needed. After Vera Thiessen left for furlough I took her place playing the organ for Sunday services. Of course, things didn't always go as planned. One week I was playing a song in sharps. The horn player arrived late and decided to join in—playing flats. It sure was a terrific sound.

From time to time, Benjamin, the director for the school, would be waiting for me when I came home from work. He wanted me to play songs for him so he could be sure of the notes in order to teach the students. Sometimes he stayed with us for supper. He seemed to be a good fellow and had a nice voice for singing. He taught the folks well, and I was delighted when they sang beautifully in four parts for a Sunday service.

I sought out Mrs. Uhlinger to help me with the language. After Acholi and Latuka, the Kingwana (Swahili) seemed strange to me in spite of having worked on it whenever I had been stationed at Oicha. I was remembering the vocabulary again but became stuck on the grammar. Since it appeared I might be here for a while, I thought I might as well get the language solid.

Information from Sudan was sketchy. I heard that the men planned to go back on February 3 for a quick trip. The road was opened to Juba, and the government wanted them to go soon. For several weeks, the only information I had from the men was that they had gotten through to

Juba. At the end of February, I had word through Barb that the men had flown or driven to all the stations and found the leaders "on top" but very cut off from news. I thought it must have given the Sudan folks a shot in the arm to know we hadn't forgotten or forsaken them.

On February 27, Sudan hit the news, and I found out that all missionaries were expelled from Sudan. We would not be allowed to go back in to work. It looked like I'd be a sidekick to Jewell for a while. I didn't know what would happen to all our belongings. I still hadn't had direct word from Don or Jerry, but Barb passed on a few more bits of information about the earlier trip back. The men were glad they had gone. Though they had seen many burned out huts, the leaders were at their task in the churches at Opari, Katire Ayom, Torit, and Logotok. Rebels were strong all around the Logotok hills. The police escorted the men and watched everything they did.

Mrs. Becker shared with me a note she kept in her Bible to remind herself through the years: "God is debtor to no man." What seems lost is nothing to what He will supply in His way.

Life on the station was busy while I awaited more word from the men. Jewell had quite a full schedule of teaching junior church children as well as teaching English to some of the hospital workers. She also went out to villages when she had a free Sunday. From time to time I borrowed her bike and went out myself. I also liked to greet folks in the large leprosy village near the station. I worked mostly in the pharmacy and took my turn at night call. We had a visit from Mrs. Atkinson's sister from the southern Kivu area. Her husband was a doctor down there in the Baptist work. She told us they couldn't get drugs so they weren't able to do much. Even when they could get them, the price was terribly high. So we were thankful for what we had to work with.

At the end of March, I finally saw a copy of a letter, written mid-March, sent from the Amstutzes to Don Fonseca and Jerry Rineer. Don and Jerry were planning to go back to Sudan again to get our things out.

The Amstutzes had gone in on Sunday, March 8 with the military governor by military plane because the MAF plane had been refused entrance. They arrived at their home in Torit and found three bombers in front of the house. One shed and two tents on the property were full of bombs. They didn't know how extensive the bombing had been, but there were four jet fighters flyning around and terrorizing the area.

They had arrived by noon that Sunday with Major General Tigani, and he told them he would let them know when it was time to leave. At 7:00 a.m. Tuesday, Major General Tigani met them again, and they flew to Juba. They had heard there was much ruthless slaughter—especially on the East Bank. The Amstutzes told our men there was no advantage to going into Sudan at the moment because no trucks or military convoys were available. The Greek merchants were all confined to towns. We had thought the government would pay expenses of deportation. Now they told us we had to pay and nothing could be exported by way of the southern adjoining countries. The Amstutzes had tried to get our men's guns which were at Juba in the police storage. Even with the proper papers, they were not allowed to take the guns. The Amstutzes flew out with the Ogdens and Cooks (CMS), the last six missionaries to leave the Equatorial Province. The commanding officer in Torit, the Inspector of Police, and the Inspector of Local Government all wanted Pastor Simeona and Fiobe to stay at Torit and they—Simeona and Fiobe—agreed to do it. They needed our prayers.

David Amstutz told me when his parents arrived safely back in

Simeona, Karen, Fiobe

Nairobi, Kenya. Things had moved fast, and it didn't look much like we'd get anything out.

By this time, I had my visa for Congo. The Fonsecas and Olsens, now in Rethy, did as well. We heard that any deported Sudan missionary could not go into Kenya or Uganda. I told Jewell that we were not really deported because we had left before the order. So it went. Jean Olsen wrote me that they were happy in their assignment and invited me to visit. Ruth Fonseca looked after twenty-six small children in the school, and Dan and Jean were in the younger dorm. She said that Karen fit right into dorm life. That was nice news.

In April, we began hearing terrible reports from other areas in Congo, and I knew the news in the States was giving much the same information. I wrote to my Mother that as she heard of the things in Eastern Congo, she should remember that Oicha was on the Northern border of Kivu province. The things she might be hearing were a distance away. Her letters told of her trust in the Lord for me out here. I prayed she would know the confidence anew each day as the things were not pleasant to hear. Yet everything was quiet where I was, and we carried on for the Lord. Whatever the Lord had in store, I would not fear, for He said, "I am with you." The Lord said all these things must come to pass, and then He would return. Maybe today! We have a great and blessed hope.

The children's return to school was delayed for a week to let things quiet down a bit more. I wrote to the Central Field Council asking for a formal transfer to Congo, though they would not meet until June. I wanted to get my letter in early. I was not in need and didn't want much because the days were so uncertain everywhere. News of Zanzibar and Tanganyika surprised me. (Tanganyika and Zanzibar united to form Tanzania.) What would it all mean?

We were busy in our work. Over 40,000 were seen in the dispensary during the month of April. We had a Catholic Sister who had been badly burned—something about the fridge and her clothes catching fire. Dr. Becker, another nurse, and I worked over two and a half hours, dressing her whole body. Then I worked another hour finishing up. She was in shock and didn't have pain. They took her on to a Catholic hospital further away, and we heard that she died. Dr. Becker hadn't thought she could survive.

We had another boy who had broken his leg when he fell out of a tree. He was in traction and cried and cried to have it taken off. I spoke to him for quite some time, telling him of my brother who had also broken his leg, and because he had listened to the doctor, he walked and played ball again. A half hour after getting half an aspirin, the boy was happy again.

A Greek mother delivered at Oicha, and her baby girl got malaria at only five days old but eventually recovered. Her parents were young and so happy with her, their first baby. The mother reminded me of the Greek girl Athena I had met in Athens on my way home in 1960.

I heard that Uganda had asked the UN for help to care for the Sudanese refugees pouring into the country. From reports, it seemed as though the Taposa people came with all their cattle and needed places to graze.

Dr. Becker returned from Field Council. There had been some discussion of my moving to the northern Congo field of the Azande tribe because they needed nurses so badly. Many places needed nurses. It didn't make any difference to me as long as I could serve the Lord as He desired. Then the talk turned to furloughs. Jewell Olson, Mary Heyward, and I were due about the same time (if I stayed five years). Doctor thought they might just keep me to fill in for furloughs, so we had to wait to see what seemed best.

By the end of May, I finished my Kingwana course with Mrs. Uhlinger and passed my test with an A+. I continued on with the medical work, and the Lord helped me. Once I tried passing a tube through the stomach into the intestines. When Dr. Becker finished in the OR, he checked my work under the fluoroscope and found the tube was just curled up in the stomach. He looked at the charting I had done and said, "You did it alright, but. . . " the "but" meaning it didn't go into the intestines.

We kept busy with so many sick folks that 2,000 a day became routine. Dr. Herb Atkinson, who was only thirty-three years old, looked very tired. Dr. Becker was not a young man. We should have had more help, but no one was scheduled to come out.

I planted a garden with some dried seeds from a tomato, and twenty-two plants came up! I laughed as I thought of the hundreds I used to plant, and I told Jewell that I needed at least a few to baby over.

The Amstutzes heard news of some of the Sudan folks from Simeona. Abednego was back at Kapoeta and had permission for building a chapel. They hoped to hear from Nikolau in Opari. Lucepu and his family were in Uganda. The Amstutzes also found out that the Katire Ayom property had been disturbed. They were trying to get some word from Khartoum regarding the state of each station. Although they had nothing definite to report regarding our goods, they were happy that the work in general seemed to be going on well. When I was able to say hello to Don and Jerry on the radio, I found they were planning to go with the Amstutzes to Juba for a meeting with the American Embassy, the Sudan government, and the mission to seek more information about our things.

Dr. Becker had plans for a trip to Rethy, but his car met with an accident the day before he traveled. Mr. Uhlinger had used it to take some folks to Bunia. When he returned that night, he put it in the garage. The next morning, upon backing it out to unload it, he caught the bumper on the frame of the garage without realizing it and pulled down the whole garage on top of the car. The windshield was completely broken and the top of the car badly bent from the bricks falling on top of it. Mr. Uhlinger wasn't hurt, but too bad for the car. Dr. Becker used Dr. Herb's truck.

The government examiners for the student nurses came two days earlier than scheduled. All but one of the men and women earned their state certificates. When the examiners arrived, we had to quickly call everyone together, and Dr. Becker had to cancel scheduled surgeries. But it was better to have it over with so Dr. Becker could head off to Central Field Council with it off his mind.

Field Council officially assigned me to the Congo along with the Rineers and Fonsecas. By the Fourth of July, I was glad to hear that Don and Jerry were given two weeks in Sudan to get the eight households taken care of. Although, between the homes broken into at Katire Ayom and the men managing all the things needing to be packed, I didn't hold out hope to get many of my things.

I enjoyed my letters and photos from home. The pictures told me of changes in fashion that bypassed me here in Africa. I tucked one photo into the mirror and remarked in a letter home as to how the styles looked so different. I also received the news that Dr. Doug and Kim Reitsma had had a baby boy in June.

One Monday in July I had a call to help Dr. Herb with a delivery. Oh the way of things! I had to give the woman ether, and she was so scared I'd kill her. After I calmed her, she fought off the mask and asked, "Will you resurrect me again afterward?" There I was holding the ether cone with my left hand and wiping Doctor's brow with the right. Then he asked for help pushing the baby's head out—so again the left hand to the ether cone and the right to push. Not always the easiest position. We delivered the baby with difficulty, and while the mother was fine, the baby couldn't be saved.

Possessions can become a great part of life. When I received a letter from Don Fonseca at the end of July, I gave thanks that I had Eternal Life—life that could not perish nor could be taken away or destroyed. I thought of Matthew 6:19, 20 which says, "Do not lay up for yourselves treasure on earth . . . but lay up for yourselves treasures in heaven." Don wrote:

> We had quite a trip up in Sudan! It was very difficult in many ways, and something I never want to do again. Had sixteen government lorries [trucks] with us, over sixty armed soldiers. Had some shooting on the Juba-Opari road, but no one hurt. Had an auction at Kapoeta of Harvey's stuff. Went Juba to Kapoeta in one day, sixteen hours. Dust—no rain. Ate Sudanese food, American Vice Counsul from Khartoum was with us. Then to Logotok, everything done in one day, one night, had to leave quite a bit there. Auctioned Rineers', Battye's, Amstutz' stuff in Torit. Very poor prices for most. Then to Juba for a few days, and on to Opari.
>
> Arrived there, heard that Katire Ayom was looted, etc. so we went right to K. A. and what a mess!! Except for your fridge and Olsens', which weren't in too good shape, all else is a total loss. What the mutineers didn't or couldn't steal, they destroyed. Everything!! Even cut mattresses to pieces. Wrecked Olsen's VW [pickup], stole Jean's accordion, emptied all drums, boxes etc. belonging to Olsens, Beattys and you. Ripped Olsens' *Encyclopedia Britannica* to shreds. Stoves, washing machines wrecked. We were thankful that none of the K. A. folk were there to see it. Very sad.

There are no Acholis living in Sudan. All gone to Uganda. Every village around K. A. is totally deserted or burned. So—that's the sad news. The American Embassy is going to try to get compensation, here's hoping. We got to Opari at 6:00 that evening and I got everything packed and loaded by 9:00 the next morning, working all night. Opari was just the way we left it, all normal. About 150 people were there to say goodbye. Nikolau might come here to Rethy to do some translation with me this fall. Hope so. Had rain on way to Juba, all our beds, chairs, etc were wrecked. So we sold all. No furniture came out of Sudan, all sold. All we brought out was dishes, personal things, etc.

Andreya moved into our house after we left, same at Logotok, Riwoto and Torit. The church seems to be doing well, all has been put in their custody for the time being.

We sold your fridge and a couple other things for a total of 92,000 pounds [$300.00].

So I guess that's about it. It sure was hard to leave the stations and the people, but their spirit seems to be good. Of course, we saw no one from Katire Ayom. They are all in Uganda. We hear Martin is working with CMS in Palabek or Padibi or somewhere like that. Abednego seemed happy at Riwoto, Tomaso at Logotok, Simeona at Torit.

It was heartbreaking. I couldn't understand the destruction. Yet, I had enjoyed the use of my things for fifteen years. I was not now in need. I had enough. I could pray for whoever destroyed and stole all my belongings. I trusted they had taken some things of the Word of God and that in some way it would speak to their hearts and bring them to the Savior. The Lord was willing to forgive them, and I would too.

A few days later, when Dr. and Mrs. Atkinson returned after picking up their children from school in Rethy, they called me to my room. What did I see? My two microscopes! I ran to hug them like old friends. They had been in Torit and Logotok and were saved along with some clothes and old shoes. So after thinking all was lost, I began to feel quite rich. Above all, I was so rich in the Lord for I had eternal life, and no one could steal or destroy it for me.

I thought I might visit Uganda (if I could get the permission) to find out how the Acholi refugees were doing. I also had a long talk with Dr. Becker on the future of the work. The Congo field was planning to expand the nurses training program. I wasn't due for furlough for another year and a half, so we talked about how I might fit into the work. I felt the Lord would have me stay in Oicha, but I went each day with Him.

In the beginning of August, Jewell and I made a quick two-day trip to Kasese, Uganda and brought back supplies. Jewell joked that after all we had bought, I might have to leave some things again. I was glad to not have many possessions. Even so, I felt like I had too much should there be a quick exit.

We began hearing more conflicting reports of the Simba rebel activity in various areas. We listened to the radio, and, of course, it caused concern when big cities fell because that would affect us. I knew my mother was troubled by all she heard. I hoped my letters would get through to assure her everything was fine for the time. The Lord knew what my next step would be, and I went a day at a time. He knew all about my past moves and losses. He knew about the moves or stays to come. All we wanted was to bring praise to His name.

Jewell had planned a vacation, flying from Stanleyville to visit friends at another mission. Before she could leave, the planes stopped flying in that area, and she couldn't go. Then we heard that the rebels had overtaken Stanleyville. She was so glad that she hadn't gotten caught up in the hostilities, and so were we.

I wrote to Mother in a letter of August 17:

> We keep listening to the radio, but things are quiet in our area. But of course, you were just writing you were glad I got my mail, but we don't know when the mail might come again with the one big city enroute out of the running. But the Lord will take care of us and we keep praying that you will have HIS peace about this all. We are where the Lord has placed us and in His place He takes care of us. We are safe with Him even if danger should come, for He is with us at all times.

Our medical work continued. I took call for the hospital. I babied over

my garden and the tiny tomatoes growing on my meager sixteen plants.
On Sunday, August 23, I wrote home:

> Decisions to be made these days seem hard. I have no desire
> to leave the work here. I hope it will not come that I must if
> things continue quiet in our area. It is not that I want to be
> counted brave—or some might think stubborn or wanting to
> do something different. But there is work to do at this time
> and if the doctors would have to stay there are so many
> avenues that they need helping hands.
>
> It is hard to think of leaving when there are those who
> want our help. Of course, we know that Satan is busy and
> would be happy. Then again, we are wanting to be led by
> His Spirit so that when HE says it is time to go we know the
> voice of our Master.
>
> I know these must be hard days for you but remember
> I'm safer here in His place than anywhere which is not His
> place for me. We want to be obedient to all in authority but
> then we need to know the Lord's will above all. I know that
> the Lord gives you peace as you pray for us and me. In many
> ways I'm sure it must be much harder for you than for us, as
> we are here and see the quiet in our area and have the work
> to carry on. Please do not get upset in my staying here at this
> time. I'm so thankful that I know you have committed me to
> the Lord long ago and He gives you His peace anew each
> day. I certainly will try and keep in touch with you, but of
> course, as to my receiving your mail that is not so certain. I
> have peace in our being here and have no leading as yet that
> I'd like to go out. We are sitting tight, carrying on, and
> seeing how the Lord leads day by day.

We gathered together Sunday afternoon to see what we might need to
do—evacuate or stay. At about 3 p.m. word came that the rebels were
near and we should pack one suitcase apiece in case we had to at some
point abandon vehicles and walk out. Everyone was to travel together and
go immediately. We sat in the car ready to go. Then at about 5 p.m., new
information indicated that the previous reports were probably false. We

went back to the house to get something to eat and drink in case we left later. By 7:30 p.m., we gathered together for a prayer service. Just at the end, eleven men of the local authorities arrived and expressed their desire that we stay to carry on the medical work. While they were willing that others could leave, they did not want to give Dr. Becker his exit papers and claimed they would help him in any way. I couldn't blame them. What would happen to the medical work if we left? Each of us went to our room alone and prayed for direction—leave or stay.

I wasn't brave, neither did I want to be stubborn, but there was a need. The task here was so great. I had no dependents. I did think of my folks so much and wished I could have them understand that things were quiet at the present. I knew they were concerned, and I prayed they could rest in Him and His best for all.

By the next morning, Monday, August 24, some decided to leave and some to stay with Dr. Becker. The Uhlingers were going. Mr. Uhlinger had fallen the day before while putting his things away and was not well. Dr. Atkinson was leaving with his family. In all, fourteen missionaries and eleven children evacuated. The Beckers, Victor Paul, Mary Heyward, Jewell Olson, and I were staying. Dr. Becker hoped we weren't staying just because of him. Really, the only time I felt funny was when they said go. I was in perfect peace to stay.

In spite of our plans, by Thursday those of us who had stayed were crossing the border into Uganda. Yes, I was a refugee once again. Just a pilgrim and a stranger on this earth traveling toward my heavenly home. I didn't know which way the path would turn, but I did know where I was heading. Praise the Lord.

After receiving more information of the Simba rebels heading our way, the authorities finally gave Dr. Becker his exit papers. Jewell and I had to be called several times before we left Oicha at 10:45 a.m. Thursday morning because we were trying to hide away as many things as we could. It wasn't easy driving away, and I felt so sorry for those left behind with the big task before them. In our prayer meeting the day before, Dr. Becker had prayed, "Make the leaving as soft as possible."

We got through the border without too much difficulty. Victor's car had trouble with the steering on the Congo side, but a Belgian man came along and helped fix it to some extent. We arrived at the Uganda border after dark and with only a few delays we were finally through by

7:40 p.m. We drove on to the Kasese Hotel and settled in by 10 p.m. their time. After a good night's sleep, Jewell and I went back to Lake Kative for mail and then met the others in Fort Portal for the police papers and to fix Vic's car. Vic and Dr. Becker went ahead to Kampala, and Mrs. Becker traveled with us in the jeep. Mary and I took turns in the back so Mrs. Becker could have a comfortable space. She remarked that she supposed one had to be seventy years old to get special seating! I told her I'd wait for the privilege. We pulled into Kampala by 10 p.m.

With a meal set before us, Doctor asked Victor Paul to give the blessing. Vic prayed, "Thank you Lord for the good trip and that the Beckers could have a fairly comfortable trip—so to speak . . ." At this point, Dr. Becker burst out laughing, and Vic decided he'd better write out his prayers ahead of time.

We depended on the radio for news of those folks still in Congo. Dr. Wilcke and Stanley Kline were still at Rethy. The local authorities, promising protection, wouldn't allow Dr. Wilcke to leave, but his wife Wanda and the children were safe in Uganda. We had no news from the personnel at missions near Stanleyville. The folks in Zandeland were safe, but they were cut off and unable to get out for the time. Sixteen Plymouth Brethren missionaries in Nyankunde were cut off but did eventually manage to get out through Leopoldville. No one had word from Mrs. Kleinschmitt, who had not wanted to leave her station. We heard some things said of planes going in to get people out.

Don and Ruth Fonseca were in Kampala and planning on going to Kijabe to help in the Academy there. Many of those with children were trying to get planes to go home.

By Sunday, Dr. Wilcke and Stanley Kline had not gotten out according to what we heard. The last message on the radio was that Rethy was very bad. We found out a few days later that they had left Rethy after operating on a Simba soldier with a ragged arrow head in his abdomen. They then drove out in a white VW Kombi with big red crosses on the roof and doors. Along the way, government soldiers boarded the vehicle and were able to get them through numerous check points to Bunia. In Bunia, Dr. Wilcke offered to navigate for a UN pilot, which is how they finally flew out in a small plane to safety in Uganda. Another missionary brought them to Arua where they walked into a service on the lawn, surprising the folks praying for them and the others trapped in Congo.

Zande folks were not on radio at the time, and we found out later that they were all into the Central African Republic. Mrs. Kleinschmitt made it out. Most of the UFM folks were in bad places. Last we had heard from them before radio contact went silent was that food was rationed. We had no definite word on so many people.

On Tuesday, September 1, the big men in the mission met in Eldoret, concerning all the problems that had crept up so quickly. I more or less settled on the idea that if I couldn't get back into Congo soon, I should take furlough. I couldn't make myself feel ready. I had not been gearing up to go on deputation work this quickly. Folks were looking into chartering a plane, but many were undecided about taking it. I would have liked to take a slower route home and visit friends in Europe rather than a quick two-day flight on the charter plane.

Victor Paul, who had evacuated with us, went back on a plane to show the way to get others. They were unable to land because of gunfire from the rebels.

Once the men returned from Eldoret, I planned furlough with the understanding that I might fly back fast if the door opened. I felt the church would stand behind me in this matter. Upper Kenya had a place for me, but I didn't have equipment, and Harold Amstutz wondered on the wisdom of spending money so close to furlough. It seemed best to go home first before starting new again. In my heart I had felt I would probably be going home, but I was not looking forward to the deputation work with such a vague challenge before me. My feelings were so mixed and my heartstrings pulled both ways.

By September 5 we heard the rebels were on the road to Oicha. That was to be the graduation day for the students at the hospital. I wondered if they had the graduation or if they were running for their lives.

Dr. Becker was trying to make contact with Yonama, the hospital administrator. He hoped he might be able to help in some way. We prayed for the people, especially when we thought of the lack of medicine or vaccinations. The days were evil, and we looked to the Lord.

I began my preparation for furlough, fixing up clothes and preparing for the fall weather in the USA. I even bought a *red* coat (after going back at least three times to look at it). Everyone assured me it was nice. At least the folks at home would see me coming.

By September 9, two weeks after we had evacuated Congo, I finalized my travel plans. I would leave Kampala on September 12, flying Kampala, Brussels, Amsterdam, Brussels, and finally to New York on September 15. I wrote home, "Lord willing this is how I'll travel home unless Congo opens before! I wish it would. "

Furlough

Jesus Christ is the same yesterday, today, and forever.
(Hebrews 13:8)

The Congo missionary staff scattered, some on furlough, others helping in the Uganda, Kenya, and Central African Republic fields. We prayed the doors would not close. For a time, Yonama and Tomasi continued the hospital work in Oicha. Meheteberi and other graduate nurses carried on their part of the work faithfully—Yohosabeti in the operating room, Alice in the Bureau, Yarusi in the delivery room. Joshua manned the pharmacy, Benjamin and Manoa on the dispensary porch, Fanweli giving needles, Abisi in the lab, Big Benjamin in the Leper Camp, and there were many other helpers and workers.

At the end of September, staff and patients had to flee into the surrounding forest as the Simba rebels overtook the station. Many of the staff and their families eventually made their way to Uganda.

By the time the tide began turning against the Simba rebels in November of 1964, they had slaughtered thousands of Congolese and foreigners. Many missionaries had been caught up in the rebellion. Men, women, and children were held captive or killed—many killed as the troops were coming to their rescue.[2]

Nearly a year later, by August 1965, the door to Congo began to open, and I looked forward to getting back into the work. We had permission to occupy four of the stations around Bunia. Other stations would be visited by Missionary Aviation Fellowship. This would give encouragement to

---

[2] "Simba Rebellion." *Wikipedia*, en.wikipedia.org/wiki/Simba_rebellion

Pastors and the Christians in those areas and help for the educational and medical work.

The Christians in many areas had gone into hiding in the bush and forest. Some were now returning, and stations were in the process of being cleaned up. Mr. Langford, General Secretary, and Dr. Becker were able to visit eleven of the Congo stations. They found the spiritual activities being carried on in worship services and prayer meetings. Sunday services in Bunia and Oicha were packed out, and a quickly arranged service at Aba had about 200 present. The hospitals and dispensaries carried on with limited drugs and supplies with as many as three to four hundred patients coming in daily.

Just a short time after their arrival in Oicha, Dr. Becker was doing surgery on a woman with a strangulated hernia. Surgical cases were waiting to be cared for.

I had no direct word from the Sudanese Christians.

My early furlough turned into a blessed time. It was a joy to meet various churches and groups to tell of His work being done and what we were still being led to do.

I began the formalities of visas and paperwork and planned to leave for Africa before the end of September 1965.

Term Four

1965 - 1971

1966

Trust in the Lord with all your heart, and lean not on your own understanding; in all your ways acknowledge Him, and He shall direct your paths. (Proverbs 3:5-6)

I headed back to Africa and my new assignment at Nyabirongo, Uganda in November of 1965. After a layover in London, I boarded my flight to Rome and then finally on to Entebbe, Uganda. I was glad I had eaten a hamburger in New York before flying to London because supper on the plane was not served until 9:45 p.m. It seemed that cheaper rates meant less food.

By the time I landed in Entebbe, I was well smoked. I almost felt sick from so many people smoking and so little ventilation on the plane. Other than the smoke, flying wasn't so bad—just trusting the Lord the same as any other means of travel. Pray and enjoy it. That was my motto.

As I flew over Sudan, I prayed for the troubled land and the needs of the many who had fled. I saw the winding roads, rivers, and mountains, but there was no sign of metal roofs shining in the sun. I knew there should be buildings along the way, but I couldn't see any.

As the plane came down in Entebbe, I looked out and saw a house with anthills to the side and surrounded by banana trees, and I knew I was back home in Africa. How good the Lord was to me in bringing me back again. Because I had never stayed in Uganda before, I didn't have to pay anything at customs. I also got all my things through without paying overweight, although my arm was stiff from carrying the overweight of it.

Harold and Jane Amstutz picked me up at the airport. They now lived in the house where Jewell, Mary, and I had stayed before I went home. After a brief stop at their house, they drove me to Kampala where I settled in the little prophet's room in the mission guest house.

The next day, Jane took me to a storeroom filled with things left over from Sudan. I found dishes, silverware, and some boilers and gratefully crossed those items off my shopping list. The Reitsmas had left a bed behind in Uganda, and the Amstutzes had already sent it out to the station for me. I felt like I had a little bit of Sudan with me even though I was out of that land!

The Amstutzes and I spent the following day going from one shop to another—one time for their business and another for mine. I found a secondhand fridge for eighty dollars (compared to two hundred dollars for a new one). It was a little beat up, but some spray paint would fix that. I bought blankets, pillows and sheets. I forgot about a mosquito net until the man in the store mentioned it. I also found a little stove. Since I had saved money on the fridge, I bought a small radio as well.

I booked a first-class sleeper room on the train for Kasese so I could sleep as I traveled through the night. Catherine, a mixed-race girl from Congo, traveled with me. She wanted to go to Nyabirongo, and it worked out well for us to have companionship for the trip. Our room was filled with boxes and a few surprise packages from the Amstutzes.

Victor Paul met us at the train station in Kasese, and we helped him finish the food shopping before heading to the station in the foothills of the snow-capped Ruwenzori Mountains. The government had abandoned the facility and turned the work over to Doctor Becker. The Beckers, Victor Paul, Jewell Olson, Mary Heyward, and others of the displaced Congo staff had built up a medical work which served the needs of the people in the area. Two other doctors were also at the station. Dr. Keith Waddell was a young man from England, unmarried, and in some ways still learning. Dr. Brown and his wife were also on the station but expected to go back to Congo. As soon as the Congo opened up again, the Beckers,

Standing on the porch of my new home

Nyabirongo

Jewell, and some of the African workers planned to move back as well.

We lived in Nyabirongo in what used to be the government homes for the hospital staff. The well–built houses had a porch, living/dining room, bedroom, a tiny kitchen, and an aluminum roof with spouting to carry the rain water to a cistern—a cement, above-ground affair. Citrus trees and flowering shrubs surrounded the homes. There was also a maternity hospital, the operating room, and quarters for the female nurses on that side of the work.

Down one hill and over another, about two miles away, was the other part of the work in Kagando which had previously been a leprosy camp. Now it was our dispensary, pharmacy, and wards for patients. We had a ward with twelve beds for women and children and another with twelve beds for men. We also had eight houses up on the side of the hill. Four were for patients and two for people from far away who needed a place to stay. One was used for storage and housing the two fellows doing the carpentry work. A few leprosy patients stayed in another. All very nice homes—but what a climb up to them!

When I first arrived at Nyabirongo, Vic immediately showed me around. I started following Jewell the very next day. Since I would be in charge of the pharmacy, I also began working with Mrs. Becker. At one

Kagando dispensary—arrow points to Nyabirongo

point, I wanted to retype the direction book for making drugs because it seemed so worn, but Dr. Keith asked me to wait because he wanted to change some things. So I held off on that job.

I began settling in. Even after running my refrigerator overnight, it didn't cool down, so Dr. Keith worked on it a bit the next day and eventually got it to run. My bed was comfortable and I was sleeping well. Because the houses were very close together, I tried to be quiet if I worked late at night. Some folks had nice gardens and chickens, but I didn't know what I'd get into yet. (I did eventually plant a nice little garden—of course.)

Everyone seemed to think I should have a car because of the distance between the two sides of the station. I thought about using a bicycle which would have been wonderful going downhill, but not so great going uphill. I would have had to push it for half the trip. Dr. Becker felt a car was essential. We had an occasionally-working station car, and Dr. Keith Waddell had a car which wasn't working at all. I had never had the expense of a car in Africa and felt somewhat reluctant about the idea.

After some discussion, it was agreed that I should buy Dr. Becker's 1961 light green VW Bug. The Amstutzes, who were leaving for furlough, had sold their larger car to Dr. Becker, and he sold the VW to me. Dr. Brown had been putting some of his medical money towards the

My new car

VW with the thought that it could be the station car. In general, a station car would not get the same care as it would if one person owned it, so the car was put in my name. I paid back the money, though Dr. Brown still planned to use the car.

When I drove the car for the first time I jumped off a bit with the gears but soon got the feel of it. The very next day, the Browns took my VW to Kampala to get their daughter and take care of some business. I suppose I could have used the extra station car while they had mine, but I didn't like driving it. I was nervous something would happen to it. I wanted my VW back.

Early in December, I received a registered letter dated August 17, 1964. What a surprise! It contained my nursing license that Mother had sent out to me before we evacuated Congo. Someone sure held onto the mail.

The Congo folks planned to depart on December 8, and I hurried to get an inventory finished before they were gone. I was also busy in the pharmacy making medicines. Things didn't always go as smoothly as I would have liked. I lost time because I put soda bicarb into the gel I was making for lubricating examination. When I put it on the fire to gel, it began to bubble up. I was surprised because it had never done that before. Of course not—I had added soda bicarbonate instead of boric acid, the correct ingredient. Not only did I have to start over again, but I had wasted the glycerin. I also made some Blue (methylene blue) for use on sores and ended up with blue fingers too. I had a time getting it off my thumb nail. So it went.

The Beckers, Jewell, and Vic began packing to leave. There were two other doctors here so Dr. Becker was ready to move on and go back to Congo to set up a training school in Nyankunde. I had quite a weepy time during the Africans' farewell service the Sunday before they left. It was hard to see them all go without me. Yes, I knew when I came that I'd be staying in Uganda, but I guess I held hope that I might work with the Beckers again. The Lord strengthened me by our final goodbyes on Monday.

The days were busy and I was tired. Even though Mrs. Brown began helping in the pharmacy, I had so many things to do that it was hard to keep ahead of it all. We heard that the folks had arrived safely in Congo. We hadn't really needed so many here, but going from fifteen staff to five was a big change. Some new African fellows and girls came in to learn, but they were helpers, not able to give medicines and such things as needles.

Doctors Brown and Waddell were different than Dr. Becker who of course had more experience working with the Africans. The doctors had a different way of doing things and sometimes seemed hard to follow. It didn't make work easy. Mary Heyward (who had stayed in Uganda and was due for furlough soon) found it particularly difficult as she had worked with Dr. Becker for so long. I began to see more what Mrs. Becker meant as I was weeping my goodbyes. She had told me, "You have a big job here to help these other people." They were praying for me, and I needed the Lord's guidance.

After sixteen years on the field, my role was changing. I was no longer one of the "younger" folks and I held a different perspective on the work than many of the newer missionaries. It seemed that many were used to security and were afraid of a money shortage. I tried to show that if we use our money wisely, the Lord takes care of His own. I sure didn't count on getting a car this term, although I had had a feeling it would be necessary. In it all, the Lord supplied and I didn't lack anything. I might wish I had a few more shelves or cabinets in my house, but that isn't everything, and so I would not put my heart on it. I didn't want to accumulate too many possessions again.

Our weekly sixty-mile trip to Kasese for supplies seemed unnecessary to me. I wasn't used to shopping so often. My car made three to four trips to the hospital and back daily and for a time was the only working car on the station. I didn't like to complain; however, I wanted to go out to villages on Sunday as well, so I felt I should do less traveling during the week. I needed to rest in the Lord and do it all for Him.

Christmas arrived. The Browns, Keith, Mary, and I ate dinner with the women hospital workers, who did the cooking. The service here in the Church of Uganda was formal and long. Mary had been up early (5 a.m.) to go caroling with some of the women. I went along for a bit but came home because I didn't feel up to that much of a hike followed by work and then church.

I was so busy that I began sending carbon copy letters to my parents and siblings because I didn't have enough time to write individual letters. A bus carrying the mail bag came by every day. That was nice, but I didn't have time to read it all. I was too tired.

Musa, the man who helped me in the house, was ill for several weeks in December and not able to work. Though we feared it might be TB, it wasn't, and he eventually recovered. Musa was a slow worker. I didn't know how anyone could do the dishes so slowly, but I was glad for his help. He was honest and that meant a lot.

My little VW bug sure got a beating on the roads. Once I had to take it to our town to get the back bumper fixed because some bolts had come loose from all the bumping. It only cost me seven dollars for the welding and an oil change, and they finished it quickly. I was happy because the Browns needed the car that day to get their daughter to the train. The very next day, I had a surprise trip to Kampala—almost 300 miles. Over half of the way to Kampala was tarmac so we could travel faster and safer than on dirt roads. As a whole, Ugandan roads were better kept than in Congo or Sudan. On that trip, Dr. Keith's friend Mary Morris drove most of the way.

Mary had been visiting but couldn't get a place on the train the day before because of the crowds of school children heading back after vacation. She was a tiny girl, and at the train they asked if she was going back to school—a trained nurse and midwife! We left for Kampala at 5 a.m. the next morning to get her to work on time. (For a while, it seemed some were pushing for a match between Keith and Mary, but in the end Dr. Keith was not ready to take a wife and she married someone else.)

I got along fine after my first time around the city of Kampala. Driving on the left side of the road was so different, but the steering wheel on the right side made it easier to remember which way to go.

Dr. Peter Williams (brother to Dr. Ted Williams) and his family were also staying at the guest house in Kampala. I hadn't seen the four girls in years. We had a nice visit, and I heard all the news about Barb and Martha who worked with them at the same Kuluva station. It was the next best thing to seeing them.

I also walked around the town and bought some books. When I stopped to put my umbrella down under some roofs, someone said, "hello." It was Nikolau of Sudan, and what a greeting we had there on the street! Everyone just stared at us. He was in town trying to get a passport to go to Kenya to attend the Scott Theological College of our mission. We went back to the guest house and talked and talked until supper. I didn't even try Acholi because he spoke English so well. Nikolau had been to Opari back in November and told me that nothing was going on there. A few people lived here and there in the bush, but elephants had taken over the property and gardens. The future for that land seemed dim.

Though some were standing well where they were, Lucepu was discouraged. Lucepu's son Martin was with some Acholi people in Uganda. Monwelli and Erasto were out of Sudan as well as Onesimo and others who had worked for me. Simeona, his wife, and five children were also in Uganda. Seeing Nikolau was the blessing of the trip.

I settled into the work back at Nyabirongo. One night I was gazing out at the sky and saw a satellite traveling across the heavens like a star. Voice of America brought me news from home. I listened to speeches from the president about the bombing in Vietnam. I also heard of the snow back in the States. Washington D.C. had been hit with the worst blizzard in forty-four years. I felt cold just hearing about it. It took that blizzard of '66 for my Daddy to write a letter to me. I couldn't wish folks to be snowed in too often, but I hoped I might get another letter from him sometime. It was nice to hear the man's side of the story from time to time.

I certainly didn't have much time to think of the snow. Days were busy and on Sundays I usually went out to various villages. At the end of January, Mary, Yonama (the displaced medical director from Oicha), Israel (the assistant to Malona the hospital evangelist), and I went to the Lake George area for church. Twelve adults and two children came to the service. After church, we went by the lake through the game area for a picnic lunch. We didn't see many game animals because it was too dry, but we saw the nets, boats, and some birds.

Boat on Lake George

The previous week, Mary had news that her sister had died. Then a few days later she had another letter telling of her brother's death. It was very hard on her. We encouraged her to come along anyway, and Yonama was quite a tonic. He was lively and loved to try out his English. He just laughed at his own mistakes and always tried again—that's why he learned so much. In the end, Mary was glad she had joined the trip.

The next Sunday, a hospital woman Mehetebela and two other men went out with me. The men each went alone to an area and Mehet and I went to another. We had a good visit, and one of the men in the village told me he wanted a Bible. Even though he said he would buy one next time I came by, I doubted he would keep his money until I came back again.

We did about forty-five miles that Sunday which totaled over 200 miles for the week. Driving ten to fifteen miles a day for work trips added up. Dr. Brown had taken the car to Kampala, and then there had been one trip for me. I was shocked to see that I had driven over 2,000 miles since I had bought the car from Dr. Becker. It just didn't seem possible. I was thankful the car worked well and only had a few rattles from the roads. Yonama told me that when he first came to the area, before Dr. Becker, it was all just wilderness—no gardens. Now it was a lovely place with fairly good roads and more repairs all the time.

Dr. Keith returned from a short vacation he had taken while the Browns were still in Uganda. Once he was back, the Browns went to Kampala for two weeks to check on the arrival of their car. While there, Dr. Brown found that he would not be able to practice medicine at all until he got his Ugandan license. So we were down to two nurses and one doctor.

Dr. Keith looked better after his needed vacation and seemed to have gained a little weight. He had his ideas and was eager to get them working. Patient numbers were increasing and he couldn't get over how many came in. He had never seen so many before. Of course, travel was opening and the name of the place was better known. One man who had found help the year before returned with nine other patients.

At the end of February, Mary and I had a flat tire on our way home from Kasese. We had started off quite pleased with ourselves that we'd be home before dark, then I felt the right back tire go flat. So I thought— here goes my first time of changing a tire myself. I figured I'd prove that I could. I soon proved I couldn't. The bolts were so tight that I couldn't budge them. Not one bit. At first, I wasn't so sure which way to turn them. I tried the front wheels which had been changed recently and found I could turn those but not the back. Soon—Praise the Lord—we saw a man coming down the road. He couldn't loosen the bolts either. We were about six to eight miles from home, in an area where we usually saw animals. Further back we had passed a large herd of elephants looking as if they were waiting for dark to cross out of their reserve for greener grass. The Lord didn't allow that old nail to get through the tire until we were away from them.

Mary found some other men to help. The second man couldn't turn the bolts either, but the third man tried and succeeded. By that time it was dark and we were working by flashlight (so relieved I remembered to bring it along). We ended up with four men helping, and we needed them. I knew how to get the jack up, but I couldn't get it down again. I referred to the book but just couldn't make it work. The four men took hold of the car, and with a shout in unison they lifted it while I pulled out the jack. That's the story of my first tire change on the VW.

I heard from the Beckers at Nyankunde. They were staying one week at a time on the station setting up a medical training facility for Africans and then one week out to dispensaries. He was the only doctor in the area. Though it seemed to keep him thriving, Mrs. Becker wrote, "Oh,

Kagando dispensary

this safari life is hard and not what I thought of for my older days, but the Lord gives strength."

We could have used more people for the work in Uganda. Dr. Brown was eager to get back to his area in Congo. Mary was scheduled for furlough in June. Dr. Keith wanted to see the work continue, but we needed help. We had the full African staff, but they were folks from Congo and Dr. Becker would want some of them back soon.

One night as I headed for a lemon from Mary's tree to wash my hair, Dr. Keith stopped me for a chat. He was very concerned about keeping track of the drugs according to the requirements of the law. I wanted to be in the right, but I couldn't see how we would be able to do all the paperwork. Each of us had so much to do, and when the staff left we would all have that much more. I prayed about the matter. Even little things, when they are hard to do, could cause real problems.

We began March with a few tough cases. A boy of about fourteen was brought in about 9:30 p.m. He had been attacked by some folks going around making havoc, and his right arm was badly cut and his abdomen pierced. In surgery, they found the wound to be into the stomach. He came through the operation, but he had lost a lot of blood and died the following noon. We had heard him say he knew Christ as his Savior. Malona, the station evangelist, told us that when he visited in the morning and got up from the bedside, the boy looked up and called, "Baba" (father). Malona read the Word and prayed with him. By the time Malona walked back to his house, the boy had died.

The next Sunday, I sat typing at my desk about 5:15 p.m. I had just completed the hospital rounds and was finishing a letter before prayer meeting when men passed my house carrying something. I didn't know what it was for the cloth was covered in blood. As I found out, a young man had been out hunting mountain rats—they are big, more like a groundhog. We got the story that he threw his spear and missed. Then the animal turned, and when he ran after it—somehow the spear had fallen in such a way that he fell into it and cut his left thigh. He must have severed the artery for he bled terribly. We took his blood type, but before we could get a donor, he was going out. Dr. found his own type was possible and he gave some direct, but it was too late. What a wail went up outside as they were told he had died. They were from the hills just above us and the men got the corpse tied in a blanket on a pole and went quickly back up the mountain, wailing as they departed. We watched them climb up and around until we couldn't see them anymore—less than half an hour. How short life could be and so quickly gone.

Back in January, eight wounded Ugandan rebels had come to the hospital. Dr. had operated on one, but the man died from his internal injuries. Three with broken bones were sent on to the government hospital because we had no traction at ours. The others were badly injured but recovering. They certainly had something to think about in seeing other folks come in and die. Mary was teaching them, and they listened. We prayed they would continue to read the Word and come to know the Lord. Once, when she missed a day, they asked why she wasn't there. It seemed they were really forsaken. Their letters for help had brought no answers, and they had sold clothing to pay their fee. Mary then learned they had sold their watches to buy food. They were more or less lost, and we didn't know what they would do when they left. They didn't really want to go back to the same thing. What a life without the Lord. I asked folks at home to pray for them, and at the beginning of April I was able to report home that they had accepted the Lord Jesus Christ as their Savior.

One Sunday I awoke to a rumbling something like the subway going under a house in New York. I didn't think much of it until that evening when I heard the report of an earthquake on the radio. The next day, our mission came on the radio and Dr. Becker's son Carl said, "I heard that a lot of our missionaries were doing the rock and roll and thought it needed to be explained." Every station—Rethy, Linga, Blukwa, Bogora, and Nyankunde—had walls cracked and ceilings down. Blukwa suffered the most damage. Congo wondered about us, but we couldn't answer on our radio to tell them we had no damage here.

By the end of March, I was still working through answers to Christmas cards I had received. The second group of workers departed for Congo—eight men and thirteen women plus all the wives and children. They had their own bus to go to Goli but had to stay there a week until they could get word to Dr. Becker. They all arrived safely back into Congo. We heard that Jewell and Margaret Clapper had moved to Oicha and were manning the station there.

Dr. Keith planned a meeting with the remaining of our men to figure out the new hours of work. He never got back over to the Kagando side to hold the meeting, so I took charge instead. What a time until each one had his say. They always seemed to have to speak in every detail or they didn't feel they had said anything at all. I sat and listened and tried to tie the ends together. Some had a bit of hurt feelings, but I felt we ended up with the understanding that we needed to work together. We had six men and six women of trained help and seven very young men and six women helping as aides but not giving medicines. Every little bit helped.

We didn't lack for patients. Mary was due for furlough in the beginning of July, just about twelve weeks away. The Field Council would meet in June to decide whether to keep the work opened or not. Dr. Keith didn't feel it could be closed because of our obligation to the people.

Things were hard, and we had some very sick people. One Friday they brought in a fellow about fifteen years old. He was some place where people were shooting guns, and when he ran away a bullet hit him in the right femur. The bone broke and rammed into his hip, shattering all around. The x-ray showed his leg was about six inches shorter than it should have been. He had been in his village for two weeks after the injury and then finally came to us. Dr. Keith drained the sores and was

Musa and helpers. Tub is for both laundry and bath

able to pull the bone back to almost the right length. Because we didn't have the equipment for fractures, Dr. Keith made a ring from some heavy iron and a splint and frame from some wood to put traction on the leg. After that we came back to the Nyabirongo side with the mail, but before I could get to it, Dr. Keith said we had a retained placenta to remove first. Retained placenta — it was a second baby. The first had been born in the village and was small but ok. The second one was dead. Mary carried quite a load on the maternity side and was exhausted.

On a typical day, my alarm went off at 5:30 a.m. I tried to read my Bible and be dressed and having my breakfast by 7 a.m. Then I was off to Kagando. If Dr. Keith's car wasn't working, he came with me. Sometimes he wasn't ready and then I'd come back for him and the African nurses. We usually finished seeing patients by 12:30 p.m., but sometimes we went as late as 2:30 p.m. Then I drove back to Nyabirongo for lunch and a rest. At 4:30 p.m. I headed back to Kagando for evening rounds and checking patients. If I had time I taught English classes. By 7 p.m. or a bit later when it was starting to get dark, I would get down to having supper. Our electric lights were on until 9:30 p.m., and then it was back to the lantern light during my nice hot bath and finally off to bed. I didn't get called at night (which was such a help) and I got my rest every

Yoanni cutting grass wearing a box on his head for shade

afternoon. Musa was a big help in the house, and a little fellow named Yoanni worked in the garden. I didn't miss any conveniences.

From time to time we heard of unrest in Uganda. Musa moved his family and built a house over on the other side. I guess he felt safer being among the strangers of the area. The men weren't walking after dark for safety's sake, but it was mostly quiet in our area.

What did the Lord have for this area or for Congo? We couldn't see ahead, but He did and He knew. We were called to follow in His steps and allow Him to work. I thought of the verse from Hebrews 4:15: "(He) was in all points tempted as we are, yet without sin." The Lord went through some hard places with those of His own who denied Him and those who couldn't understand. But He went right on loving and even dying for them on the cross.

One morning Big Benjamin, as we called him, led in our prayer time before work. He prayed for those in Congo who had fallen away and for the fathers to be kept from temptation. He prayed for Jewell and the other workers there, and he prayed for the church that it might stand for the Lord.

I marveled and praised the Lord for men like Benjamin. He gave Scripture in the evening service and talked about how Jesus called the disciples to Himself and yet how quickly they went aside when they didn't understand what the Lord was doing. They went back to fishing again when the Lord had called them for something much higher. Yet, the Lord was right there calling them back. We are so much the same and so quick to doubt when the Lord doesn't seem so close by, or when troubles come. I noticed that as Big Benjamin prayed, he prayed in the first person before he prayed in the plural for us all. He was a quiet man, but he walked with the Lord. Dr. Becker wanted him back, but that was up in the air. Benjamin's wife didn't feel she could go back as some folks had been mean before and stolen everything. So many things to pray about.

Dr. Becker and Victor Paul came for a visit one Thursday early in May. I hosted the noon meal for all of us, and after a few delays we finally ate by 2:30. I had sent Musa for fish and told him to get two of the larger ones. He didn't think it would be enough, so he got a third. That one by itself would have been more than enough to feed us. I ate fish for the next few days and still had enough to give the helpers.

We had a nice visit, but we mostly talked business and not too much else. Dr. Becker gave good advice to Dr. Keith, and they spent time together with the Congolese staff. As he was leaving, I asked him how Mama Becker was doing. He said, "Oh, pretty good, but you know we are getting older and I think she'd like to retire. Nyankunde is very hard for her for it is so hilly, and when we get to Oicha she thinks this is home. Traveling is hard for her, but we go on."

Our time with Dr. Becker was marred by the bad news that Mary could not count on furlough because they had no one in sight to replace her. The Central Field Council would not meet until the end of June, and she went on—uncertain and weary. Jewell was also due for furlough. When I told Dr. Becker that I was glad I had taken mine already he replied, "Kabisa" (truly—right). We needed prayer.

Victor loaded up some of the Beckers' furniture to take back with them. Other missionaries were returning to Nyankunde, and borrowed things would have to be returned. The Beckers also had furniture at Oicha for their monthly visits. Because their house here was now used as the guest house, I'd have to find beds for Barb and Martha who had planned to come for a visit at the beginning of June.

Tomasi with a patient ready to go home on the bus

While Dr. Becker and Vic were at our station, letters came to Mary and me concerning our registration with the Nurses Council. They asked each of us to send the original copy of our state license (which I had already sent months earlier) or a penalty of L50 ($150) would be assessed for practicing without being registered. Dr. Keith didn't get upset; he just sort of shrugged. What was L50? The government had given the Mission much to do before they would consider us to have a land grant. The Mission wouldn't do those things without having assurance that the buildings on the property would be theirs after so much expense.

So the round and round went on. Although the future of the work was in doubt, we continued witnessing while we were there. Tomasi, one of the medical men in the wards, asked me what was what. He wondered if he should plant his potatoes. I told him to go ahead because I didn't know. If we were here, he'd need them; if not, then the Lord would supply at the next place.

If a change came about, I had in mind to try and visit the folks of Sudan before I got into a new work. Dr. Becker had asked me whether I would come over to Congo if this work closed. I told him I would; however, if something in Sudan changed, I would have to make a decision. The Lord would work it all out the way it pleased Him.

We switched to charging patients their fee by the month instead of by the year. That would save trying to figure out how to reimburse folks if we closed. We had many people coming in—three to five hundred a day. There were some really sick folks on both sides of the station. We went day by day.

One day, our laboratory man William became ill, and I had to try my hand at the microscope again. It had been so long, and I was thrilled that I could still find some things. I went back to my pharmacy work that afternoon and finished the day much later than usual. After working on the shopping lists for Kasese that evening, I had no time for my letters.

Dr. Keith had been summoned to a court case in Kasese for a patient, and I thought he could do the shopping as well, but he wanted me to come along. He said he didn't want to take my car without me in case something happened to it (his car still needed repair). I held out for a bit and finally just said point blank that though it didn't bother me, for the sake of testimony I didn't think the two of us should go alone. So we took someone else along. That meant we couldn't take the seats out of the back to carry more things, but it worked out. We ended up having a truck come and deliver because we needed whitewash and some other larger items. We finished the shopping, but the court case was not held that day. I wasn't surprised!

As we came back at about 2 p.m., Tomasi told us that there was a new case—a man had fallen from a building. After examining him, Dr. told them what to watch for and to let us know if any changes happened. By 5 p.m. Samsoni came biking over to us on the Nyabirongo side to tell us there were changes. We went right over and found the man needed surgery. After putting the patient in the back of the car to bring him over to the operating room in Nyabirongo, we caught Samsoni before he got all the way back to the hospital and turned him around to help. The doctor opened the skull and relieved the pressure. Because Samsoni was to have been on call that night, I went back to the Kagando side to check on things at the hospital and found someone to take his place. It was good to find ones willing to pitch in.

At the beginning of May, we had one little boy come in with a huge ulcer on his leg. Something was eating the flesh, and we gave him medicine but that didn't seem to stop it. Dr. wrote to others about it and tried a different drug. He eventually did a skin graft in hopes it would

George

improve the healing. I hadn't seen the boy for a while, and when I checked, I was so happy and surprised to see him coming along so well. I don't know why I should have been surprised, for we had prayed. The boy was one of a set of twins about six years old. I called him my brother because his name was George, the same as my own brother. He was a pleasant child—unless we were changing the dressing.

Barb and Martha passed through on their way home for furlough. We had such a nice time together, and of course it went too fast. On one Sunday we all went to the Lake George church and then to see the lake and animals. Barb and Martha wanted to get a picture of a Kob (a type of antelope), and the animals obliged and came close to the road.

At the end of their visit, Mary and I drove them to Kasese where they got the plane for Kenya. I was glad we didn't have to go all the way to Kampala. Though things were quiet outwardly, sometimes cars were stopped. We had heard of some incidents down country, but it was quiet where we were. They got their plane for Nairobi as planned, then on to the Holy Land, London, and finally home by the end of June.

They had heard about our station and were pleased to finally see it. Martha said she'd be willing to come here if needed, but of course that didn't help the present demand. Mary was still waiting for word to give her hope that she might be able to go on furlough, but it seemed impossible when you think of the time needed for someone to get their papers. But then the Lord doesn't need a lot of time for His work and could move men to do what he wanted.

After we said goodbye to Martha and Barb, Mary and I found that medicines we had ordered were at the station in Kasese. The supply came through just when we needed it most. The Lord always has things timed well. We were weighed down with packages from the railroad and the post office and had to remove the back seat and tie it on the roof of the car so it wouldn't get spoiled from the heavy boxes. By the time we had everything loaded the shops were closed, so we had dinner at the hotel. After that, we went on to Kilembe where I had a new tire put on

George and his brothers

my car and we finished the shopping. After I arrived home, I put everything away and saw some patients. I filled in wherever needed.

A letter from the Beattys brought some bad news. Dr. Barnett at Kijabe told Dorothy that she needed surgery before he even saw the test results that confirmed cancer. She wasn't sure when it could be scheduled because their oldest son Barry would graduate high school and leave for the States in August. Bill would have to look after the two younger ones with Kathy, their youngest, only two years old. Dorothy found special meaning in Psalms 84:5-7. She wrote, "'who going through the valley of Baca . . . make it a well.' I wasn't aware that Baca meant weeping, until just now. But it seems to be my turn to go through the valley and I do trust to make it a spring."

I also heard that Dr. Becker had had a heart attack. Mrs. Becker stayed by him at the side of the road for two hours until his pain lessened and they could get home. The next day, he was right back at work. Dr. and Mrs. Atkinson, who had been at Oicha before we evacuated, arrived at Nyankunde and that would be a real help for Dr. Becker.

At the end of June, Mary opened her mail to find her certificates that had been sent to the government. We didn't know what it meant until we read the accompanying letter which requested a translation of the certificate. Apparently, her University diploma was in Latin. The government also said they were sending word to the hospital to find out what courses she had taken. Good luck. She graduated in 1928, and the hospital was no longer in existence. When we told Keith, I laughed and said that she had finished her schooling before he was even born. He sort of chuckled at us old people. I wondered when I'd hear about my paperwork.

The government was in charge, and we tried to comply with everything they asked of us. If we were confused about exactly what they wanted, we simply continued on as we were for the time and trusted that they would clearly communicate any changes they required.

We still had no word on whether the government would give more of the property to the Mission. We were in a no man's land. We didn't have much contact with Congo, and they didn't feel they could keep us. The field of West Nile, in Uganda, where Barb and Martha worked, didn't want the responsibility for the station either. It was unwanted. I wondered what the Lord had in store for the work. I prayed for the Lord to make me willing for what he wanted for me. I was settled in, enjoying my work and my little house. Any moving meant getting used to new things all over again. The Lord was able and I praised Him for that.

We often had over 500 people coming in. I still went out on Sundays, visiting different churches. One Sunday we went out to a place right on the border of Congo. I found Acholi people, and one of the young men knew English very well. We talked a long time on things of the Lord. He had the idea that if man was getting close to landing on the moon then he'd be closer to God, for God is up there. I told him no one could be nearer to God than I was right at the moment because God was in my heart. He was Christian in name but not able to say Christ was his Savior. He accepted a New Testament in English and I prayed it would bring him to the Lord. He was an Acholi from Gulu in Uganda. When I tried to speak Acholi, I mixed it up so much he told me, "You may speak English."

The next week, Mary and I took a trip to Oicha. Mary really wanted to go, but I hesitated because I didn't like to leave Doctor alone. Our trip took a full eight hours. We were held up at customs because the man on the Ugandan side had gone to buy food and we had to track him down. Since we had no visa for Congo, that side was unsure what to do with us; this caused more delay. They finally gave us papers for seven days even though we only wanted to stay overnight. The first twenty miles were good, but then the road deteriorated. It seemed that every time Mary remarked that the road seemed better, or I shifted into third gear—we'd hit some hard bumps. Of course we had a car full of other folks, which didn't help. As it turned out, I was glad we had the extra help. We reached the houses in Beni and almost to the turn for Oicha when Mary said we had a flat tire. She had to repeat it before I understood. The tire was a new one I had just bought, but I had forgotten to tell them to put a new tube in it, and they didn't ask. We changed that quickly and added air to the back tire which also looked low. Before we got to Oicha, that one went flat too. I fixed one hole in the first tire and thought all was well, but then I found three more. Someone saw us by the side of the road and told Jewell and Margaret Clapper, who drove up just as we finished. Our trip averaged 12 miles an hour.

We had a nice visit, although I could see things were difficult at Oicha. So many houses were vacant, and it didn't seem as alive as it used to be. They had problems getting medicine and trouble with some of the workers. Jewell had a big task before her.

After our short trip, we were back into the work again and Margaret Clapper paid us a visit in mid-July. I had stayed with her in Rethy when I first came to Congo seventeen years earlier and was happy to be able to return her hospitality. During the time Margaret was visiting, Mary got a telegram from Mr. Amstutz. It stated, "no replacement—appreciate your staying. Will see what I can find out in Kampala, letter soon, and keep praying." I felt bad she couldn't keep any of her furlough plans. She was exhausted and wanted to go on furlough. I was glad Margaret was there since she had been Mary's friend for a long time and helped take sting out of the news. We continued on, and I prayed for our situation. Mary wasn't getting along well with Dr. Keith, and I knew she was tired and disappointed.

I had a letter from Martha saying they had enjoyed their trip home but were glad to stop traveling. Back in the USA, she and Barb visited the Rineers and then one Sunday they all went to the Reitsmas' for dinner. Kim had invited the Greens as well and what a party they had. Sixteen children. I had thought the Greens were in northern Africa and had been praying to that end. But, apparently, I had missed a letter because Dallas Green had surgery in the spring and they never went to north Africa after all. Mary thought perhaps the Lord might store up some of those prayers!

Samsoni, one of the medical men, and his wife Eudia had twins. She had been so big and Mary knew it was breech, but she hadn't figured there were two. Both came breech and one had been on top of the other which made it seem like one long body. Eudia's last pregnancy hadn't been normal and so Mary was fearful, but the boy and girl were fine and so cute. Each weighed over seven pounds. (No wonder she couldn't lay down.) The parents were so proud of them and said that God gave two— one extra to take the place of another they had lost.

When Mary should have been on the *Queen Elizabeth*, sailing home to New York, she was working full days in maternity. She rarely had a night without some calls because we didn't have enough of the experienced help to take over. We had over fifty deliveries in the month of July. The things done in the village for deliveries must have been awful because we saw many septic cases come in. What these poor women went through and survived was something.

Things were not calm at the border. Tomasi, one of our hospital workers, had crossed into Congo and was not able to get back. I suppose they were taking precautions. This poor old world was a mess. The States had its troubles too. All the riots and murders were terrible to hear about. My heart ached for the lost souls of those everywhere. Maybe it was a glimpse—a small understanding—of the pain the Lord has for the world.

The people here were in such need, and we didn't have the workers or permits or even the place as of yet. Neither Mary nor I had our registrations (government was still checking and I finally received mine in October). But, the people kept coming in for help. On our day for vaccinating children, I thought I might have to come back to the Nyabirongo side early to help Mary. By noon, she sent an SOS and I rushed over. The book work took so long that even with four of us writing we didn't finish until 3 p.m. We saw a total of 269 children that day.

We were waiting for Harold and Jane Amstutz to come and give us direction on the future of the work. Dr. Keith received a letter from Mr. Brashler, an AIM director from the Congo. He indicated that if we didn't get more help, he would come and close the work. It didn't seem possible that it could stay open, but we carried on day by day. I dreaded to think of closing the work. Border trouble would cause difficulty for moving things. All the details of importing items seemed like too great a task to me. I didn't want to think of all the effort it would take to pack up and close the work—so much easier to leave with just a suitcase (though I didn't really want to do that again!)

On Friday, August 5, I received a telegram from home. It took a while for the news to sink in. My brother Edward had died suddenly. All I could think was glory for him and all his burden gone; yet I knew the sorrow. I thought of my family and was with them in spirit and prayed for physical strength and peace of the Lord who loves us so very much. I thanked the Lord for his life, and my tears in prayer were for those left, and for those loved ones still not saved. At work the next day, I told the men and asked that they pray for my family. Benjamin prayed so nicely—that the Lord would comfort, praise that this one was the Lord's, and praise for the hope we have. I praised the Lord for the saints here.

Mid-August, the Amstutzes, Stanley Kline, and Dr. Keith went to Fort Portal to try and get some word about our station. We all felt it would be a shame to close a work when there was a need and every opportunity to give forth the Word of Life. But we needed the land grant before we could build. They were seeking the grant for the Kagando side with the plan to build homes and move the whole work over there instead of the two sites we had now. Because of the uncertainty of what the days might bring on other fields, we were glad for the open door here and would not close it easily. We were afraid the local folks might block us if we tried to leave. Mr. Bwambale, who had encouraged Dr. Becker to develop this work, was trying to keep us here, but everything moved slowly. As it turned out, the meeting in Fort Portal didn't happen, but Harold finally met up with the right people in Kasese. In spite of no firm results from the meeting, the Amstutzes told us they were trying to get permits for Jerry and Anny Rineer to come join us. Jerry would do the building and Anny could take Mary's place. Harold felt he could get the staff if we got the grants.

Labor Day came and I was labored. I was myself as much as I could be, then I was Dr. Waddell for some of the work. Later I became Joshua, writing patient cards. After I finished that, I gave some medicine before coming home. Musa was away, so I did his work. No one came for English lessons, and I had extra time to just putter around. Later, Tomasi, our hospital worker, came by and talked for a while. Just as he was leaving, a woman came running saying her baby was very bad. When I examined the baby, he looked up at me and smiled. The mother was afraid more than anything. I gave the baby more medicine then settled her into a bed for the night. So it went.

Dr. Keith hadn't been to work since the Friday before Labor Day. He had gone to bed early on Friday and had asked me to turn out the lights. We saw no sign of him on Saturday or Sunday. Then he didn't work on Monday either. I noticed he had taken medicine on Friday, but I didn't look to see what it was. Mary took food to him on Saturday and didn't think he looked very ill. He was a different sort of person, and we didn't know what to think. When I brought the mail, I tried to find out how he was by talking through the window, but I couldn't understand everything he said. By Monday, I found out he was having fevers that would ease and then return at night, so we took a slide but couldn't find anything. I had Musa cook dinner for him, and he ate a little then immediately lost it. That was the beginning of the vomiting. We suggested he go to a doctor, but he thought he'd be better soon.

On Wednesday morning, Mary and I looked in on him, and he thought he felt a little better; however, Mary sent a note over at noon asking William (our laboratory man) to do more lab work. Dr. Keith was weaker and breathing heavily, but he still wanted to wait another day to go see a doctor. I called the men together for prayer for the Lord to guide us. By the time I got back to the Nyabirongo side, William had taken the blood and couldn't get over the doctor's lack of response. Mary was planning to set up an intravenous and told me that Dr. Keith had mentioned that maybe he should go to a doctor. On that note, I went in and pushed him to let me take him to Fort Portal. At first he told me, "Oh Olive, let me wait until morning." He looked so sick, and I was quite concerned, so I stuck to the point until he finally agreed.

Tomasi and William helped him get dressed and out to the car, and William rode along to help on the way. I took out the back seat and filled the place with blankets and a smaller mattress. Though quite ill, Dr. tolerated the trip. We left at 7 p.m. and arrived by 9 p.m., just when it began to rain.

The doctor in Fort Portal couldn't find anything more than the malaria we had found but would run more tests in the morning. If he needed to get in touch with us, he would contact the hotel in Kasese. Keith didn't want me to write to his parents until he was better. I didn't know how to contact the Mission because the Amstutzes were in Congo, so I sent a telegram to Bunia. When I called the hospital on Friday, they hadn't gotten all the tests back.

That Sunday, I didn't go out to any villages. With all my work and running around, I had gotten malaria. I didn't like the effects of the medicine, but I decided I might as well take it and get it over with.

Having left so quickly for the hospital, we didn't think of things we should have taken with us. Mary went to town and bought some shirts and pajamas which we sent along with the Chief's son who was going to Fort Portal. When I called on Wednesday, we learned that Dr. Keith had been diagnosed with infectious hepatitis which would require a long recovery time. I wished I could be there to give him nursing care, but we couldn't carry on in both places. I sent out the call for prayer. He was a young man, and doctors were so needed out here.

The following week I traveled into Kasese on a Tuesday to call and check on Dr. Keith. The next day I began to hear a funny noise in my car which I thought might be the muffler going. We looked but couldn't see anything wrong. That Friday, driving back from Kasese after another phone call, the car began losing power. I decided to go straight to the garage in Kilembe, but the car stopped completely when climbing a hill. John was with me and took a note to the garage by hitching a ride on a truck passing by. While he was gone, I took my cushion and *Reader's Digest* and found a spot under some bushes to wait for the garage man. After looking around and trying some things, he finally reported that a bolt was broken off—which meant removing the engine. So out came the tow rope. A tow of six miles instead of the thirty had I broken down at the station was alright by me.

The car needed a part from Kampala, so that meant a few more days. Since I didn't want to leave Mary at the station alone, I took a taxi home to the tune of $7.00. It was a swanky Zephyr that the fellow used to haul fish. He was very nice in getting me right to my door. As we drove in, no children waved from the road. They didn't recognize me. The next morning when I drove over to Kagando in Dr. Keith's Hillman Husky, the children were out to wave again.

That car got me over and back, even if I had to giggle to myself each time I tried to shift it into the right gear. Mary thought it sounded like an airplane and always wanted to look up in the sky until she realized it was me coming home. When Dr. Keith heard about my car, he wrote a note saying I should use his car—not knowing that I already had.

Dr. Becker learned of Dr. Keith's illness a full week later. He had gotten word through New York when Sid Langford asked him how Dr. Keith was doing and he didn't know anything about it. My telegram never got through—and I had paid over $5.00 to send it. We were just over the mountain, but further away than America.

Dr. Keith was very weak; he could hardly hold a pen. He came back to Nyabirongo with the Chief who had gone to visit him and planned to recuperate with his parents in Johannesburg. The next day, Wednesday, we got him on the train, and he arrived at his parents' place by Saturday.

I hadn't planned to use Dr. Keith's car for more than driving back and forth to Kagando, but he wanted to get to his parents. On the way home from the train, I thought I was getting the feel of it and it wasn't so bad after all. But about five or six miles from home, it began making a noise and became overheated. I let it cool off, then I managed to drive to the foot of the hill into the station when the noise got worse and something snapped. That was the end. Another car came along and towed it the rest of the way home. Not only did I manage to finish off two cars in one week—I had to walk to work.

Dr. and Mrs. Becker came by the next day for a visit. He saw some patients, then wanted to talk to Harold Amstutz. I went along with him to Kasese to see if my car was finished (it wasn't) and to help him get his call through, since I already had the knack of using the phones there. We came across an accident on the way home and brought one man back to the hospital. Nothing serious, just a few wounds.

Harold arrived the next day, and he and Dr. Becker had a meeting. Dr. Becker had gone over the books and found we were not bringing in enough money to carry the staff. The future was uncertain for the work. Dr. Becker also met with the medical men. Mrs. Becker was in bed, sick for the time they were here, but took some medicine for the trip home to Nyankunde.

Harold and his son David, who had traveled with him, removed the engine from Dr. Keith's car to take with them to repair. With no cars, I tried biking to work. Even three years earlier it wouldn't have been a problem, but my legs weren't up to it. I couldn't get back to the hospital in the evening, so the man on duty had to check everything.

Sometimes I took my lunch along to work so I could stay over there, particularly if I was meeting with the women or with children of the workers. The children were so cute. They would run to get their feet and faces washed at a large pan by the side of the house and put on another dress or suit before we met. It was interesting to watch the five–year–old help a three–year–old. Often the fathers were supervising because the women were down in the garden. We would finally get it all together and my time with the children gave the mothers a break to get ready for their prayer meeting.

I took the bus into town to check on my car which was finally repaired. I didn't get to town before the bank closed, so I finished the shopping instead. When I went back, one of the clerks told me the bank didn't open again that day. How was I going to get the money to pay the men? To make it worse, I found out that the money transfer from the Amstutzes hadn't come in yet. I had money in my account, and a shopkeeper cashed a check for me. That, along with some money I was holding for two Africans, covered the need. The next day, a check came in the mail from the Amstutzes, so all was taken care of.

By the beginning of October, Dr. Keith was slowly improving but still so weak that he could only walk a few yards. He wrote to me that if I had stopped using his car, perhaps I should take out the battery. I didn't like to tell him that not only was the battery out, but the engine as well.

We felt a few earthquakes in the area. We heard a loud noise and the house shook, but there was no damage. The wind was another story. It took down a tree by the hospital and the roofs off the patient houses. They told me the string used here to tie together the grass for the roofs didn't last well, so the grass blew off quickly.

We had a little light to our situation in hearing that the Rineers were ready to come back to the field. They were just waiting on their permits for Uganda. We carried on. We had some meningitis cases and were so happy to see them improve. A child came in so very anemic after her treatment for worms. I was afraid I had treated her too quickly. Later I learned the family had given her medicine from the store, then came in and we gave her more medicine. She passed over 100 worms. No wonder the poor girl was so sick. I praised the Lord that she responded and improved.

With no surgeries, I moved the man who helped with the operations to evening work, but what a time. He took more time to say over and over what he wanted—to get out of work. The other men more or less gave in to him. I was finding difficulty every time a woman had to take over what a man had been doing. Was I harder on the men than a man was, or was it harder for them to take assignments from a woman?

We were expecting a visit from Jewell and Nina in time for Mary's birthday at the end of October. On the day they were to be here, we heard by radio that they hadn't even left Oicha. Mary was so disappointed. I put two pillows on chairs and labeled one "I am Nina" and the other, "I am Jewell". I had gotten her a cosmetic bag in town and put a few pictures inside from *Time*—one of a smart woman in one of the new pant suits. I told her it was just the right thing for her furlough. She enjoyed her birthday celebration, and we had a long talk.

One Sunday in mid-November, Mary, two men, and I traveled out to a little church about four miles from our station. I had never known it was there. When the man pointed it out as we were driving, I wondered if I'd be able to climb up to it. After we went around another bend, it didn't look so high. We parked and walked up the foot path between gardens. It was quite steep, but not nearly as far as it looked at first glance. The mudded walls of the church were damp (whether from rain, or having been freshly plastered, I didn't know).

In this church, the men sat in front and the women in back instead of the usual side by side division. Most of the folks were refugees from Congo. The singing was good (maybe better to me because it was in Congo Swahili and I could sing along). The order of service was more familiar as well. The Church of Uganda had a formal service which was not in Swahili.

They asked if I'd speak, and I used the wordless book which I had brought along. Each different colored page represented something different. First I showed the gold page. It was gold to remind folks of our loving God in heaven. The next page was black to represent our sinful hearts—so unclean that no one is righteous enough to be with God on his own. Next came the red page—the blood of Jesus. God loved us so much he sent His Son Jesus to earth to die on the cross and pay the price for our sins. Then He was raised to life again. The next page was white to show folks how Jesus makes hearts clean when we confess our sin and invite Jesus into our lives. Last came the green page to remind folks to pray, read the Bible, and obey in order to grow in Christ.

The adults enjoyed the book just as much as the children. This was a poor group of people, clothing patched and wearing through, but that didn't dampen their spirit to worship the Lord who had died to set them free from sin. These were people who knew the Lord. Though they had had to flee their homes, a place of worship was what they wanted. They loved the Lord and came together for Him. We were all encouraged by remembering God's great love for us through the death and resurrection of our precious Lord and Savior Jesus Christ.

We still had no word on the grants for the land. We were in the government buildings, but we couldn't build more until we got those grants. Some local people were upset because they had paid taxes for those buildings and they wanted their free medicine again. We tried to explain that we needed the grants and the folks thought they would come. Without a doctor on the station we couldn't do as much for the people. The Lord knew all.

The African world was surely uncertain and needed much prayer. I heard of uprisings in Rhodesia, an attempted coup in Togo, and a plot by an American to blow up a bridge in Zambia over its copper industry. We looked to the Lord for guidance and took the days to tell of the love of the Lord to as many as He gave us to teach.

Harold and David Amstutz stopped by and reinstalled the engine in Dr. Keith's car. They had delayed coming in hope of having some word of the Rineers, but there was no news as of yet.

Some of the younger men came to me and wanted a time together for training and a time around the Word. Dr. Keith had worked with them, but since he became ill, they had nothing. I began meeting with them on Monday evenings, and we had a nice hour together: some about medical work, some around the Word. Mary told me I was never home, but I felt I hadn't come over here but to give myself to His work. I was over at Kagando anyway and was glad to give them time.

At the beginning of December, Betty Wilson came to stay with me while Mary went to get work on her teeth. She had had pain and swelling for a time and finally had to take care of it. Betty and I caught up on all the news of families and happenings in the four years since we had been together.

While Mary was gone, I was looking after both sides of the work, but the Lord was good and maternity patients came in such a way that allowed my rest at night. That first weekend, I had an evening case on Friday, then another on Saturday at noon. Early Sunday, before I was dressed, the call came for a woman having twins—her third set with only one of the children living. The babies were born and were alive, although the second one was weak and shaky because of the work he took to start breathing. After that I had breakfast, went late to the other side, then late to church as well. But I fit everything in!

Praise the Lord. On Saturday, December 17, the Rineer family arrived at Nyabirongo. The previous Thursday, Betty left and Mary arrived on the plane. Mary thought the Amstutzes would bring the Rineers on Monday, but they came a few days early.

The Rineers settled in a small house and put two double-decker beds in the room next to the maternity house for the boys to sleep at night. We heard Dr. Keith would return around the first of the year, although he needed medical clearance from the British Home Council first.

My house and the Rineers' house at Nyabirongo

Once everyone was settled in, we would need a good look at the running of things. We were not able to meet expenses at all except by the extra gifts given to help the work. So many things were needed— mattresses, rubber sheets, blankets, new toilets dug.

We celebrated Christmas with nine missionaries and children on the station. The children had fun making gifts for everyone. Many of their things hadn't arrived so they asked me for paper, string and jars. They gave me a pretty oil-painted vase, a handmade Christmas card, and a Pan Am wash up packet.

We heard the Christmas message in several languages, so familiar yet always so wonderful. "For unto you is born . . . a Savior which is Christ the Lord" (Luke 2:11). I thought of the wonder that the message is for ALL people. I praised the Lord for his provision in giving health and strength for the added tasks of the previous months. We praised the Lord for continued fruit in the hearts of patients. An added gift was a quiet day—a break on Christmas.

1967

Therefore do not be unwise, but understand what the will of the Lord is. (Ephesians 5:17)

A blizzard at home in Pennsylvania resulted in a letter from Daddy. How nice the Lord sends snow. I think my parents would have liked to visit me in Africa, but it never worked out.

Mary returned by train to Kampala for surgery on her face. We expected Dr. Keith back soon but hadn't had word from him. The Rineers and I began talking and praying for direction in carrying out the non-hospital work. Jerry found Uganda so different than Sudan. He had been out to one of the lake areas and people came around, listening and expressing their desire to accept the Lord. Follow-up work was difficult because we weren't familiar with the area churches. Fruit needed to be nourished, but we struggled to know how to direct the people.

The Rineer children headed back to school on January 8. Jerry took the train with them from Kasese to Kampala where the children would go on alone with the other school children back to Kijabe. Jerry was a big man but very soft of heart, and it was hard for him to see the children off to school—especially his little girl. Anny, Mickey (their three–year–old), and I stayed back in Nyabirongo.

We heard Mary had come through her operation well. She wrote that Dr. Keith was in Kampala and had stopped in to see her. She told us that he looked well and had gained weight, but he still didn't have medical clearance from London. The dispensary at the station carried on with three to four hundred coming in. Happily, I had only one night call for maternity during the time Mary was gone.

By mid-January, Dr. Keith was back, and I was glad he was there to take responsibility for many of the patients. He had his ideas for changes, and I prayed for the part I would have to help work some of the things out. It began to look like both Barb and Martha might be coming here and be able to relieve Mary for furlough. I looked forward to the time we would have things running smoothly and I could get away for a little rest. Anny was ready to get into some work, but had her little fellow to look after and couldn't go to the Kagando side so easily.

By the end of January, Mary was back with her face healed. The growth they had removed was not malignant; however, she minded the paralysis very much even though the doctor said it would go away soon.

The rains came. We mopped water that came in under the front door then mopped the water that came in through the back door. I liked the rain. The garden took on a new look. The hills were so pretty just freshly washed and clean—such a picture. I had tomatoes, carrots, and a few ears of corn coming in and began to think of what to plant next. Previously I had planted both celery and parsley. Only the celery survived to transplant into the garden. All along I thought it to be different as the stems weren't getting thick. I cooked some for a meal, then I told Catherine (the girl who had come out with me on the train back in '65) to take some if she wanted it. She told me she thought it was parsley, but I insisted it was just a different kind of celery. I took some more that evening for my salad, and after I ate it I woke up to the fact that it was parsley. What did I taste when I had eaten it before? I suppose I often ate without thinking of the food.

Mary began preparing to take furlough in April, and I prayed she could keep her plans. She really needed a change and rest. Anny began working in surgery and was doing fine. I finally cleaned out the pharmacy and felt so good about that.

One night I had just begun reading the newly arrived minutes from the Congo Field Council when Mary came dashing in to point out the minute about me. "Miss O. Rawn: That in view of the prospective provision for nurses at Nyabirongo, Miss Rawn be reassigned to the Congo as soon as replacement is available."

Surprise—as much of a surprise as when they reassigned me to Logotok. I knew someone had to go, but didn't think they would send me. There was much need in Congo. Jewell was overdue for furlough and carrying on a big job at Oicha, but I thought I was here and that was it. Dr. Keith believed that some of the solution for the financial problems at Nyabirongo would be more missionary staff paid from home. I had told him that I didn't think he could count on the mission giving many people to one place when there were so many gaps elsewhere. Little did I know I was talking about me.

The Congolese women were not planning to continue on at the station after Mary left. They were like her children. She had trained most of them, and they stayed to help, but didn't want to continue on without her. Folks leaving would help Dr.Keith in terms of money, but the work couldn't be done without people to do it. I didn't know what would happen.

My feelings were mixed. When I heard of how Mrs. Becker could only get around with crutches and her leg brace—I wished I could help her. When I thought of Jewell alone with so much to do—I wanted to help her. We had the potential of three to four nurses here and I didn't want to just put in time somewhere.

Perhaps it was all the Lord working and I didn't even know it. There was nothing to do put pray and wait. It gave me a different view on walking day by day with the Lord. I couldn't put down roots, but I kept working for my Lord each day at the place He had for that day.

When Jerry read the news, he came over and said, "Well Olive, it was nice knowing you!"

Dr. Keith had been away at a meeting and came right to my door as soon as he arrived back. He asked if I had read the minutes. I told him I had. He replied, "The one about yourself?" I told him that I was just as surprised as anyone. Dr. Keith didn't think we had too many nurses for the work. Martha would soon join the team, but Mary would be leaving. A new couple from Canada were to come as well; however, Benjamin and many of the Congolese staff wanted to return to Congo, so time would tell.

I didn't expect to be leaving soon. There were many bridges to cross before I crossed into Congo again. The Lord knew what was begun by that minute. We were not indispensable anywhere. I went where I was assigned to labor by those in charge. The Lord would settle each heart.

I decided to take a long weekend away at the beginning of February. Since things were piling up, I thought I might not be able to get away for my two weeks this year. A short getaway seemed like the thing to do. All the others agreed I should go. When they asked what I would do, I said, "Go away and hide." The African staff couldn't imagine where I'd go to hide.

I hid at the Hotel Margherita in Kasese. The room was lovely with a private bath and a tub big enough to lie down in. I rested, read, prayed, and enjoyed the meals in the hotel dining room. It was lovely to be on my own—no entertaining or being entertained. I felt extravagant staying in a hotel room that cost ten dollars a day, but I would have lost time in travel had I gone all the way to the rest house in Kampala.

After the few days away, I came back and felt exactly the same as before I left. I could only see the difficult places and everything that was wrong. There was so much entailed in keeping this place running. So many avenues to keep check on, and Doctor didn't make it easier by scheduling so many operations. Then at our prayer time, Catherine told of the family so thankful for what Dr. Keith had done for their baby and how they had looked to the Lord. I felt I had been impatient. There was so much I needed to pray about, and I didn't want to allow Satan to destroy any of my work in witnessing for Him.

Mr. Brashler, the Congo Field Director, stopped by for a visit. I didn't know what he had on his mind in coming over, but I prayed the Lord would guide him in all things. There hadn't been understanding between that field and this station—we were on our own. Margaret Clapper thought I'd be over to Congo just as soon as Martha came, but that would leave one married and one single woman here. When would people begin to realize that a married woman never can carry the same workload here as a single person? Perhaps a few did, but not many. Children and husband needed their help, and so their time on duty was always less. All the women workers would go when Mary left for furlough. There would be no one to deliver patients except Catherine and me. Anny hadn't ever delivered a baby.

While the Congolese staff had been trained, our young local staff were green. Either we hadn't taught the procedures, or hadn't given enough supervised practice for them to do things well. As I went around, I saw problems and had to teach on the run. Sterile forceps set down and then put back! Saving supplies never entered their minds. I asked for folks at home to pray for us in every way that the Lord would be magnified and lifted up.

Jerry Rineer often went out on Sundays with many men in his big truck. One Sunday Mehetebela, one of our women workers, and I went along and visited a village we had not been to since the previous July. Two women in one home said they didn't understand Swahili well but did understand Nyoro. I found the gospel of John in that language and began to read. One of the women could read and came close, following along. At least they heard the Word even if not all was pronounced properly.

I had blessed times with the children in various areas. I went to the chief's village for a children's meeting and had a real welcome there. I gave out seventy-seven Sunday school papers, and eleven boys and nine girls stayed afterward to accept Jesus as their Savior. This was the first time I asked at this place. Most of them seemed sincere, and I trusted that they understood.

Harold and Jane Amstutz came to discuss the work, and I felt we were able to get across some of our concerns. Even though Martha and Barbara were coming out in April, we simply could not carry on with so few staff. Harold felt the work could stay open with some changes and planned to meet with Dr. Becker about the medical side. So much had fallen on Dr. Keith's shoulders and we stood with him to help. I felt some strain lift after the meeting and the spirit seemed better. The Lord was able to help us all.

I made some medicines ahead because once Mary left I would be mostly on the Nyabirongo side to care for women coming in for delivery. I hoped that not too many would come at night. The Lord knew and cared, and I trusted him for this too.

Mary planned a visit to Oicha on her way home. She and the hospital women left for Congo on March 22 with a fully packed truck. I didn't mind this departure as much as when Jewell and the Beckers moved.

Maternity building and operating room at Nyabirongo

When Mehetebela came to say goodbye the night before, she told me that she and the others thought that both Dr. Keith and I would soon be over too. I thought I'd see what kind of prophets they were. Of course I had been asked to move, but I couldn't see how that could work out. What would happen here? In many ways, Harold Amstutz would be just as glad to close the place, but with the instability of the present government, I wondered how it might affect the Mission as a whole.

Musa, the man working in my house, wanted to leave at the end of the month. He had a big coffee garden in Congo and needed to go back and help the man looking after it. One more thing, but I wasn't too upset by it.

With Mary gone, I worked mostly on the Nyabirongo side. Because I had been out of maternity work since Opari in 1957, I began reading up on prenatal clinics. Anny and I worked together. One morning, Anny did the sterilizing while I went to check the Kagando side. When I got back, she told me she had learned two things. First, fill the kerosene at the beginning; second, be sure enough water is in the autoclave. When she had checked the autoclave, she smelled something burning and found one side of the bundles scorched. So it went.

The Lord was good in my first week without Mary and the Congolese women. The verses in the *Daily Light* at the beginning of the week started out, "He is faithful." I told the Lord that He knew what kind of rest I needed and how He would give strength.

Tuesday morning after the folks left, the day went well. I took care of the babies, then towards evening one patient came and shortly afterward another. I went to bed and at midnight was called for one of the women. Within fifteen minutes we had a baby. That was fine for the first day.

Wednesday was prenatal clinic day. Before clinic, I took care of the babies and then the mothers who were in the ward. It was raining that day, and the women arrived late for clinic. I had to break for an hour at noon when I delivered a baby, and I finished clinic by 3 p.m. The medical girls and I had our prayer meeting, and we ended with a quiet evening. I slept well that night and dreamed we were packing quickly to leave.

A case came in at 4 a.m. Thursday, but they waited to call me until 6 a.m. and I commended them for that. We finished seeing twenty-three at baby clinic, and the patient hadn't delivered yet, so I took my dinner early. Anny came to tell me that another woman came in, and that the first one seemed to be getting somewhere. I was going to finish my fruit, but I got the call to run. She was on the table, and I got there just in time to deliver the baby. After prayer meeting at 2:30 p.m., I was resting, dozing off with my shoes on ready for the next case. The call came but they had the baby delivered by the time I ran down. I was glad the maternity building was downhill.

Friday began with a call at 1 a.m. for a delivery and back to bed by 2:30 a.m. I had told the girls to let me know if I had to come fast or else I'd take the time to put my shoes on. They had called a bit early so I'd have time.

Saturday was supposed to be my day off, but I told Dr. Keith I'd do the babies. After sleeping in until 7 a.m., I went to do the nursery work with one eye watching a patient on the delivery table. By the end of the morning, we had two babies delivered and a third not progressing. When Dr. Keith came back at noon, it was decided to do a cesarean. That was the first surgery for Anny and me. She set up and I prepared the patient. Sadly, by the time we were ready, we couldn't save the baby. It was the woman's eighth.

The next day, Easter Sunday, was Anny's day off. That morning I put on stockings and my more modern style uniform — not to be sat down in too much! I thought that once I had finished the babies, I'd dress for Easter day and have lessons with the patients. I took off my uniform at 10:30 p.m. That morning, Dr. Keith had stopped by to see if there were any needs for patients and in came one-two-three. All of them were quiet and it didn't seem that Dr. Keith needed to stay. He and Jerry were preaching for the morning. I taught in the maternity building, and at the end of my lesson the fourth patient came in.

By then, the first one looked like I needed to get her on the table. The fourth one was on the second table in the other room so I could see both. Each of the two girls working that day was with one patient, and I was scrubbed and ready for whomever needed me first. The first woman had her baby. The third woman to come in was waiting in bed while I was in the delivery room with the others. I got the call for the woman in bed, and by the time I got there she had already had the baby. One of the girls caught it. It was quick anyway. The second woman to come in didn't deliver that day. The fourth woman finally delivered at 10 p.m. with the help of medicine to bring the pains. We had a time to get the baby to breathe, but she did well. Dr. Keiyh had malaria but stayed with the woman while I slipped away for supper. He was done for by the time Easter day was over.

My days were busy, and I caught rest whenever I could. I had so much to do. We had thirty-one come to prenatal clinic the following week. Anny began helping by checking the women who had been in before, and I handled the ones on their first visit. We seemed to be having a run on women having their first baby. Some came late to clinic, so we had a second round of teaching from the Word. In the middle of seeing the first lot, we had a delivery. Anny handled it with me nearby in case she needed help. This was only her second time to deliver a baby. She had five children of her own, but to help another deliver is a different thing.

We started seeing the second group of women. I finished one case and went to find the next. In the meantime, a woman came pushing ahead of another saying she was in pain. Next thing I knew they were calling me. There she was, squatting on the floor with the baby's head showing. Anny ran for the pack and I delivered the baby. Just at that moment, Dr. Keith looked in on us to say he was heading to the other side. We looked at him and said, "We have them everywhere!" It kept us on our toes. At least the woman made it to the clinic and didn't have to pay the fee for delivering without coming to clinic first.

Anny and I became quite a team. In addition to the babies and mothers, I also went to the Kagando side for rounds and the pharmacy when I could. Catherine was taking a real interest and became quite a help. Dr. Keith learned more about the pharmacy now that I was not over there as often. He came and asked questions about the making up of some of the drugs.

One morning I had finished the babies and caught up on charting. I thought I'd head back to my house. "Wapi?" (where?) The bus came and we had to run for a patient. The woman's water had broken on the bus, and I guess they got scared and came right up to the door. An hour later, we had a fine baby boy. I thought I could go home then, but another woman arrived at the delivery room door. In between things, I tried to read up on how to sterilize our vacuum extractor. It was a new instrument for us, in some ways easier than forceps and less dangerous on the whole.

Mid-April, we had Dr. Sally, an American medical student, visit and see the work. She stayed in Mary's house but ate with me. One day as I was finishing at Kagando, I heard a car blowing the horn. Barb and Martha had arrived. They were driving through on their way to Kuluva to pick up their things. I said to myself, "Okay, two more to feed." They went on to the other side, and I gathered my things and followed. When I pulled in to Nyabirongo, I saw an extra car with two more people. It was one of the Australian missionaries from Kenya and his girlfriend (who was heading home to England for Bible classes before they married). Who knew what a day would bring forth. The first thing I did was to go into the house and take two aspirin. I ended up feeding six of us for supper. Anny had her whole family home from school, but she made dessert and got the beds fixed up. We all worked together.

Two letters came from Mary while she visited in Congo. She told me the need was terrific there, and they were looking forward to my coming. What would the future hold? I was needed here too.

By the beginning of May, Martha was into the work, and I was not catching as many babies. I was still busy. Really there was plenty for the three of us to do. I helped in maternity and sometimes in surgery. Occasionally, I made dinner and Martha, Barb, Keith, and I ate together.

Anny, Martha, and maternity staff

I had a good garden. Once I had bacon, lettuce, and tomato sandwiches with fresh celery—and it really was celery.

Sometimes when I went out to homes to visit former patients, they gave me gifts of food like palm fat or a chicken. I didn't like the gift giving and always told them I hadn't stopped by for a gift, but they gave it anyway.

Undernourishment was a big problem in the area. We gave venoclysis to a small child who was over one year old and weighed only six pounds. He had no teeth, really just a skeleton with skin over him. The children had food, but often were not given the right kind in the right balance. The cassava flour just didn't have the right food value and many times that was all they had. Of course, the malaria and worms worked against them as well. Unless they had treatment, they went down fast.

I planned to take a vacation in Kampala in Mid-May. Before I left, Martha came with me to the Kagando side so she could see what was done and carry on some. It was a big task to have calls in maternity and keep the medicine made up in the pharmacy. I hoped to get ahead on the medicine so she wouldn't have as much to do.

I drove off to begin my vacation at the rest home in Kampala. The Zimmermans, Weisses, and Pearl Hile greeted me when I arrived. They were all leaving the next morning, but we had a good talk together. Pearl Hile was a nurse with the UFM work and had been through much before she evacuated Congo. Dr. David of Tanzania, a national doctor, was also there. The two of us had an inspiring conversation late into the night of his zeal to heal the whole of man.

I spent time with the Amstutzes. The weather was nice and everything looked so green and pretty. That's what I needed—some sun. I had been inside all the time and was so pale. Of course, I read a *Time* article about the danger of sun, so I guess I shouldn't have desired to be tanned.

I took my car to the garage for a going over and I went to the dentist. I couldn't get an appointment with my usual dentist, so I visited the national dentist. He cleaned my teeth and couldn't see anything wrong. One and a half years and nothing wrong. Much to be thankful for.

A book about Dr. Becker's life had just been published. I read half the book one day and finished it the next. I enjoyed every bit of it.

The Beattys and I had planned to spend some of my vacation together and I met them at Kampala. They would soon leave on an extended furlough because of Dorothy's health problems. We traveled together up to West Nile to visit the Booths in Ringili, near Kuluva. While we were there, I was able to see Fiobe and Simeona, the pastor from Congo who had worked in Torit and now helped at Kuluva.

Our time with the Booths was lively with little Peter Booth and the two youngest Beatty children Bob and Kathy. I called home to my parents and the other relatives gathered around their phone. I began the call in the office, and the operator told me it would take half an hour to go through. Then we went back to the house, and no sooner were we in the house when the call came through, so I took it there. The operator in Nairobi was such a flirt. He told me he liked the name Olive and talked on and on until he got my brother Raymond on the line. Bill and Harold both teased me about that. The phone was around the corner from the living room. Everyone tried to be quiet, but I could hear them tell me to say something another way when my parents didn't understand what I said. When I finished the call, I asked the men how long I had talked. Bill said, "Harold pulled the page off the calendar some time back." Anyway, we all had a nice hello together.

The Beattys and I went on to Gulu, the closest to Sudan you could get at the time. We saw Andreya and Lydia for a short time before we went to the Beattys' home in Ogada, Kenya. I had my visa for Kenya, but someone messed up and didn't give me my reentry to Uganda, and I hadn't thought to check. When I stopped at the immigration office in Kisumu, they almost said I had to go right back. Then the man told me two to three days but changed it to be out by June 4. When they finally brought my paper, he told the other man to write June 6, which is what I had wanted from the start. They called me a prohibited immigrant because I came in without exit papers, and they were afraid I wouldn't go back to Uganda again. That would be trouble. The border business sure was something. I wrote home that folks could be glad the USA was all one and not a check at each state.

The next leg of my vacation was to Kijabe to see the Olsens, Fonsecas, Gehmans, and Bakers. I stayed with the Olsens who were looking forward to furlough at the end of the term because they had adopted another baby. She had been born the beginning of May in Virginia, and a friend of theirs was taking care of her until they got home. They had planned to go home through the Holy Land but changed that because things were not very good there at the time.

I had an extra blessing from a visit at Scott Theological College. I saw Nikolau and Abednego and their families. They were so glad to see me. Nikolau's newest baby was three months old. They had four girls, all very sweet. Abednego had three girls. I caught up on the news of the women from Sudan also. Tabita told me that she and Maliam (Abednego's wife) read the Word and prayed the way she and I did in Sudan. I praised the Lord for that.

I went back to Kampala for a few days before finishing my vacation and heading home in the middle of June. I often ate as I drove and had just put a roll that I had bought in my lap. In a split second, I was off the road and in a deep ditch. I got out of the car and just sat on the grass and looked at what I had done. I didn't even understand what happened. It sounds ridiculous to say that I went into a ditch for no apparent reason.

My knees hit the dash and my left side on the gear shift—remember we had the right-side drive. I was glad no one was with me for the left side was damaged and I'm afraid they would have been badly hurt. I had the car loaded with Bibles and other books and some drugs. Nothing broke that I could find but the hood of the car had opened and some

Standing in the ditch months later at the site of the accident

things flew out. People came around quickly and helped me. They warned me to not leave the things around or they would be stolen. Soon other cars stopped and some men (after they found I would pay them) took hold of the little bug and just lifted her up and back on the side of the road. We pulled the fender off the wheel and I managed to get back to the town of Masaka where the Plymouth Brethren work was located. They were gracious and helped me call through to Mr. Amstutz. So the car went to the garage and I stayed put until it could all be straightened out.

A few days later, I got a ride to Kampala and stayed in the rest home there until I could deal with the insurance. While I was there, a Central Field Council note was made thus: "That Miss Olive Rawn be considered a member of the Congo Field and that her transfer to Congo be approved upon the agreement of all parties concerned." Some folks move from their station because they are not happy in their work, but others move when they are happy. It seemed I only moved or changed when I was happy. I was glad about that, but it didn't make it easy. I remembered back to my first experience of change when I bawled as I left my job at the factory for nurses' training!

I still didn't know when the transfer would be, but I knew I'd have to start preparing to leave. Jewell was having difficult back problems. In May, she had been riding on the back of Harold McDowell's motorcycle when it hit a bump. She had had such a jar that she had to stay in bed for a bit. I told her she should watch out for these young men—he was our baby, born when we first arrived back in 1949. How the years marched on. Jewell's back still bothered her. I told Harold Amstutz that Jewell and I were saying the same thing—"Why did I do it?"—she for riding the motorcycle and me for running the car into the ditch.

My car needed two weeks for repairs. I went back to Kasese by train and would get my car when Jerry came for the school children at the end of July. I thought I would take the VW to Congo with me. Jewell's jeep would be there for me to use, but that would cost more to drive. I would have to see how the roads were for driving with the little VW.

No one met my train. I waited an hour before I hired a waiting taxi to take me to Nyabirongo. On the way out, we went by the post office and there I picked up the telegram I had sent to let the folks know I was coming. I spent as much money on the taxi as I had on the train.

I got myself settled back into the work. We had a good discussion on how to turn my part of the work over and to whom. As I came back, Jerry asked me where I would like him to build my house—he had a site picked out. He sure didn't want me to leave, but he was resigned to it. Jerry and Dr. Keith had begun to build houses on the Kagando side with poles, mud, metal roofing, and cement floors. The Rineers needed more room for their family, and we had been assured we'd get the land, so they put up simple buildings to begin getting the work in one place.

On July 2, I began my letter home writing, "Praise the Lord with me that I can write to you again."

Four days earlier at 2 a.m. on a Tuesday, a thief broke into my house. I wouldn't have known anything was going on had the man not pulled back the mosquito net and hit me on the face. I'm glad the Lord gave me a good voice—I let out a scream. My first thought was that the house was falling on me. Then I thought it was an animal until I heard the back door close and I knew an animal wouldn't close the door as it left. Jerry and Anny came running to see if I was alright. At first I didn't see anything missing, then all of a sudden I noticed my typewriter and Anny's sewing machine that I had borrowed were both gone. They called

Jerry Rineer and his "toy"

Dr. Keith and he went down the road but didn't see anyone.

Martha had heard the scream too. At first she thought it was a maternity case and the woman had come to have the baby in the front yard.

I had forgotten to lock the back door. When Barb heard the details the next morning, she told me that she often forgot to lock that door when I was away. Jerry bought some extra bolts and put them on the doors. After the "horse" was stolen, we locked the door.

The Amstutzes arrived the next morning on a scheduled visit. I told them that I was their problem child now—always giving concern.

A few days later, Carl Becker sent a general message on the radio that a British worker had been killed in Kinshasa when a robber shot him as he tried to call the police. The Lord took one but spared me. I felt more and more my dependence on the Lord and what HE had for me in the days ahead. I prayed I would not fail Him at all.

I read the verse on the Scripture calendar the morning after the robbery. "Let not your heart be troubled. . . I will come again." The robber? No, the Lord would always be there with me. He would not leave me. It was really something to see that verse.

Congo became unsettled again, and I didn't know when I would be able to move. The borders were closed for travel. Missionaries still broadcasted on the radio, but only in French and only at certain hours. They all seemed fine so far. Samsoni had been over and brought back some letters, getting through the border on the very day it closed. Dr. Becker's letter told me that when I could get over, they would like me at the Oicha work.

One Sunday Barb and I went to visit a church further out. On the way, we found a washed-out bridge. Folks had put some logs across, but not over the deepest place. A new iron bridge was in progress but not yet complete enough to safely walk over. We didn't feel like wading so we went back to Kabiri to the Congo church I had visited before. No one was actually meeting there because leaders had returned to Congo, but the men with us got some folks together and taught them. We were able to meet in the building, but if someone didn't take care of it the white ants would soon finish it.

I thought of Camp Meeting going on at home. I had written a letter of greeting as I did every year. I even had a dream that I was at services at camp meeting but was staying in some poor folks' humble home in town.

Dr. Keith took a two-week vacation while I was still at the station. Jerry was busy getting the buildings finished. The others began taking over more of my work, and I filled in everywhere I could. I continued teaching the medical workers, and Barb learned more of the pharmacy work. She had a difficult task because many of the medicines and the purposes for doing things a certain way were foreign to her.

I still held the children's classes and had about forty-two boys and girls out to class. Eight stayed behind to take Jesus as their Savior, but it was sometimes hard to know how much they really understood. One boy said he stayed to kneel before God, another to pray, and one girl said she had believed since before she was born. How they needed teaching.

Sometimes I wondered who was safer: the folks at home, or those out here. I heard about riots at home, the latest in Detroit. We had little word of the Congo folks. Those with children had gone to Kenya to pick them up from school and were staying out until things settled down. Dr. Becker said the situation was still in the uncertain stage. They were not to use the radios, and the MAF planes were not flying. The Rineers had gone for their children and said the headlines in the Kampala paper didn't make Uganda sound very wonderful either. There was much need for prayer. I thought that surely the Lord's coming was near.

Dr. Keith returned from his vacation the first week in August and immediately took a patient for surgery. I had thought he might bring my car back with him, but he didn't. I continued filling in, teaching the medical folks and taking night call for Martha. One night I had a call at 3:30 a.m., and by the time I was home again I had delivered three babies. I had to use the vacuum extractor on the second baby and worked over half an hour to get her to breathe. She died the next evening.

As soon as Dr. Keith had moved to the Kagando side into his lovely new house, we had a nice big question mark before us again. A letter came from Fort Portal saying the government was interested in both Nyabirongo and Kagando. Day by day.

I still didn't have my car back. With Dr. Keith living on the Kagando side, I often rode over with Barb in the morning and walked back in the afternoon. The VW was repaired, and I could have gone to get it, but that meant more time away. I told the Amstutzes that if someone was coming out this way they could bring it. I still didn't have my papers for Congo.

I couldn't understand all the ways the Lord was leading me, but I wanted to be used by Him. I found that I needed the Lord to help me keep my thoughts on Him and not on the ways of fellow workers. I reflected on Ephesians 5:16-17. ". . . redeeming the time, because the days are evil. Therefore do not be unwise, but understand what the will of the Lord is." I needed to make the best use of my time, despite all the difficulties of the days, not being vague but firmly grasping what I knew to be the will of the Lord. It was difficult. What was the will of the Lord for me or any of us in these days? Barb and I went out and found people interested in the Word. We praised the Lord, for here was every open door for us to talk with the people.

At the beginning of September, Harold Amstutz and his son David planned a visit and would bring my car with them. That day, I had the five Rineer children over for supper just as something special for them. It wasn't all that special, but I did make a pineapple upside down cake, and we played some games. After they left, I was stacking the dishes and heating the water to wash my hair when they came running back saying the Amstutzes were here. I looked out, but I didn't see my VW. They had been on their way with my car but stopped about a hundred miles from the station when smoke started pouring out of the engine. After a push to

Bible class with the children

get it started again, they drove slowly into Mbarara, a nearby town, and left the car at the VW garage there. The Lord was good in that I wouldn't have known what to do had I been driving. Everyone was glad that I wasn't stuck like that.

The Lord knew the next step. I filled out the papers for a Congo visa that the Amstutzes had brought with them. The folks in Congo were trying to get permits for the radios, though a few were transmitting among themselves. We overheard the pilot give a message from Mr. Brashler that the American consul informed him that everyone should be ready to leave if he gave the word—even if their area seemed quiet. The consul felt that if the south worsened, the unrest would most likely spread. The planes were now free to fly, but since not all in the military were aware of that change it wasn't safe. Those out of the country were advised to stay out.

When Jerry took his children to Kampala to get the train for school, the escort never showed, so he went on to Kijabe with all twenty of the waiting children. He came back with the bad news about my car. The man at the garage told Harold that the whole engine needed to be gone over. I would have a new car and an empty pocketbook by the time this was all over. I needed the car for work, and I figured it should do me a long time after this. Earlier, Jerry had offered to buy the car if I wanted to get rid of it. Now he was glad he didn't have it. The Rineers were low in funds too—some of their support had not come in and the schooling was costly. All I could say was that my vacation was a nice time, and had this car business happened before, I would not have been so free or gone so far.

The work went on. I taught Anny and Martha how to make the iodoform gauze. The medical fellows needed supervision, and I took on more responsibility for their training. Some tried to do things without guidance. I was very upset to find an intravenous set with air in the tubing. My time was full, but I needed to find even more time for classes and further supervision.

September 9 was Independence Day for Uganda. The Rineers moved to the Kagando side and Barb made dinner for Martha and I. Jerry began work on houses for Barb and Martha—a duplex with a carport in between. They also had a camper they had brought out and would have to decide whether car or camper would be in the carport. Building was progressing, but the government was still uncertain about giving the land. It was an independent country, and they wanted to run their own things. We were after all foreigners and we had to remember it.

I had left for vacation on May 15 and on September 18 at 8:30 p.m. my car came home. Dr.Keith took the bus to pick it up for me. I didn't get to drive it until the next morning because when Keith brought it home, Jerry drove him over to the other side. Jerry told me it never drove so well. The repairs came to three hundred dollars, but no fenders shaking, a nice paint job, and four good tires on it. Except for the inside seats, it looked new. We only found a few things to fix. First, the horn wouldn't blow and the front signal lights were opposite from the back. We found the wires had been put together wrong. Then when I went for children's class, I stopped for some children and the car wouldn't start again. I checked the battery and one cable seemed a little loose. After I jiggled it, the car started. Later, Jerry took a look, and sure enough, he found the battery in backward. It was all minor things we could fix. The engine had new parts, and the front had been fixed up quite nicely, so I felt it would serve me well.

I celebrated my forty-sixth birthday still waiting for word from Congo. Only two stations were on the radio and still no planes flying. We heard the Oicha missionaries had to move away for a time due to local danger. As it turned out, the four women there never left. They felt that if they pulled out, the place would really go bad. The unrest was a distance from them and the local Pygmies would come and give warning if anything was happening or more soldiers were in the area.

Jewell, Jean Schram, and Vic Paul came for a surprise visit. Vic went on to Kampala for a part for the generator engine at Oicha. His car was still at our station and he also hoped to get it running again. Jewell and Jean stayed for a few days then went back. Jewell was waiting on me to know when she could go on furlough. I began thinking about what I needed to finish up before I left for Congo. When my visa came, I wanted to be ready to move. I boxed up some old letters and sent them home with a few other things. Maybe the Lord would come and I'd never reread those letters, but if I ever wanted them I'd have them saved.

Through the home office, I learned that the Mission Board of the Bible Fellowship Church approved using some of my housing money to replace things that had been stolen. I bought a new typewriter—a deluxe model. While Vic was in Kampala, he had gone with Jane Amstutz to purchase it. The typewriter had more features than my old one and came in a zippered case. At first I wondered how I was ever going to type because the top didn't go back far enough. Vic came to the rescue and informed me that the typewriter came completely out of the case. Did we ever have a laugh. Jerry said, "It takes a mechanic to know what to do with such things!" The type seemed smaller than my other one, so I could fit more on a page. I felt that I might not have enough news to fill up a letter. Could that be possible?

Victor got his car running, and he loaded up and left for Congo. It had been sitting here since the work opened two years ago. This was the car he and the Beckers had used to evacuate Congo back in 1964. The steering wasn't working back then, but the Lord had undertaken until they were safely out.

I enjoyed my work with the children. About fifty children would come and hear the word of God. One week we had rain, but they came running when they saw my car. The children didn't think much about the rain anyway. I wished I had more time to follow up with the children in their homes. I felt I was unable to do the full extent of the task. When I left, I would truly and completely miss the children.

My visa came through at the beginning of December, but not the reentrance for Uganda. I sent my passport right back to fix that. It looked like I'd be moving soon. I wasn't excited about it if I am truthful. Surprising since exactly two years ago I had been weepy because I wasn't going with Jewell and the folks returning to Congo. Now I was weepy because I was going. I felt sorry for Martha and the work that would fall to her, and I thought of all the things that wouldn't get done here. I kept praying for the Lord to keep me from thinking or saying anything that I shouldn't. I didn't want to feel I was the only one for the work. I was glad the Lord had given me joy in my work here.

I packed my personal things and supplies for Congo and continued filling in wherever needed. I didn't have that many possessions, but boxes sure can pile up. I helped in the operating room and delivered babies right up to the night before I left for Oicha. I didn't cry until Martha gave me a big hug before I left.

On December 21 at 8 a.m., I began my trip. Jerry loaded all my things on his truck and went to the border with me. There we transferred everything to the truck of a Greek man that Dr. Becker had sent to meet me. Everyone at the border was as nice as could be. I didn't have to open a thing. The name Oicha was like an open door at that time. If they knew you were going to help them in the medical area, they forgot other things.

Dr. and Mrs. Becker were at Oicha when I arrived, and I took my first meal with them. It seemed like old times around the table. I was amazed at how much was left whole in the work. The station hadn't been destroyed as was first reported.

I stayed with Jewell and began following her around, getting the feel of the work. Jean Schram would take the operating room, leprosy camp, and dispensaries. I'd take the pharmacy and maternity. I also took care of the money end with the wages, pension reports, and drug bills. We had Benjamin who had been trained by Dr. Becker and was able to do emergency cesarean and hernia cases. Paul and Padona oversaw the workmen and upkeep of the work, and Matiasi cared for the motor and generator as well as helping on the weekly dispensary trips. Barnaba carried on in my house and meals. Margaret Clapper and Nina Smith worked in education. Jean didn't know much about maternity, and I was glad for all the practice in the previous year. We would work things out as we went along. By the end of the year, Jewell finally was able to leave for furlough.

Thus, the Lord led through another year, and I praised Him that the Word of God continued to go forth. I looked forward to the new year. Maybe this would be the year of His return. What a blessed hope we have.

1968

Great is the Lord, and greatly to be praised; and His greatness is unsearchable. (Psalm 145:3)

My first days hadn't seemed so busy as I trailed Jewell, but now I was on my own and had plenty to do. I sorted through bundles of donated clothing. Pharmacy required a large portion of attention in getting things ready for our Friday travels to other dispensaries as well as for the daily needs for Oicha. Sometimes I lost time hunting for medicine because I was unfamiliar with the pharmacy. Sometimes I couldn't find the medicine at all. Our pharmacy was not as freely stocked as I remembered.

The very next weekend, we took time away for our annual conference at Rethy. I felt worn out before we started our trip. At first, I thought it was due to the tension of the last weeks in learning the work and the books here. We also had a cesarean case die. I hadn't slept well and was achy as we drove to Nyankunde. The first thirty miles took three hours because of the deep ditches on the road. At three places we had to hunt for stones and logs in order to build up the road enough to get through. One time the road was dry at the deepest spot so we could go down then up the other side.

At Nyankunde, I took my temperature and received orders from Dr. Becker to start medicine for malaria. Before we left for the conference, I toured the station. What did I find in one of the wards? My microscope! I didn't see my first one, but the one Bethany had purchased was there and in use.

I left my car at the Beckers' and rode with Margaret in her VW while Jean and Nina drove Jewell's Land Rover (dubbed the "pray and push"). The meetings were good, and I could see myself in the message about Jonah. He was having it easy when God called him to go to Nineveh just like I had myself settled and satisfied at Nyabirongo.

Back at Oicha the next week, I tried to organize my house and my work. We had a fairly routine schedule. A doctor came to the station about once a month for surgery and consulting on difficult cases. We also prepared boxes of medicines for the dispensary visits. Three out of the four Fridays in a month, following a rotating schedule, we drove to the dispensaries at Mwenda, Lume, Mangina, or Luanoli. At each dispensary, we consulted with the national staff, checked the books, and saw patients.

The first Friday we were back from the conference, we took the Land Rover out to Mwenda. After loading the Land Rover with foodstuff and donated clothing, Jean, I, and two others left at 6:45 a.m. for the dispensary. I realized that I'd never be able to drive my VW to this dispensary. The last seven miles had too many rocks for the little car. The road was also steep, but that wouldn't have mattered if it was passable. No one took care of that part of the road anymore.

We got to Mwenda about 9:15 a.m., stayed until about 1:00, and then left for our next stop near the border. It was 8:30 p.m. by the time we returned to Oicha. Margaret was relieved to see us as she was beginning to think something had happened to the car.

We were turning more control and management over to the nationals. Oicha had a medical committee made up of fellows representing the medical works in the district. Jean and I attended a meeting that would decide on the fees for the medical cards for the year. Nyankunde had fixed theirs, but we still had to decide what was what. That meeting took over two hours of hashing the same thing back and forth. We started at 5:00 p.m. and didn't finish until after 7:00 p.m. Jean and I tried to let them do the talking, but after two hours I said it was about time they moved on to another point or we would never finish. A lantern had to be lit before we completed our business. I was finding out that my days were full, but not so much with nursing. Books and more books needed to be kept up for all the work. The nationals should have been doing it, but they needed help and the know-how, and first of all I needed to know how.

Jean and I discussed the need to increase the spiritual part of the work. Sometimes we felt that the things of the Lord were done because they had to be and not because of hunger for the Word. I knew it was the same at home too. I prayed there might be a desire for the things of the Lord. By the end of January, I began visiting villages whenever I had a free Sunday.

We had the help of a good midwife, Yerusi, and some other women for the deliveries. Jean began learning the maternity work, and I stayed close by as she did more and more. Often we could not save the baby. One day we had a patient who had a bad infection and a dead baby. Jean tried the vacuum extractor with me encouraging, but it didn't work. A cesarean in this case would have been a long hard pull for recovery, so I decided to do a symphysiotomy. I had seen Dr. Keith instruct others, but I had never done the procedure myself. I referred to my book and began with Jean encouraging me this time. About halfway along, I was getting cold feet, but finally I heard the pop and it was done. The baby's head began to come down and we delivered the baby. The sewing up took a while for I couldn't keep from tearing the thread. So many people were watching—five others beside myself and the patient. I praised the Lord, for He enabled and I trusted all would go along well since we didn't have to open the abdomen.

I started calling the symphysiotomy "my operation." It was the next step if the vacuum extractor didn't work. We tried to avoid opening the abdomen with a cesarean because of the increased potential for infection. A cesarean also complicated a woman's next pregnancy as we were well aware she might not have access to medical help for her delivery. We were faced with many complicated decisions.

I often felt overwhelmed by the daily pharmacy work. Because we didn't have the quantity of medicine as we used to, we could only make up a little at a time. I tried to have the medical people see that they couldn't order as before, but they didn't seem to understand. There was much to learn. Dr. Keith gave less medicine sometimes, and I saw it worked just as well. It was hard to communicate this since I wasn't the one writing the cards.

The book work at Oicha was something. I didn't understand it all at first. The laws for labor had become more complicated, and we had to comply with the law. There was a wage limit. If anyone worked more than thirty days in two months, they were to have the pension book and all the extras that go with it. They received a certain amount extra for each child and all medical fees taken care of. It wasn't like the old days when we simply paid wages.

The medical workers were not always happy with their pay. At the beginning of February, they refused their pay but continued to work. That's the way they protested. They had had a pay increase the previous May and didn't like it so the Medical Committee gave them a raise again, and they still weren't satisfied. It was a labor problem that could be found most anywhere. I prayed for guidance and diplomacy to meet the situation in the right way.

Once when I had time, I walked around the area of the hospital where the tuberculosis patients lived. I hadn't been there before, and I noticed that many of those buildings needed repair. Our airstrip also required work in order to meet regulation. The name Oicha was to be on one side with letters four meters high. The airstrip had to be kept cut down so if there was an emergency it would be ready for the plane. Roads were often cut off because of the rain, so the airstrip was an important way for the doctors to get here.

Austin Paul passed away at the beginning of February at Nyankunde. He was the father of Vic Paul and Freda Atkinson (Dr. Herb's wife). Years back, Austin Paul had started teaching some nationals to play the horn, and they had toured different countries including Sudan. At his funeral, fourteen men played, and it was a radiant testimony for the Lord. Austin Paul had been back in Africa only a short time before he became ill. The Africans said it was right that he came back even for this short time for this was the place for him to die and be buried.

Days were full. Even when there was a stretch of no emergencies and quiet maternity, there was plenty to do with the pharmacy preparing the medicines to take out to dispensaries. The roads seemed to be getting worse, and if they weren't repaired we eventually would not be able to get to some locations. We always used the Land Rover. It ran on "pray and push" but rarely did it let us down. We spent so much time driving to the dispensaries that we decided to write our letters on the way. I typed one of mine, then Jean dictated one to me as she drove.

Mid-February, Vic came and worked on our light plant then went on to help Jerry with electric wiring at Kagando. We had been without electricity for a while, but I had my battery powered radio. I began hearing more about Vietnam, and the news wasn't so wonderful. President Johnson was seeing more of the young men off and also those coming home.

A week later, Dr. Wilcke was here for the surgeries with Dr. Murray, who was visiting to see the work. They left for the next station on Friday morning at 8 a.m. Margaret had gone out to a church meeting, and Jean and Nina went to town, so I was the only missionary. At 10:30 a.m. I heard a voice behind me in the pharmacy asking for some sandwiches for the path. The doctors had been on their way and found a big truck stuck in a hole, so they came back to go the other way around (longer, rougher, but no deep holes). Of course, I didn't get my pharmacy work completed.

While the doctors were here, we had all eaten dinners together including Fanweli their chauffer. Dr. Murray thought the corn on the cob from my garden was the best he had all along the way. He kept saying that we missionaries had it pretty nice. What was hard when we had such good food? After seeing the roads, he told a different story.

In March, the men who had refused their pay the previous month declined it again. Strikes worked a different way out here. On pay day, Benjamin set their wages aside and told them that if the rats ate the money they couldn't blame him.

Rats were a problem. We had been in desperate need of adrenaline and finally obtained a bottle. One morning we found the broken bottle on the floor of the pharmacy and figured a rat must have caused the trouble. Once when I was in my house, a rat came from the bedroom. It ran back just as I turned to see it. I followed it and run it did—right up the window and out the torn screen. It had visited my house before and was quite determined in seeking a way in. I figured I had to find a handier spot for the poison so the rat would die instead of making new entrances.

Vic came back through Oicha after finishing the lights at Kagando. He walked into my house looking like Santa Claus carrying a whole sack of mail for me. I had thirty-four letters and Christmas packages from my mother, my home church, and two other churches.

We had a busy time the week of March 17. Mr. Brashler flew in at 8:30 a.m. with guest speakers. About 3,000 folks attended the meetings to hear Mr. Dawson, a black man from Camden, and Mr. Bell, recently from Brazil. Mr. Dawson was a good speaker and would have liked to come back for a longer time if the Lord opened the way. After the service Margaret made a quick lunch, and the men were off to another place. They came back just in time to have tea with the local men then dash off to the plane. I had given Mr. Brashler the keys to my VW, and he enjoyed driving the men around. He had owned the VW when it was new, then he sold it to Dr. Becker who in turn sold it to me.

The pilot, Ernie, said they had to be back in the air by 5 p.m., and they just made it. They might have been up earlier, but Ernie had to swing the propeller by hand to get the engine to turn over. I was always amazed to see all that needed to be done before the plane could take off.

On our Friday dispensary day, we hadn't gone far in the "pray and push" when something went wrong. We found the bolt at the front steering had broken so we took one from the other side and limped into Beni to get it fixed. We made the second try for the dispensaries on Saturday. On our way home in the rain, the tire went flat. Jean didn't notice until the tire was ruined and she was sick about it.

The Beckers came for our doctor visit, and I enjoyed it so much. We had twenty-six operations and saw all the dispensary patients. Many folks came when they knew Dr. Becker was here. Later, I went with Doctor to see the needs in the leprosy camp and hospital grounds.

After they left, some of us began thinking ahead and wondering whether Congo's Independence Day (June 30) would stir up problems as it had in years past. Then we received news that Martin Luther King Jr. had been assassinated. At that point, I had more concern for the welfare of the folks at home than they had need of concern for me. I kept praying for my homeland and for many to turn to the Lord Jesus Christ.

As Easter approached at the beginning of April, the girls called me to come quickly to maternity one evening. The mother was having baby number twelve, and they thought the foot was presenting. Examination found it to be an arm, and that meant she couldn't deliver. We went to the operating room calling for Benjamin to do a cesarean. He wasn't home so I had the other fellow give the spinal to try and turn the baby and get a foot. Just as I was all ready to begin, Benjamin came and scrubbed but said he'd stand by, and if I couldn't turn it, he'd go ahead above. I was able to get a foot and deliver a baby boy. It turned out to be twins. The boy was not good and didn't live, but the little girl came and let out a scream almost right away. She was small but did well. The mother had been sick with malaria which must have brought her into labor. It was about midnight before I saw my bed at the end of that day.

I tried to get rest when I could, but I really felt ashamed of myself because as soon as I sat down, I'd get sleepy. Once at evening prayers, the girl ahead of me was praying, and next thing I realized she had stopped. I later asked Jean if I had gone off long, but she said no. In the men's prayer meeting the next night, just as I went to speak after the Scripture was read, we heard snoring from the corner. Benjamin was asleep. We all got the chuckles, and someone must have nudged him because he soon stopped. I figured that I'd eventually fall asleep in the wrong place too.

Barnaba, the man who helped in my house, came back from a vacation, and what a difference to turn the housework back to him. My garden was doing well. The man kept planting more seeds, so we had a good supply of vegetables all the time. Corn, carrots, peas, peppers, and spinach all grew well. Usually the chickens got the lettuce before it was big enough for me. We had the avocados growing on the trees and palm nuts too.

At the end of April, the women of the area held a conference of sorts that lasted two and a half days. The theme of the conference was "Awake." I missed some of it because I was out at the dispensaries, but I sat in on Saturday afternoon. They had a good message and then a testimony meeting. It took them a little bit to get started, but then they didn't want to stop. I was glad to see the young women as well as the older ones asking for prayer for their husbands. We were praising the Lord for the way couples were standing for the Lord now.

I had another big job when the CPRA, a church work, brought some food and twenty-two bales of clothing. The clothing distribution was quite a headache for me. Who is poor or not poor when nice clothing comes in is another story. There was pressure from many sources as to how it should be given and to whom. I handled it slowly. I wanted to be led of the Lord to do the right thing and seek to keep peace among the brethren.

Dr. Herb Atkinson was the doctor for the next monthly visit. We did over twenty surgeries in three days. I wasn't sure how I would handle it all next month when Jean was on vacation. While Dr. Herb was at the station, Dr. Becker came in on the plane with the American ambassador from Kinshasa and two others. The ambassador had gone to Bunia and Nyankunde for a visit and wanted to see Oicha too. The school children greeted them at the airstrip. They held signs of welcome and another one to say they wanted their doctor back right away. Margaret took the group to see the Pygmies, and Dr. Becker came back with me because the other car wasn't big enough for more than the pilot and the three folks from Kinshasa.

When they came back, Dr. Becker gave the tour of the hospital. Dr. Herb and I were taking a case over to surgery when Jean said the others were ready to go to the plane and needed my car. We quickly switched jobs. She took the venoclysis out of my hand, and I saw the folks off just three hours after they had arrived. Never a dull moment.

Jean and her friend Irene from Nyankunde left for a month-long vacation in the beginning of May. Shortly after they drove off, they came right back through the station. The road they had planned to use had been closed because of some plague cases in the area. We laughed about her nice vacation and how quickly the month had gone.

That Friday when I was at the dispensary in Mangina, I found a maternity patient bleeding. I kept an eye on her while I was working then put her in the car to bring her back to the station. About nine miles out, she went into labor and delivered in the car which I had padded pretty well, so we didn't have too much of a mess. The fellow I had brought along with me helped out by handing the knife to cut the cord. She was only seven months along, so the baby didn't live, but the mother was fine. Since there was nothing more we could do for her at the hospital, we took the patient back home again.

The local elders at Mangina had put one of the certified midwives out of the work because she was not walking right. She had been in trouble once and had been accepted back into the work. The fellow came back around and she wouldn't listen to the elders. When I returned with the maternity case, I said she could come along since her family lived near Oicha. She wanted me to take her things and said she'd follow by foot. I told her nothing doing—she had to come with me or I wouldn't take her things. I couldn't be a part of her running her own way. I was sad to lose another of the local trained girls. The area needed more, but they tangled up their lives by not yielding to the Lord.

Dr. and Mrs. Becker came to Oicha and held a meeting with the committee men of the various dispensaries. I wasn't there for the whole meeting, but things certainly didn't drag out as when they had met before. After the meeting, the men decided to take their pay. I was able to talk with Dr. Becker about a few other things. I guess I could have been called an accountant. Dr. Wilcke enjoyed that kind of work, and when he was the doctor for the monthly visit, I always had a list of things for him to check.

I often requested prayer from the folks at home for the leadership that was mine. It was hard to know how to cope with some things. I had changed the way we gave out medicine because those above me asked that it be done a new way. The men felt I had asked them to record things because I thought medicines were missing. I knew they'd feel that way. They didn't like it, and not everyone wrote down the information, so the count didn't come out right. I was discouraged: they just wouldn't bow to authority—a trend the world around. Pastor Zephania had a good message calling for the church to come to Christ in surrendered lives.

By mid-June, I was counting the days until Jean returned from her vacation. I planned to go out to Kasese to get my car fixed. I had to go out of the country before June 28 if I wanted my papers to be valid for my vacation travel in August. If I didn't, I'd have to get a new paper, and that was costly. I wouldn't have planned trips so close together if I didn't have to.

That week had been something for my home country again. Voice of America reported on the death of Robert Kennedy. I arrived home from a delivery at 1 a.m. and took a bath and washed my hair while listening to the live program of the funeral train traveling to Washington. They were running so far behind schedule that I didn't hear the end of the burial.

Information regarding Sudan wasn't positive either. North and south Sudan were still very divided. The radio news carried denials from Khartoum about the slaughter of the southern people. The world went on with no peace anywhere.

Jean arrived back on a Thursday evening, a few days later than planned. On Friday we went out to the Mwenda dispensary in her new car. It was just like her old one except it had only a canvas top on the back when she bought it. She switched out the top with the one from her old car and called it a good deal all around.

I took my car for a quick trip to the garage in Kasese. Nancy Houser, a Canadian medical student who was heading for Kampala, rode along with me. I hoped she might be a prospect for the mission field, but of course she had several more years of schooling.

While in Uganda, I visited Barb and Martha at Kagando. Martha was carrying a load but the station was moving ahead. The houses were nice, and they had begun building an operating room. The son of one of our medical men was returning from vacation, so I had someone to drive with me back to Congo.

Martha's house   *Barbara's house*

Mary Heyward returned from furlough to work at Nyankunde. She had been able to visit with my parents in the States and brought a surprise for me—two dresses from my mother. I had to get used to the shift style. I liked them better after I added pockets to the one dress and a belt to the other.

After all the trouble with the pays had finally settled a bit, the government in Congo raised the pay scale again, and we had to make the change. I was late with the next payday. All the details needing attention before my vacation wore me out. The clothing distribution alone was a real headache on top of the bookwork and medical things. I feared I wouldn't get it all done.

We had an interesting communion service one Sunday. Our hospital evangelist was asked to pray for the bread before giving it out. As he was praying, his alarm clock began to ring. Apparently it had been wound tight and rang all the way out. He just kept praying and finished some time after the clock stopped. I didn't dare look up for fear I would laugh. He carried that clock everywhere, but who wound the alarm is to be wondered.

Here in Africa, we used what we could find for communion. We might use broken cookies and whatever juice was available. Once, the head of the school, who was also an elder, asked Jewell to look for pens with red ink when she went shopping. She located them and was quite pleased that the teachers would have their red pens. "Oh no, madam," he told her, "that is to color the communion juice."

The Lord was good to us in so many ways. One Thursday in July, we were finishing our work and planning the dispensary trip for the next day when Benjamin told me that we had another case. We connected with the doctor on the radio even though we knew it was too late to fly that evening. We planned to call back at 7 a.m. the next morning to update him on the patient's condition. At 8 p.m. that evening our lights gave out, meaning we would have no power to call. Matiasi worked but couldn't get the lights back on. The next morning, Jean went on the dispensary visit. I stuck by Matiasi and finally he found a loose wire. He fixed it, and we were on the radio by 10:30 a.m. I talked to Dr. Herb and gave the weather report to the pilot Ernie, and they arrived shortly after noon. We finally did the surgery. As we were on our way to dinner, we were waylaid to see a maternity patient with a ruptured uterus. We quickly ate while they prepped her for surgery. Of course, the baby was lost, and by noon the next day, the mother had died as well, but Dr. Herb was here to do the work. If all had gone as planned, the doctor would have been here and gone earlier and not been around to take the case. It was a full day, and the plane took off with just fifteen minutes to spare before it would have been too dark for safety.

My vacation began on August 3 with a stop in Kagando on my way to Kampala. I met the Haweses, a new couple who had arrived to help on the station. Barb and Martha were preparing to head off for their vacation, hoping to see some Latukos to check on their translation work.

Once in Kampala, I called my parents from the Amstutzes' house and had a wonderful visit with other missionaries in the area. I also had a close call on the road. I was driving on the right side and for a few seconds couldn't understand why a bus was coming straight towards me. I quickly got over to the left side—all the surrounding cars were good and gave me space.

I left my car at the garage for some work and took a train to Nairobi to stay with Dick and Flo Gehman. They took me to Kijabe to see all the changes going on there, and we enjoyed a big meal with the Bakers. With twelve of us around the table, it felt like Thanksgiving.

We went to the airport one day to meet up with the Olsens and the Fonsecas who were on their way back to their stations. The Olsens had adopted Erika, who was so sweet, and their other daughter Karen helped care for her. Cindy, Sandy, and Diana Fonseca were growing so fast. It was nice to visit even though it was just for that short time.

At the end of August, I took the train back to Kampala and then headed with the car to Kagando to finish my vacation. I had to stop at Masaka for more repairs to the car. Yes, it had just been in the garage in Kampala. I had only driven about thirty miles when I heard an awful noise. A man stopped to help me and found the shock absorber broken. He took it off and said he would fix it for me in the morning. I had a memory from way back of folks telling me that a man who helped drill the first well in Sudan lived around this area. I discovered that my helper was the one and told him that I had enjoyed that water until 1963. We eventually got the car fixed, but I arrived back in Oicha a day late. Just keeping up my reputation—late again.

My first week back at Oicha was full because Dr. Herb Atkinson was down for the monthly visit. He had a talk with the medical men about tracking the medicine and some other things. He gave pep talks all week about being faithful. Ernie checked our lights when he came back to pick up the doctor. He had also brought the doctor's two sons along, so we had eight folks for dinner.

As they left for the plane, two English medical students named Stanford and Paul arrived. They had an eight-week research project in Uganda and were taking a little holiday before going back to school. We found out that Stanford was having a birthday, so Margaret made a cake. He had surprise written all over his face and left us saying he had never had such a nice birthday party. It changed his first impression of Congo.

Dr. Ulrich, a new doctor, came along with Dr. Herb for the October visit. Dr. Ulrich did the surgeries, and Dr. Herb saw the office patients. We thought the Beckers would be coming, but Mrs. Becker had such weakness that she couldn't make the trip. Fanweli brought Dr.Becker's truck, hauling rocks, sand, and poles for the work down here. He stayed by as they put a new door on the pharmacy which had been weakened by the rebels and never fixed. Fanweli put it right.

Work went on, sometimes busier than others. One Saturday night, I was so sleepy; I washed my hair, and as I went to bed I thought—oh to not be called out. Then I thought that I didn't need to be concerned because I didn't really get called out that often. At 12:30 a.m. I thought I was dreaming that a horn was honking. I didn't realize it was not a dream until I heard a call at the window. It was the night medical man asking if he could start up the lights. A man had been in a fight, and they had to sew up his badly cut hand. I gave him my pressure light to use instead and off they went. I fell back to sleep until 3:30 a.m. when the night girl came saying a baby in maternity was crying and would not be comforted. I went to check and ordered medicine. I was to be off on Sunday, so I went back to bed and didn't set an alarm. At 6 a.m. the night watchman came to return the flashlight he used. I fell asleep one more time until 7 a.m. when Jean came for the keys for the day's work. She didn't need to feel bad for waking me up because shortly afterward the night medical man was at the door with my pressure light.

By the end of November, things had slowed down a bit. We had lost some children to measles. Those who were weak before couldn't overcome when measles hit. We had three long-term accident cases. A tree had fallen on one young man and mangled his forearm. The doctor had taken the arm off, but infection set in. Another man, a soldier, had been cleaning his gun and shot his leg, shattering the bone. We also had a woman with an open fracture of both bones in the lower part of her leg and one in the upper leg from a tree that had fallen on her house. Her young son also broke his leg, but his would heal more quickly because it was closed. He was cute and we had a nice time with him while the family was there.

Dr. and Mrs. Becker came for the next monthly visit with some others to fix up our generator. We were limping along until a new one came from the States. The Beckers were doing well again. Their daughter Mary was planning to come out for a visit sometime before Christmas. She had not been out to the field since she left as a child. When the doctor first heard she was coming, he was perplexed and said, "We don't understand why she is coming, certainly not for us, we are feeling better!" His son Carl told him that of course she was coming to see them.

It seemed like each week had something special happening in it. I was sure folks at home thought I was making things up. The second week in December started with the rats in the clothing bundles. As I sorted through the donated clothes, I found rat carcasses. Some were too smart to eat the rat medicine and were running around as I worked.

Later that week, which was a rainy one, we had to turn around before we got to Mangina for the weekly dispensary trip. The next morning, I found Paulo (our man in charge of the outside maintenance) and others looking at our dispensary roof. The rain had weighed down the tiles, and the roof began sliding off overnight. We knew it was going bad but had thought that propping it up would save it. I checked in by radio with Dr. Becker, and he asked that we try and save the louver windows. All hands on deck and we soon moved everything—medicines, laboratory, and the windows. We all slept well that night and praised the Lord that, in spite of the quick exit, we had everything settled into such good order.

The next week the Beckers came with their daughter Mary. She hadn't been home to Oicha in almost thirty years. She looked good and everyone was glad to see her. Richard Dix came along, and he and Dr. Becker went around the station to look at the buildings and decide what should be done. At that time, most of the good buildings were close together, and that saved on walking. Things would be put up as needed, and we would fit in as the changes came. Dr. Becker still enjoyed making plans and was alert to all the work. They had some things to talk over, and then the Field Council would decide what should be done for the future of Oicha.

My fourth Christmas in this term passed with four Christmas babies, three of them born between 5 and 6:30 a.m. The woman with the broken leg was recovering. Her son was out of traction and up and walking around. He wasn't going outside on his own yet, but he followed me around. I gave him and another little fellow plastic scraps of packaging from medicine that looked something like a big watch. They had such joy with those leftovers. That was the way I spoiled the children.

Before the end of the year, Ernie, our pilot, came with Bob Zimmerman who brought us a new radio. I had to keep it in my house because the battery and charger had to be checked more often than our old one. We also hoped there would be less chance of someone stealing it from my house than an empty one.

1969

You therefore must endure hardship as a good soldier of Jesus Christ. (2 Timothy 2:3)

I turned my days and nights around by working twenty-nine hours and then sleeping all day. On the way home from Mangina dispensary that week, we looked up an Indian maternity patient in Beni and found her beginning labor. After the formalities of greeting, we were given tea, cookies, popcorn, some noodle-like things, and candy before we could head back to Oicha and set things up for her arrival. She seemed to move along well, but she was scared and like so many in saying she was going to die before it was over. Her pains continued through the night, and 'Olive the anxious' got concerned and radioed to Nyankunde. As I tried to connect, Margaret came in and took over for me, but we were unable to get through. By 7:30 a.m. things progressed enough to move to the delivery room. By 10:00 am, we had a healthy little boy, though we did

265

use the vacuum extractor at the end because she didn't seem to have the strength to push. We praised the Lord that all went well, for she had lost two pregnancies before. I went home and slept the rest of the day.

The next week, I went to Kagando for a long weekend and stayed in Barb and Martha's camper. I felt like I was at camp meeting. I

Camper guest house

suppose that our outdoor life brought camp meeting to my mind so often. Martha carried quite a heavy schedule. About 800 women came each month for baby clinic. Because so many people were in one place, research teams came from Kampala to conduct studies. I hoped that might influence their chances to stay, but nothing had been settled yet—so they carried on.

When I came back across the border loaded down with supplies, the Congo side officials asked me to take everything out of the car. Not the usual border men, and looking to charge duty, they thoroughly examined everything. I didn't have papers for the medicines, but they allowed those to pass. They charged me for Nina's car pump, and I had to pay for a radio battery and charger. I kept quiet as to its use because officials often got ideas when they heard about radio contact. They didn't know what to charge for the battery and spent a long time paging through their book. They didn't know what they were looking for. I just sat it out until they made up their minds. In all, I was there for two and a half hours.

Back in Oicha, we had some hard cases. One baby died, and another was failing. Our generator gave out, so we didn't have lights. I had a set of someone's false teeth to send up to the dentist for repair. Glasses, teeth, deliveries, generators, buildings, and pipe fittings—name it and I probably had something to do about it. I asked the Lord to give me the time, wisdom, and strength to get the pension report finished and all the other things waiting for me.

At the end of January, Benjamin called me to help with a case. The man had been speared by someone waiting for him in some affair of long standing. The wounds didn't seem too serious, but by the time we finished bandaging he went bad and we couldn't get him back. So the next morning I had a different sort of trip. Since the government had a concern in deaths like this, I took the body to Beni for them to take over.

What a crowd of people gathered around my car, looking and repeating, "He really is dead." One wife came up to the car, and his other wife was on the ground holding her child. They both went into wailing together and kept it up a long time. I didn't know how they knew when to stop, but they finally did. During all of this, another younger woman came and stooped over and took off the shoes of the wife who was standing and tied the sash around her waist tighter. I wasn't sure what that meant, but I thought it must be the sign of sorrow. Finally, I had permission to take the corpse to the morgue. When I reported to the big man at the office, he gave his thanks for helping his people—in the name of the government, the population, and on behalf of the family. Very proper in all things.

The needs of the work were great. Two of our certified men moved to other dispensaries. Those were needy places, but we felt the pinch of less help here. Then another new thing came into the picture. Through the years we had trained young girls (fifteen or sixteen years of age) to be midwives. Dispensaries sent the girls for training and then they returned to work there. We learned we could no longer carry on that way. The girls now had to finish six years of school and then two more years of advanced work before they could go into the medical training program with the men to earn a certificate. There were very few girls who continued their schooling that long because marriage was thought of rather than such a long training. The girls working for us here reacted in disappointment. We had trained them and they could work with us, but they could no longer go out. They became girls with a job that might help them personally in their future homes, but they had no certificate. It was cruel and hurtful for these young girls to feel they had no value because they couldn't get a certificate. These were the burdens of the work.

At the beginning of March, Ernie came down with the plane to pick up some visitors and brought a pile of mail. It seemed like the days back in Sudan when we would get mail all at one time. I had a stack of

Christmas mail and other letters. By the time I finished it all, I felt caught up on the news from home.

We heard that Jewell planned to come back from furlough sometime in May. Jean had plans to leave to take training in India for leprosy rehabilitation. I told my mother that she had better not count on me to be home by December of 1969 because I didn't see anyone to replace me. I thought I'd certainly be home by the next Christmas because my visa for Congo ran out at the end of 1970. I didn't want to extend it before I had a furlough.

How fast time went by. One patient with tuberculosis had a baby, and the lesion broke down after delivery. She was spitting blood and needed to be watched. Dr. Herb told me that pregnancy was wonderful for a woman with tuberculosis, but the delivery was not. During the pregnancy the baby pushes up the diaphragm, but delivery causes the lesions to all open up again and that caused the bleeding.

In the middle of March, I felt good that I was caught up on the pharmacy work; however, I was discouraged about two difficult cases in maternity. We lost both babies. Then the one woman needed fluid in her vein and eventually died. May the Lord help me when I should have helped her sooner. If one of our doctors was at the station, he made the decision for a cesarean. If not, I had to decide. In these cases, I should have made the call sooner, but the possibility that a woman who had a cesarean might not have access to medical help for her next delivery weighed on me. Although I struggled to study with all the other things needing to be done, I began reading my obstetrics book to check some of my mistakes. These were times of leaning on the Lord.

I fixed up my house, repairing some cracks from the earthquake some time before. I painted the walls and waxed the floors. Jewell was due back in May, and I didn't know how we might arrange things as far as housing, but I wanted her house to be nice. I was uncertain how we would divide the work. She had been the one in charge here. After she left, I had been the one. With both of us here — that was another story yet to be learned.

We had a man painting the hospital too. Everything was taking a new look and what a help. It certainly brightened things up.

The hospital remained busy. We had another woman come in with her lower leg bones broken from her house falling down in a storm. She was from the same area as the woman who came in with the broken leg back in November. We had amputated the leg of that first woman because of infection.

We looked to the Lord for all things. Near our Lalia station, some Pygmies were injured by rebels. Margaret and Jean went out to get them. War can be awful.

Some folks of mixed race background came in with their little girl in convulsions. She quieted down when I gave her the injection. When cases like this turned up, I just had to call upon the Lord for His strength. I always held the image of Ricky Beatty just going from one convulsion to another. The parents called on the Lord for their child. I pointed them to Christ who is always with us when we trust Him. Whatever God did for their daughter was for His glory.

We missed our April visit from a doctor. Dr. Ulrich had hepatitis, and Dr. Wilcke had an infection in his foot. Dr. Becker was going to come, but neither he nor Mrs. Becker were fit to travel. The gasket on the generator engine that ran our radio gave out, and Matiasi worked to get the thing fixed so we could at least talk to a doctor. We found tin foil worked long enough for a short radio transmission before it gave out again. The next day one of the Greek men told us to make the part of tin. Margaret cut a piece from her roofing and it worked. We had a new engine, generator, and water pump, but they were in Nyankunde. The men were planning to bring the big truck with those things and also the lumber to fix the dispensary roof. The big trucks were getting through, but not without some difficulty.

A husband and wife from Switzerland visited us, and Jean took them out to see the forest and the Pygmies. The husband, who had traveled around the world before he married, had a guitar, and at night we sat around and sang. They knew more of our American folk songs than we did. I could remember the tunes but not the words. Jean enjoyed the visit of the younger folks, but I felt like I might have gotten too old and too much into the work—no time for play. When they were ready to leave, the husband just couldn't believe they wouldn't be able to get through the roads. He went out to inspect the holes for himself and came back convinced (he hadn't even gotten to the really bad places). The wife was expecting, and they planned to be in Africa until September and then go back to Switzerland.

At the end of April, Jean took a week in Kampala to get the Land

Rover fixed. I would have to go out of the country again in May. I had gotten a permit to travel, and it had to be used within the first three months or it wouldn't be good. If I went out, it would renew for another ten months. I planned to go across to Kagando and visit the girls there for a few days.

The woman with the amputated leg was back in bed once again. She had been up on crutches, but fell and re-broke the upper part of her leg. We all wanted to weep with her. Once the pain was gone she cheered up and began to get around again. Her husband stood by faithfully. We praised the Lord.

We had the people who come a long way for treatment stay in houses provided by the hospital. I lacked the time to visit with them as much as I would have liked. I often found the Pygmies needed encouragement to stay for treatment because they didn't like to settle in village life for a long time. Once, I found a young boy needing some food and clothing. He finished the food I had brought for him and was soon in my pathway calling me "Mama."

"Peanut" one of our premies ready to go home

In April, all our beds in maternity were full and two women were waiting to deliver. I looked around for someone that might be able to leave and found one of the tiny babies weighed two kilos on the button which meant he could go home. The mother was so happy. She hadn't wanted to stay at first, but I wouldn't let her go. Now, after forty days, she left with a live baby. We had two sets of twins too small to leave and one other small baby. Two other babies had died in the womb and were born in sorrow. Such a mix of happy and sad, but we kept going.

April ended with a week full of visitors. Dr. and Mrs. Becker came for two days, and it was so nice to have them again. The Crossmans and the Paul Stoughs visited as well. It was the week to go to the Luanoli dispensary fifty miles out. How thankful we were for a dry road. It was a beautiful trip, and we stopped to take pictures of the Ruwenzori mountains. Think of a mountain with snow and palm trees in the foreground. Animals were everywhere—baboons, birds, and the black and white colobus monkeys jumping from tree to tree. We saw places the elephants had been but not the actual animals.

May was busy and Jean took some of the maternity work so I could get other things done. I was working to get ahead in medicines and to finish the pension reports to cover the time I would be in Kagando.

In the middle of May, just before I left for Kagando, I took a young girl home who had had an affair with the pastor's son. She said she was not pregnant, but time would tell. She wanted to run away, so I had to make a special trip with her.

As I drove back into the station, Margaret ran to my car to tell me that Dorothy Beatty had died while at home in the States. Hearing of her sudden home call hit me hard. Margaret sure was broken up as well. She had worked closely with the Beattys in Kenya before she could come back to Congo. I wrote a letter to Bill and the five children, but I hardly knew what to write. It just seemed impossible. The Lord alone knew the end from the beginning.

I took my trip to Kagando and stayed with the Rineers because Barb and Martha were in Kampala. Dr. Keith joined us for supper one evening, and we had a nice talk together. Things were moving along in all they were doing.

After several days, I returned to Oicha and had no problems at either border. They stamped my passport and barely looked at the car. I had brought back fabric for dresses and aprons for the medical women, paint, and food supplies. As I pulled into Oicha at 12:30 p.m., I saw the plane and knew dinner would be at Margaret's house. They had a plate set for me but had started eating. Dr. Becker was along with the men who were setting up the light plant. As soon as I finished my meal, I was in uniform and working. Something blew out on the new plant and the men couldn't finish setting it up. They left shortly after 5 p.m. (the limit Ernie had set for getting off the ground) and returned on Saturday to finish the job. We had nice lights and a generator that started with just the push of a button—no crank.

That Saturday was a full day. I helped Jean in maternity. We had a line of patients and a backlog in the pharmacy. It seemed every time I turned around someone else needed something. I thought I could get to the wedding of one of the teachers but was called to the hospital instead. Then I thought I'd get there but just a bit late until the men came to show me what I'd need to know about the light plant. I missed the wedding completely. The others told me it was very nice.

We missionaries were invited to the feast afterward, and this is how they did it for us. They sent a chicken and rice for one of our cooks to make. Since most everyone brings his own dishes, we took our plates and food along. At the feast, the men's choir sang, then the teachers' choir, and then the women sang for the bride. They sang beautifully in parts, but at times a bit too loud for my taste.

Times were changing, and at this wedding the bride and groom both ate food even though the bride didn't touch much of hers. At African weddings, the bride always had to look so sad. This bride did some talking to the attendants, and though she wasn't weeping as some did, she did keep her head down a lot. This day, the pastor tried to have the people change it up and sit together as families.

Dr. and Mrs. Becker and their son Carl came to the station the first week in June. I couldn't help but call the Beckers "Dad" and "Mother" sometimes. It was nice having them that week. Dr. Becker did all his work so easily, it was like play to him.

Some of the certified men had refused their pay again. The teachers in the school were also upset and wanted some direction. Carl met with the teachers, and things seemed better at the end than before. Dr. Becker talked with the medical men, and the next day they gave him a typed letter with seven names of men who wanted to leave. If they really wanted to go we'd let them, but they were the younger men and I didn't know what they'd do if they left. I'm afraid the ring leaders of the troubles didn't give their notice. All this was hard on Dr. Becker; after all, he had trained these men. I prayed the Lord would guide us for His glory.

While the folks were with us, we had a birthday dinner for Mrs. Becker who was about to turn seventy-five. The Beckers were so sweet and the Lord had given them to us for a long time.

Keeping the books was an ongoing challenge. Dr. Wilcke checked over my books whenever he was the one for our station, and I usually needed help with them. When I went out to dispensaries, I checked over their books. Often they needed help. The folks would add incorrectly and then try to say it was accurate. In one place I checked the totals and had three extra zaires. Finally one fellow said, "Yes, there was some left over but we couldn't see where it was supposed to fit in and so we said there wasn't any." I knew it wasn't easy keeping books, but it had to be done.

Jean planned to leave at the end of June, and Jewell was to arrive sometime in July. Then Jewell sent word that her mother was sick in the hospital, and her return would be delayed. Dr. Becker didn't know what to say as to how the work would carry on. We didn't understand all the ways the Lord led, but we followed. Sometimes I felt as I had in other fields—that the days were short. We lacked enough personnel, and I didn't know where the unrest of the wages would end.

We hit the jackpot in the nursery with a new set of twins. The mother was a very young woman who weighed 100 pounds pregnant. We suspected twins but couldn't be sure. As we began to prep her for the cesarean, I checked on the fuel in the generator because we would need the lights for a longer time. As Benjamin cut the skin, the lights began to flicker. I ran to check again and found it was not a quick-solve problem, so I went to the house for my pressure light. By the time I got back they had a small lantern and the twins were born. I checked back with the fellows at the engine, but we gave up when we found a welded part had broken off. Benjamin finished the woman by the pressure light and told us that this was the first set of twins he had delivered. Each baby weighed over four pounds. That little girl would have her hands full. She seemed like just a kid herself, but all went well and we were glad for that.

We had seventy-seven deliveries in June and in the first six days of July were already up to seventeen. We had some premature babies, and they took up space. Women were in the ward, in the labor room, and two on the floor. I knew a woman was close to delivering one Sunday morning but wasn't sure when, so I began my usual reading Scripture and teaching in the ward. When I heard a different kind of noise, I ran and caught the baby in her bed. After that, I finished reading and teaching.

I had a letter from Bill Beatty telling more of Dorothy's death and his plans to return to Africa. I didn't know how he would manage, but David and Barbie wanted to graduate from Kijabe so badly. All the children seemed to be that way, and it meant so much to them to be able to graduate on the field. I trusted it would help Barbie for it all must have been hard for her.

Dr. Wilcke and his wife Wanda came for the monthly visit. Wanda was a big help in the pharmacy and I appreciated it. Margaret was with her for most of the time, learning some of the work. The pharmacy was a lively place the whole week, and they ended up with everything finished and labeled better than it had ever been before.

We went to Luanoli dispensary that Friday, and the driving fell on me. I was the one who knew the way, but I told Wanda that perhaps Dr. Wilcke would help if I got tired. I never asked, and he didn't offer—in fact, he dozed off some of the time. At the big hill, another Land Rover was ahead and I didn't get going fast enough. Matiasi got out and directed as I backed down, and thankfully we made it all the way to the top on my second try. Coming home, it started to rain. I didn't see a hole, and we got a bump and a shower out of it. Dr. Wilcke did not enjoy travel on the roads—he had some kind of phobia. It was bad enough for him to be on the roads, let alone driving, so I did the whole trip. When we got back, he told me I did well. Our week was a busy one, but Dr. Wilcke did have one evening to sit with me and the books. He gave me advice on some things I should do differently. I tried to fix the problems, but the money and the books didn't always work together.

Jewell sent word that her mother had died and she was looking to the Lord for direction. Her father was weak and everyone had been surprised that her mother died first. Margaret planned to stay with me until we could hear more of Jewell's plans.

I enjoyed my radio news and heard the astronauts were on their way to the moon. Later I read all the details of the trip. About this time, Sudan was in the news again, and all the Americans were out of the country.

August was busy with many visitors. Dr. Ulrich came for the monthly visit along with a medical student from Canada, which of course slowed things down. We only did fifteen surgeries but had many patients to see in addition to the leprosy patients. The medical student did some little things with Dr. Ulrich and some on his own. It took him about an hour to amputate a finger, but he finished it and was pleased for the chance to operate.

During the week, two men from Eli Lilly came in with Dr. Ruth Dix as well as a photographer to take pictures of Dr. Ulrich, the flying doctor. Dr. Ruth sent him off for photographs and she took over his work. We finished by 5 p.m. that day, the earliest time for the whole week.

The government in Kinshasa gave word they were checking on all the foreigners and their activities. Nina took a trip to Beni with our passports to fulfill their requirements. We heard more and more said of the nationals taking over the work. We went on as the Lord gave us each day.

Martha's mother died suddenly early in August. The next week she got a letter from her mother that had been written just the day before her death. By the end of August, Martha had still not received details. That happened so much out here. Something occurs at home and the family forgets that those on the field are waiting for details. I was happy to hear that Martha took a needed break for a week in spite of the heavy load at Kagando.

I often worried about my own mother, whose health was not good. Many of my letters urged her to please take care of herself. I asked her to stop trying to do things she couldn't do. If she had to sit and rest, that was just what she should do. My mother was such a prayer warrior for the work and we wanted her around us for as long as the Lord allowed.

August came in with a record of eighty-nine births with ninety-two babies—three sets of twins. One day, I delivered a twin born twenty–four hours after the first one. Then Yerusi, our midwife, delivered another pair. They were premature and one died. Of our three sets of twins, one pair went home, one set died, and one of the third set was still alive, small but doing well. We had difficult cases. One day I did three of my operations in one day, all with good results. We did have birth control available, but not many took advantage of it.

I was glad for radio contact with doctors. A woman came in from the Mwenda dispensary whose baby had been delivered legs, arms, and body. The head wouldn't come. I did my operation but still no success. After I spoke with Dr. Ruth Dix on the radio and followed her advice, we were able to save the mother.

I hoped that some of the men and women would soon finish their training and be on the job. We needed more folks to work at Oicha, and it was a big disappointment when some men who had earned their certificates at Nyankunde were found leaving with drugs from the pharmacy in their luggage. Of course, they were not allowed to go out and work. The men were given a chance to come back and do manual jobs to show repentance. One who had the brains and could have gone for more training refused and so was lost for the work.

A few weeks later, Dr. Helen Roseveare, from the training program, wrote regarding the fellows. They had taken their punishment in a good spirit. I prayed they would keep faithful and humble.

We had another busy stretch in maternity. Several of the Greek women were in to deliver. One of the women had a baby weighing nearly ten pounds. Sometimes, the Greek women would refuse the help of our African workers which made more work for me. One woman stayed for a week before she had her baby. I had hoped she would deliver while Dr. Becker was here for his monthly visit. Dr. Becker told me she would deliver okay or the Lord would have had it come earlier. Benjamin was concerned that something would happen to the Greek babies or mothers when they came in, and I tried to stay close by to ease his worry. The baby was born without incident and all were doing well. The only difficulty was in talking with her. She was new and didn't know much Swahili.

Another day, Benjamin called for me. We had a man who had been speared, and the stomach was out. Benjamin thought he had found all the holes, but the man began vomiting blood and went bad. We couldn't save him.

We also had a German man come in who had climbed Mt. Ruwenzori alone and had fallen, broken his clavicle, and badly bruised his leg. It had taken him eight days to come down and get to Oicha. After staying for a time, he went on to friends in Butembo.

By the end of October, Jewell had plans to return sometime early

December. Margaret hoped to go with her friends to the Holy Land on December 7 and prepared to leave. I began to make tentative plans for my own furlough. My mother had hoped I'd be home for this Christmas, but I had known that wouldn't happen. I thought that if someone could be found to take my place, I might depart Africa by April. I had to be out by December 1970 or I would have to renew my visa. I didn't feel I could leave until Jewell had someone to help her.

The days slipped by rapidly. Dr. Keith and Martha arrived for a visit. Dr. Keith had originally been assigned to the Congo field. Because that was at the height of the rebel hostilities, he worked in Uganda instead. This was his first visit to Congo and he was with us when Dr. Ulrich came for the monthly visit. Then Dr. Becker came for a day with two doctors from the American Leprosy Mission. All the visitors kept me stepping.

I had a sadness in the work when the one young fellow working for me had to leave. He stole clothes meant for the children in the leprosy camp. I had stored them in my bedroom and hadn't found the time to give them out. I never suspected anything and felt awful that I had put temptation in his way.

As Margaret prepared to leave at the end of November, she had many come to her door to give her gifts. One fellow came and wanted to give her a little money. She didn't want to take it, but he told her, "I want to give it and you can buy some bread along the way." Just to have some bread to them was a special treat—like candy or ice cream for us.

On a routine call to Nyankunde on December 7, they told me Jewell had just flown in and would arrive at Oicha in the afternoon. My heart beat in leaps and bounds. Help was on the way! Everyone was eager for her return. I moved over to Margaret's house, and the next Sunday was the first in five months that I was not responsible for calls.

We had word that the David Downings would join us after they finished their language training in Switzerland. Diane Downing was a nurse and could take my place, but I suspected I would not be on furlough by April.

I had much praise for the Lord's continued help in the year. Without Him, I could never have done it. Surely the Lord was good. I prayed for Jewell and me as we were about to go on in the work.

How quickly the year went by. How wonderful to enter another year and know Who was going before each of us.

1970

You will keep him in perfect peace, whose mind is stayed on You, because he trusts in You. (Isaiah 26:3)

We arrived at annual conference in Rethy after the cleanest, fastest trip of all my twenty years in Africa. An hour from take-off to landing.

Back in December, a military truck had overturned near Oicha injuring fifteen men. By the time we should have been heading out for our conference, this unruly lot of soldiers was well but refused to leave, so we sent for their leader in Beni. He arrived around dusk, just as Benjamin was suturing the head of another person who had been beaten by these men. Benjamin finished the job then took off to hide. These men had no respect for their leader and refused to leave until the next afternoon when trucks arrived with reinforcements to take them away. Once they were gone, Benjamin came back on the scene, and we missionaries quickly handed over our keys and flew off to the conference.

Because we weren't putting down at Nyankunde, our pilot Dave took a different route over the forest. Flying at about 1200 feet instead of 3000 as in a big plane, I looked out in amazement at the dense forest. We flew low over Lake Albert and could wave to the folks on the shore and those in their little hollowed-out log boats. They stood in awe as Dave dipped his wings—then they bravely waved back.

I enjoyed a wonderful week of meetings at conference. The Lord blessed me through the messages and fellowship. A Congolese teacher recently returned from the States also spoke. It was good to hear his opinions of the future challenges and needs of the mission. He stressed the need for further training of Congolese doctors to carry on the work.

Back at the station Jewell and I settled into a routine. She had an easy way about her and could quickly finish all the little things that took me so long to accomplish. I suppose things fell into place for her because she had been on this station through all the years (except for the time out because of the rebels).

At the end of January, just as we came out of church, the local administrator drove up with the army general and his secretary. The general wanted to make an apology for his men. His secretary, who had studied in the States for two years, translated the apology into English for me. They didn't realize Jewell could understand French, but it was diplomacy. I recognized the apology and thanked him. I was to convey the apology to Dr. Becker as well, but by the time I talked to him on the radio, I forgot.

We had five new girls: fifteen to eighteen years old and as green as they come, but they were enthusiastic. They were sure epilepsy was contagious. We started at the basics of how to take a temperature and what a time we had until some of them learned to see the mercury in the thermometer.

Mr. Epp came in to fix the dispensary roof that had collapsed the previous year. Because the new roof was metal, they had to make a new support for it. The work was progressing when Mr. Epp developed a fever and had to stay in bed. Even though it was the dry season, we had a heavy rain and I hoped they could get on with it quickly.

One Sunday on my day off I went out to a church service in Mbau. The pastor had a good message, and when he asked for a word from me, I took my Bible and told of the importance of it in our lives. They didn't often have white folks and had set a special chair in the front of the church for me, but I didn't sit in it. I asked that they forgive me for not sitting on that chair, because I had come to worship the Lord with them. I didn't want them looking at me and not hearing the message the Lord had for us.

I took the "pray and push" to Luanoli for the dispensary visit. There wasn't too much work there, but it was a long trip. The exhaust had been broken on the Rover, and what a noise—I sounded like a big truck. Coming home, something didn't feel right so I stopped to check it out. We shook this and pushed that and started off again. The Lord put his power in, and we climbed the hill home. Later, Jewell took the Rover to The Greek's garage pit. She casually remarked, "Hole in the exhaust?"

He looked up, eyes popping, "Hole! You've lost half of it!" The exhaust had rusted and fallen by the wayside. Just like many Christians in the fallen-by-the-wayside condition.

I planned a trip to Kampala for March and wrote home to arrange the details for a phone call. I also hoped to see some of the Sudan folks as well. Barb and Martha were planning a trip out that way in June, but I didn't know if I could take a second trip to join them. As the translator of the Latuka New Testament, Martha had just received the first copy. The printers had done a nice job with it, and Barb and Martha were hoping copies would come in time for their trip to the people.

I drove to Kagando for the first weekend of my vacation. There was no trouble at the border. In fact, because they wanted to send someone over with me to the market, they pushed me through at the noon closed hour. Then on the other side, they didn't give any trouble either. They sent a man along to go for their mail.

Before I left Kagando for Kampala, a Land Rover that looked like Jewell's pulled into the station. It was Jewell's. She brought Anne Cowell, a missionary from Rethy, who needed to get to Kampala to catch her plane for furlough. Apparently, the upper borders were having some kind of petty happenings. The only way Anne could get out was to go on a plane to Banda with a doctor, then back via Nyankunde to Oicha to finally get over the border to me. She had gone 600 miles to get 200 miles from her starting point. I dropped her at the Amstutzes, and they took her to the plane. I supposed Jewell and Nina would have a big time of overnight guests with others coming out via Oicha.

I enjoyed my vacation. I caught up on letters and had my yearly phone call with my parents. I mixed up my times and got through at 7 a.m. instead of 8 a.m., but we had a good connection.

I headed back through Kagando on my way to Oicha with my things plus thirteen other boxes and the muffler/tailpipe for the Rover. On my way out, I stopped to greet the Laurences who had helped me at the time of my accident the previous year. As I left, Mr. Laurence told me, "No ditches!"

Jewell and I continued on in the work. We traded duties each month. I seemed to get more efficient in my book work and managed to send in the pension report on time. That was a first.

It was really something to see how much use the MAF plane was to so many. In March, the plane completed eighty-one flights totaling over 13,000 miles. We could have used two planes and pilots. I always waited at the airfield, praying until he was off the ground and I prayed extra hard if it was wet. I thanked the Lord for His provision for us at these times.

Our airstrip at Oicha was quite an attraction. People always came running to see what was happening. Children stood in the breeze as the plane warmed up and would throw grass in the air and watch it fly away.

In April, Dr. Wilcke came in with his whole family. The children (Keith was thirteen and Karen fifteen) hadn't been to Oicha since they were young. Dr. Wilcke wasn't feeling well, so we had less work than usual. We enjoyed the children. One afternoon Jewell, Wanda, and Karen went to Beni. Karen drove most of the way and it was quite a big deal for her as she was a relatively new driver. When she came back she told her dad that even though they complained of their northern roads—here they were really bad. I used to think that going to Beni was a pleasure, but not anymore. I didn't know which vehicle was worse: the Land Rover that jumps around and is harder to handle or my VW that might hit the bottom.

Keith took his BB gun and went out with the Pygmy men to hunt. He shot some birds, and when they came back the men told Wanda she should give him a bigger gun so he could get a monkey for them.

Early in May, I arrived at my house after the medical women's prayer meeting and found a window screen slashed. I felt weak when I saw the front of the locked dresser drawer torn off. That's where I kept the hospital money and the money box was gone. The thief got away with about zaires 282 ($470.00). He must have left in a hurry because nothing else in the house was touched. I couldn't imagine how he knew where the money was, or how he could leave with so much and yet so little.

Benjamin felt we had to report it to the government at Mbau. The chief came out with some men and they took Arubeni, my cook. I was fearful for him and prayed with his family when they came to tell me he was taken. Arubeni was not beaten or even held long. An hour after he was in prison, the headman went and took him out, but about six other men were held. Arubeni had a good spirit all along. He said that he knew they would come and take him because that was their way. He wasn't surprised but was glad he hadn't been held long.

A few days later, someone threw a roll of money at the pastor's door with a note. It was about a third of the money, and the note said the men in prison should be released and that he was repenting to the Lord. It was signed "Somebody." We gave the note to the government man but didn't hear much more.

The families of the men still held made terrible accusations against our working men. Matiasi, our former mechanic, who we had asked to leave in November, and two of our painters were among those held. Matiasi's young wife came saying her husband wanted me to go see them. I wasn't sure what to do and sought the advice of others. I wished it all hadn't happened. I looked to the Lord, for He doesn't allow anything in our lives but that we are to see what He has to teach us and what we can learn of Him.

A little over a week later, the men held in prison were released because there wasn't enough evidence. We had our night watchman with his two dogs begin patrolling around the side of the station where we had our houses. Later, the two painters came to me saying they were told that I had accused them. They were very bitter about the whole thing. I told them I hadn't accused anyone because I didn't know who stole the money. They had some clothing stolen while in prison and thought I should replace it. I gave them some shirts from the bags of clothes, but trousers were another thing—there weren't any. We never recovered the rest of the money.

I had to make a trip to Kagando to get our new battery and charger. Because it was getting harder to take Africans across, I went with Nina in her car. Fifteen miles before the Congo side of the border we hit a rock. The differential cracked and all the oil came out. After we saw what was wrong, we asked the Lord to lead our next step. Soon a truck came along and agreed to tow us. What a dirty time until we were over the border, but we didn't want to leave the car unattended in Congo. In the process of towing, the brakes went as well. We decided Nina would stay with the car and I would go on in the truck to a town where I could get a taxi to Kagando. Jerry Rineer and Martha Hughell drove back for Nina and the car. It was decided the best thing would be to tow the car to Kasese and then put it on the train to Kampala because it was too big of a job for the locals. They found someone to take it all the way to the train and we told Harold Amstutz that it was coming. Poor Harold. We gave him so much to look after.

So our trip of two days stretched out. I was so glad Nina had been driving and it wasn't me this time. What a sinking feeling when you ruined a car.

Dr. MacClure was now at Kagando, so Dr. Keith would soon be leaving for furlough. Barb also planned to leave, going to north Uganda to visit the Sudanese folks, then home.

We found a ride back to Oicha on a truck, and Barb took us to the border to meet up with the driver. He was late to our meeting spot, so we sat and waited and I caught up on my reading. He was a very good driver, and because his truck was empty, I thought it too bad we didn't have a load of things to bring back with us.

Jewell and I carried on in the medical work. I still had no plans for furlough. We were busy, but it was not anything in the way of difficult cases. In May when Jewell handled maternity, she had twelve cesarean cases. By mid-June, I had only three. By then, Nina had her car back and in working order.

We had one mother in Lume who had delivered one of her twins but two days later had not delivered the other. I finished the work at the Lume dispensary then brought her along back to Oicha. The second baby wanted to come hand first, so I turned him and delivered him. I had to give the mother ether. All was well except that his leg broke. After we set it, he was happy and doing alright. His sister was tiny but seemed fine. They would be with us for a while, but I was glad we didn't have to do a cesarean. She would have been a bad risk because so many days had passed.

Jewell took a two week vacation and came back with news about the Beattys. She said that Kathy was a doll. Bill was trying to get her into school, but they didn't like to take such young children because they had to live away from home. He hoped there might be an exception since she no longer had a mother. (As it turned out, neighbors stepped in and Kathy was able to stay with her dad that year.) Barbie planned to go to Lancaster School of the Bible. Dave didn't know what he was going to do, although he was almost twenty and the draft could take him. Barry thought he might be called up and was considering enlistment in the air force.

We missed our doctor visit in July. Dr. Wilcke was to come, but he was stranded in Banda. The plane never arrived to pick him up. Somehow Dave Voltman, our pilot, strayed into Sudan during bad weather and had to land. They wouldn't let him take off again without investigating everything. He was able to tell his wife where he was, but there was no other contact. The embassy worked on it and somehow found out that he and the two other missionaries with him had been taken to Khartoum.

Dr. Wilcke made his way back slowly by car—which he hated. We looked to the Lord for everything. On Monday of the week the doctor should have been here, Benjamin had to do a cesarean. Wednesday we had an ectopic pregnancy. We talked with Dr. Becker on the radio, and he gave Benjamin the go ahead to try and do it. When that one was successfully finished, I told Benjamin we had another case that I was sure was ectopic. I was getting afraid to wait too much longer as she had so much bleeding internally. We did her on Thursday and all went well. In both cases, we were able to get blood from their husbands and that helped give them strength. We had all kinds of cases at Oicha. If you wanted to find abnormal cases, I said come to Oicha and stay around and you'd see them.

The next week we had a man with a badly injured leg from a falling tree. Benjamin questioned himself as to how he could help this leg. Then Dr. Ulrich drove in with Dr. Becker. The Lord answered before we called. The leg couldn't be saved, but Benjamin was relieved to have a doctor work on it. The man seemed quite cheerful. I guess he was glad to be alive.

The doctors did at least thirty-five operations that week in addition to seeing patients. We had to go into the highways and byways to find enough beds for the patients. They did three more surgeries for ectopic pregnancies which made five in two weeks. That was a very high count for such things.

After two weeks, the plane was still not out of Sudan. I knew that Mrs. Voltman was feeling the strain. We thought for sure he would have been back by now. By July 20, we heard by radio that they were back on one of our stations and had been treated well. Dave said it had been a real lesson in patience, and he also mentioned that he had found some Christians in Sudan standing for the Lord.

We had many guests stopping by our station, missionaries and tourists. One tourist stayed with us for two weeks. She wore the new style of short dresses and there was more looking at her than the Pygmies. In the back of my mind, I had concerns about furlough. I was beginning to feel that I might not fit in well. My skirts covered my knees—not mini, not midi, not maxi. I hoped my middle of the road would be okay. Having so much company made it hard to finish my book work. Just the same tale month after month, but that's the way it was.

In August Benjamin went on vacation for a month, which meant we had to send out any cesarean cases. At the end of August, we heard the big news. Bill Beatty would marry Phyllis Spahr, a nurse/teacher in

Zambia, who was from his church back in Collingdale. The wedding was planned for December when she would be finished with her class of students. Barbie and David were planning to stay on in Africa until the wedding. I was happy for Phyllis and Bill.

Ted and Marieanne Crossman arrived to work on the station and in the district. I had new hope. He saw the work and the overwhelming amount of things that needed to be done. We had not been able to keep up with all the little and big repair jobs that fell to us. Our workers had been faithful and able to do so many things, but I was relieved to pass on the oversight responsibility.

Our electrical system was sad. Ted drew up a map showing the plan of our electricity. We weren't getting the power from the engine that we should have because the wiring was so bad. I was amazed at what Ted felt we could add with the power we already had.

I received a letter from the David Downings from Switzerland. They were eager to come and get into the work but would go to Belguim first so Diane could take a nursing course. They would get to the field sometime the following April.

I began to think of how things could be turned over to someone until another medical worker arrived to help Jewell. Marieanne Crossman

The Crossmans

Ted, Marieanne, Lois, David, Peter

285

began learning the books. I hoped to get away some time in November and visit Nyankunde before I traveled home. My mother was eager for me to get home, but I told her I felt I had to stay as long as my visa would allow. I didn't want Jewell alone more than necessary.

At the end of September, I went back with Dr. Becker on the plane to visit Nyankunde. The work there had grown so much. It really was a big station with the hospital and a printing press. At least thirty missionaries and forty children lived there. The Beckers were remarkable. Mrs. Becker still worked in the pharmacy, sitting down with someone bringing things to her. They did think of home and seeing their daughter Mary, but they both felt that as long as they could do something, they wanted to stay. Mrs. Becker had so many folks helping her here in the work and the house, and they knew going home would mean a nursing home.

I took the bus back to Oicha. Jewell and some of the Blukwa medical girls had a birthday supper for me. The girls brought some African food, and we all enjoyed the cake Jewell made. She gave me a banana fiber picture and on the back wrote "Olive, 1970 and may the remaining 40s be even more challenging and filled with His daily blessings."

My cook Arubeni and his wife had their fourth son born October 3. On Dr. Ulrich's monthly visit, a medical student with longish red hair and a beard came with him. I became used to the hair and beard. Things slowed down a bit on that visit because everything had to be explained. Students needed time to try. We all had to learn sometime.

The second day of the doctor visit, Benjamin went ahead with a hernia surgery. The student was assisting but was concerned that Dr. Ulrich wasn't there. He wondered if Benjamin had ever done the surgery before. Evidently, no one had mentioned Benjamin's work. I felt like telling the medical student that Benjamin had done more of this surgery than he'd ever have a chance to do in a very long time.

I was having problems booking flights ahead of time because the Amstutzes were not in Kampala due to Harold's health problems. I decided I would just go and get whatever I could find. It wasn't that hard for one person to get a flight. Many were using a cheaper travel company that flew out from Nairobi, Kenya, but that would have meant extra travel and a visa for Kenya. I felt sorry I couldn't give my mother definite dates, but I didn't want her heart set on a time and then have it not work out. I couldn't even tell her where to write to me. I was in the dark and could only see each of those days as the Lord opened the way.

I also had to sell my VW before furlough. I didn't know what I could get for it, but any amount would be helpful. Even though I'd never get out all the money I had put into it, it had been a joy and a help to me. I prepared everything for my final close out—paperwork finished, mail answered, storeroom cleaned out. The day before I began my travel home, the country had a big holiday. Though President Mobutu had taken over the country some time back, he had been reelected to serve for the next seven years, and they made a really big day of it. No work. I greeted the hospital chapel patients as my farewell and took some literature down to give out. They seemed to appreciate it. Receiving something from someone leaving was important to them.

Nina traveled with me out of Congo, and by November 26 we were in Kampala with ten days until my flight left for London. I hated leaving so far ahead of the flight because of all the work in Oicha, but my visa to enter Uganda would run out and I hadn't sent in my passport to get it extended. I stayed at the Campbells' home then moved over with Jane Amstutz. Harold Amstutz was home in California due to health problems. Jane had returned to Africa to take care of some business. If the doctors gave Harold the go-ahead to come back in January, Jane would stay until then. If he had a later return time, she would go back to the States. Jane said that Harold was doing well. He had to walk a mile in thirty minutes twice a day. She walked along with him and she looked good. I was surprised to learn she would turn sixty in a week, but then I remembered she was ten years older than me, and I was almost fifty!

Jane planned to go to Bill Beatty and Phyllis Spahr's wedding and she filled me in. I had an invitation, but no details. Bill had written to Harold to do the tying of the knot but of course that plan changed, and now Mr. Bisset would do it. Phyllis' mother had died very suddenly the previous summer, but her father would come out to the wedding. The wedding would be on the last day of their annual conference. Barbie was maid of honor and Dave the best man for his dad. They would both leave the very next day for the States. Barry was in the service and couldn't come out for the wedding.

While Nina and I were in Kampala, there was a disturbance downtown. I never discovered the true story. Nina and I were in a store. Crowds gathered and police came and more crowds came. As we went to leave the store, the Indian owner warned us that tear gas had been shot. I was glad he told us for we would have been caught in it for sure. The funny thing was that the commotion continued up until evening. The crowds would seem to thin out and people would run away. But then they would wander back and start the whole thing again. All the stores closed, and Nina had to go back the next day to finish shopping for her orphans.

On December 6, I began the transition from forest life to the good old USA. I flew from Entebbe, Uganda to Paris to London, then changed planes to go on to Anne Punt in Amsterdam, Holland. What a joy to see how the Lord blessed her work in the Bible clubs and Adult Bible study. Her co-worker, Annie Verboom, was now on TV each week. From there I flew back to Paris and on to Philadelphia where my family and others from church met me. A six-year-old greeted, "Aunt Olive, you don't look as old as your picture." You can know that made me feel good.

I stayed with my parents who had moved to an apartment in Hatfield, PA. It was a blessing to come home to my growing nieces and nephew and have them drop by the house often. I happily began deputation and shared the work of the Lord. The Lord blessed though the devil was busy too. I praised the Lord for His strength in a busy furlough.

Term Five and Beyond

1972

But seek first the kingdom of God and His righteousness,
and all these things shall be added to you. (Matthew 6:33)

Zaire. I traveled back to my adopted land—the same country with a new name. After taking a small plane from Allentown to New York, I waited for my luggage at the circular. First one, then the second of my large bags appeared, but not my third one. I filled out the claim paperwork, and the airline folks asked if they should hold the bag until I came back. I said, "Four years? I need that typewriter now." The small plane had another scheduled round trip that day and they managed to return with my typewriter before I left New York. I knew that I traveled with too much luggage and wrote a reminder in my diary—"Don't do that again." I hoped I would take note from now on. It was a struggle to travel with so many bags, but in those days, other travelers would watch your luggage when necessary. I guarded the bags of a Roman Catholic priest when he went off to find food, and a woman who managed a bar watched mine.

I changed planes in Iceland, then on to Glasgow, followed by a train ride into London. My London room, though quite lovely, required shilling pieces fed into the gas heater to make it work. The part of your body facing the heater roasted and your back was cold. Later when I went to the dining room, I was surprised to find Dr. Keith Waddell at my table. We met up the next day at Westminster Abbey for sightseeing.

Due to a delay in my London to Nairobi flight, I missed my connection and had to take a later plane to Entebbe. The Amstutzes picked me up, and we stayed in Kampala before heading to our conference in Rethy. On the way, we stopped at Murchison Falls where Betty Wilson, Barb Battye, Martha Hughell, and I had visited back in 1957. The place had grown so much.

At the hotel, two Acholi waiters recognized me from when they had worked at the hotel in Kasese, Uganda. The Amstutzes and I stayed in the tent area. With the Nile just below us, we could hear the hippos coughing and water splashing. Driving through the park, we saw lots of elephants and their tiny babies. We had enough time to take the Nile launch trip to the falls, and to our delight the animals all seemed to perform for us—crocodiles, hippos, elephants, waterbuck, warthogs, and all sorts of birds.

As usual, I enjoyed the conference. I met the new workers from Oicha—David and Diane Downing and Hank and Ella Shoemaker, a Dutch couple who had moved to Australia when they married fourteen years earlier. When the Shoemakers were young, they had both helped one summer at the camp run by Annie Punt. Hank would be overseeing our lab.

Some changes in the status of religion in Zaire created much discussion at the conference. We didn't know what it might all mean, and eventually some of our men went to a meeting with the Ministry of Justice in Kinshasa. We all had a challenge in those days to keep the message of the Gospel as first on our list.

Jewell Olson and I traveled in her Land Rover for the twelve-hour, dirty, dusty, bumpy trip back to Oicha (which included a short stop at

Nyankunde to see the Beckers). As Jewell was unloading the Rover in Oicha, we heard a strange noise and soon discovered air leaking out of the back tire. But we were HOME! Just think if it had happened five miles out. We would have had to unload everything to get to the jack. On the whole, our trip had been good except for the slipping and sliding of the Rover's hood. I'd tell Jewell, "Next bump should be with the Rover leaning the other way to make it go back," and it worked.

Yona (our man for the lights) and Barnaba were the first to greet me. Then many others came. I heard little voices in the darkness: "It's her. We'll be back on Saturday." And come back they did. I had close to a hundred children in Bible class that first week.

Since Jewell was due to leave for furlough and had been living in Margaret Clapper's old house (the one I had stayed in before furlough), she moved to the guest house to make room for me. Nina Smith and Jean Schram were in their houses. Hank and Ella Shoemaker lived in Jewell's old house with two of their six children (their other four were in Rethy Academy). Ted and Marieanne Crossman were still in their house. I was back into the work.

The first thing I did was fall off a stepladder. It was one we had had for years, and I knew I had to watch it. I was up and down all morning, cleaning shelves, and I must have put it on an uneven spot. Before I knew what was what, I went down, hitting my head on the cupboard which took some force off my landing on the cement floor. I did see stars, but I was in one piece.

Dr. Herb Atkinson came for the doctor visit with a Canadian couple, a medical student and his wife who had been married for only one month. Jewell and I provided supper, and at dessert time Jewell said that her coffee supply was almost finished and we should go to the Crossmans' and ask them for some. The rest of us knew what was up and agreed. The couple told us later that they couldn't imagine how we could impose like that but went along because the others did. They were so pleased with the pretty decorated cake the Crossmans served for the couple's one-month anniversary.

The poor little bride didn't see much of her hubby with all the hospital work that week. We had all kinds of cases. One woman came with a "ten-month pregnancy" which actually was a fetus of four to five months that had never been expelled when it died. We had another woman who delivered her baby, but we found a ruptured uterus. Dr. Herb did the repair, and though we thought she wouldn't make it, she survived. We had some tough meningitis cases that Hank Shoemaker said would have died had they been in Australia, but the patients were still with us and looked like they might recover. We also had some surgeries for bowel obstructions. It was a busy week.

Around the same time, Pastor Makanza, who was called the Billy Graham of the Congo, held meetings in Beni and Oicha. He spoke in French, and Samsoni, our Christian Education Director, translated. Thousands made decisions for the Lord. Pastor Zephania knew that we had a large work to follow these folks and help them stand for the Lord. We continued in prayers for our area.

At the beginning of February, 390 children attended baby clinic. I wrote the cards and gave 190 DPT shots. Jewell gave 100 BCG (tuberculosis) shots and we ran out of measles vaccine. I was glad to work with Jewell in the baby clinic one more time before she left. The chapel was well filled as folks waited on the benches, money in hand. We called the folks row by row. That was one time it was good to sit in the front of church.

Baby clinic

Job managed my outdoor work, and my garden was well under way. I had arranged to pay three boys to bring goat manure for my garden and five showed up with their pans, so I had more than enough. We had vegetables growing and also started some flowers from seeds.

I wasn't getting many calls when it was my turn for night duty. We now had an intercom between maternity and my house, so the maternity girls no longer had to come to the house to get me. Even though I wasn't woken up for work, I still had night calls from the dogs. Jewell's dog had puppies that were still in my house, and they would get out of their box and roam around. Once, one of the puppies wedged itself halfway in and halfway out of the box. One of them even scratched the door trying to get out of the room. Jewell told me that was the way of dogs. They were cute, but I didn't like all the bother. I hoped Barnaba would take her when Jewell went on furlough. We did eventually get rid of the puppies in Beni.

I went over to Kagando, Uganda with David Downing for a brief visit with Martha. At first I didn't think I'd be able to go, but my papers to exit and reenter Zaire arrived at the last minute. Martha had had a rough term and was worn out. Lois Clark, a British nurse, was taking her place and fit in well but would have a big job falling on her. While I was there, I transplanted Martha's African violets. She always had such pretty ones but had been too busy to take care of them.

I put in an offer of $1,005.00 to buy a VW Kombi that was for sale in Kenya. (Jewell advised me to add the five dollars to win the bid in case someone offered $1,000.00.) It was almost too much to think they would agree to that amount, but it was worth a try. A VW would use less gas than other vehicles and a Kombi was the only kind that would be high enough for the growing rocks in the road. Did you know that rocks could grow? The more earth that washed away from them, the bigger they grew. In the end, my bid wasn't high enough. I didn't really have the money for a car anyway. The inland freight to transport my barrels to Mombasa cost $979.00. It would be another $500.00 to get them to Oicha, and I didn't know what I would have to pay for customs. Even people couldn't cross the border for free anymore. The Crossmans had to pay $6 to travel over. Not much, but it adds up.

We still traveled out to various dispensaries, but we couldn't get to Luanoli because the road was so bad. The fellows had been out on bicycles and told us it was covered in water near the river. Jewell tried with the Land Rover but got stuck.

One day in early March, we had a storm that began with a blowing rain. Then I heard the hail. After it let up a bit, I went to the Shoemakers' for prayer meeting. As we were praying, we heard a "Hodi, Hodi, Hodi" from one of our workmen who was running up the path to the house. He told us that the secondary school, still in the process of being built, had blown down. We finished prayer time and went up to see the damage. Though it could have been worse, all I could think was poor Ted Crossman. He was away at the time and would be discouraged to see the damage.

Around this time, the government called for a detailed plan and outline of all the property of the mission and church. Dave Downing traveled to Rethy to help Carl Becker and Mr. Zimmerman make up the diagrams. I had a long discussion with one of the area Greek men on the topic. He had called Zaire his home for forty years and feared the government might begin taking things away from him. He acknowledged that God had heard and helped so many times in the past or we all would have been gone a long time ago. I prayed for him that he might trust the Lord as his Savior.

Nothing was completely clear in what the government might do. Some thought there would be changes that would challenge our ability to teach the Word. That sounded impossible, but the days changed so quickly. We knew the Lord desired to build His church and His people, and many times a challenge to our faith is necessary for us to stand up strong for the Lord. "May His Name be magnified at all times" was our prayer. "Might wheat be found and not all chaff should those days come."

I admired Jewell's ability to use objects when she taught the women's class. One Sunday she used one of those birthday candles that won't blow out to illustrate that even if trials, troubles, or temptations come into our lives, yet we are not to let them blow our light out. She blew and the candle went out. Then just like that, it burned again. The women really listened and watched as she talked and blew the flame out again and again and it came back each time.

Ernie, the pilot, brought the doctor in a new plane for our March visit. It looked the same as the other except it was green instead of red, although I didn't see it up close that day as I didn't go to the airfield. There was an advantage to not having a car—less responsibility for running people around.

At the end of March, I went out to the Lume dispensary and found the road just as bad as ever. Yona and I split the driving. He drove to Beni, then I took it to Lume because he hadn't been that way for a time. Coming back, he drove that part and I took Beni to Oicha. Ted Crossman grew worried as time passed and we weren't home yet, but Jewell told him to just wait. We finally arrived home at 9 p.m. I counted that we drove seven hours, worked six, and spent one and a half hours in Beni for various errands.

We brought back a drum of gas that was filled while we were at Lume and picked up on the way home. We had some money to spend, and even though all the shops were closed, the one shopkeeper opened for me. He had promised he would if we were late getting back to town.

The more I traveled, the more I thought that it was too late for older folks from the USA to come out and visit me. In the past, we had stretches of at least a mile where you could get up speed, but no more. Even the good areas had holes. If you kept up the speed you'd really get a jar. We would wind from side to side and miss some of the holes, but you could never, never miss them all. The Land Rover's speedometer didn't

Yona and Kasereka with our faithful "Pray and Push"

work, but what of it? You could never go fast enough to worry about going over the speed limit. The heat of the metal floor tended to increase as one drove, especially going up hills. The left door had a faulty catch and could cause quite a surprise when it flew open from time to time. I always felt bad for any patients we brought back with us. The back of the Rover had seats that faced sideways and no cushions. Usually the back was packed with all sorts of supplies and possessions, so the folks just hung onto boxes. But our faithful "Pray and Push" never let us down as long as we carried water, oil, and gas.

One evening, I went down to the hospital to do the tube feeding of a baby girl with meningitis. I also checked in on a boy with a fast–growing cancer. He had a tumor that had started in his lower face and then spread to the abdomen. The doctors said there wasn't anything we could do, and the boy was close to death. It was known as Burkitt's tumor, named for the English doctor who first described it. Our Dr. Ted Williams in Uganda worked along with him for a while in finding cases in our area.

As I came back from the hospital, I looked up at the sky and the moon and the stars. I didn't use my flashlight; I didn't need it. The big dipper was going down in the sky, the Southern Cross was too low to be seen, but the Milky Way was full of stars. I stood in awe.

We had a time of visitors early in April. The training camp for leaders of the Girls and Boys Club was in progress. Three different parties came to climb the Ruwenzori Mountains, all starting off from Oicha. Dr. Ulrich came down with his three oldest children ready to climb the mountain. Since he was here, we asked him to examine one of our patients. I was fearful of an ectopic pregnancy, and I was right. He operated and saved her life. She had not wanted us to go ahead before her husband arrived, but we insisted and she was glad. As they began with her, a strangulated hernia case showed up. Dr. Ulrich had quite a workout on that surgery and had to resect part of the bowel. (Benjamin was happy the doctor was here to do the work.) I told Dr. Ulrich that I was conditioning him for the mountain climb.

We began hearing about the most recent flight to the moon. It no longer was the only thing on the radio as in years past, but we stayed informed. I kept up with news of all places. Sudan didn't get a pact signed with the south, and we heard the Jewish people had to leave Uganda.

In our area, some of the Roman Catholic priests had been expelled from Zaire. A new sort of problem arose when I began having trouble understanding who folks were talking about. The government had declared the nationals should use African names and not foreign ones. Changes came and we adjusted to them.

I took the overnight Luanoli dispensary trip at the end of April and was well taken care of there. We left at 6:30 a.m. and arrived by 12:30 after being stuck twice for a short time and stopping three additional times. We did it in five hours coming home but only stopped twice to get out of a hole we were hung up on. So many of the cement culverts were cracked or washed away. How long we would be able to get through was anyone's guess.

At Luanoli we saw patients until about 4 p.m., and then we were served rice and beef (I think). I was ready for it. Afterward, it was back to work again until dark. In the morning, I had pai pai (papaya), lemon, bananas, rice, and eggs. Then we had rice and chicken before leaving. They sent a thermos of tea with us, and we had our tea and bananas on the road after we got out of the one hole and before getting stuck in the next one.

When I got home, I dropped my blankets outside of the house. At midnight in Luanoli, I had realized I was not alone in the bed—mamas,

Crossing the bridge to Luanoli

297

papas, and all the kids were having a feast on me. I had my spray bomb along and went to work. Some people have strong reactions to bug bites, but I didn't have too much to show for it. The chickens enjoyed the dead bugs on the dirt floor in the morning, and I hoped the spray wouldn't affect them.

The outhouse there brought another dilemma. They had a nice, newly prepared hole, but no house was built over it as yet. There were only a few blades of grass around, so I went to the others. One had a door you had to hold shut, and another was surrounded by sticks that were pretty far apart. I chose the one with the door problem.

This trip also brought an unusual meal time custom to my awareness. After they seated me, Zakaria, the medical man at Luanoli, prayed, but then he went away as I had my meal. I suppose they had done that before, but I had never been so conscious of it.

All my drums arrived by the beginning of May. I unpacked a little at a time as I could find a moment between work, medical committees, and children's class. Everything seemed to come through in satisfactory condition. I had four barrels of things for the hospital including one barrel of bandages and one of uniforms for the women. The men seemed happy when I gave out the white trousers I found in another barrel.

Mother received her usual belated Mother's Day greeting. I was so blessed in knowing that she prayed for me each day. She was a prayer warrior.

At the end of May, we hosted ten tourists stranded with a broken car. The Downings loaned their car for some of them to go and buy the needed parts in Kampala. The tourists cared for themselves pretty well, but we did have a few meals together. Some also helped Diane Downing in the pharmacy—but oh, the short, short skirts. The president of Uganda had put a ban on them over there.

Children with their instruments

Jewell began final preparations for furlough, and I didn't know how we would get along without her. She was one to keep things organized and moving, especially when the doctors were here for surgery. She couldn't leave until her passport and visa came back, and when they finally arrived in May we couldn't understand the way of things. The documents were dated the end of November yet had never been sent. The delay had been difficult for her; however, I was so thankful that we had had those months to work together before she went home.

The week before Jewell left, we held four straight hours of baby clinic. Diane came down and helped too. We gave almost 200 DPT shots, 90 small pox vaccinations, and 250 BCG shots against tuberculosis. We also gave 373 children the Daraprim pill (antimalarial) to be divided into four and given each week until the next baby clinic the following month. It was a very noisy afternoon, but we managed.

Our pastor Zephania's son Yakobo (Jacob) was also a pastor, and he taught a horn class about thirty miles out. They were thrilled to see that the present group included two girls. The pastor's other son Tito, who worked for us giving out patient cards, taught horn at Oicha. With so

Horn Players

much music, our afternoons were like a campground. When the government had some big affair, often the horn players were invited to provide the music.

We had very sad news of an accident in Kenya. Mrs. Edythe DeYoung, a widow whose husband had died some years back, was killed in a car accident. Edythe taught at Rift Valley Academy where her younger daughter was to graduate soon. Her older daughter was in nursing school. They had planned to go home after graduation, and now she was at home with the Lord. Edythe was driving her VW bug, taking some folks back to the academy after a concert (her daughter was on the bus). She rounded a corner going down an escarpment, and right in front of her was a truck that had stopped on the road with no lights or branches on the road as a warning. Mrs. DeYoung was a good driver, but with a car coming the other direction on the narrow road and the steep drop off, she had few options. The hood of the VW bug buckled under the back of the truck. Mrs. DeYoung was killed and the other four passengers seriously injured. Dr. Wilcke's daughter Karen, one of the passengers, suffered serious facial injuries. The accident happened after Nyankunde was off the radio for the night, so the Wilckes didn't find out until the next morning. The Crossmans, close friends of the DeYoung family, picked up Wanda for the trip to the hospital in Nairobi, Kenya. Other missionaries stepped in to care for Karen in the hospital until Wanda was able to reach her daughter four days later.

My first week without Jewell was the doctor's week. We no sooner started seeing patients when word came that a mother was bleeding—placenta previa. Doctor saw five or six patients and then went into surgery with her. A second patient came with the same thing. As I went to tell those waiting to come back at about 2 p.m., I was called to help Hank Shoemaker take the blood for the second patient. When I got there, I discovered that he needed me because it was Hank giving the blood for the woman. Little Jacob, one of our hospital workers, shook the bottle for me and he shook his head too. To think that this man was giving his blood for that woman! It was something hard for many to understand. Hank hadn't been feeling well, and later when we checked we found that he had malaria, so the poor patient got a dose of it. He hadn't known when he gave the blood; he just knew he wasn't quite tops. Both the women lived, although of course the babies did not survive.

The week passed rapidly. I did well, but after it was all over, my throat hurt and I had a cough so bad my toes almost came up. We had so many coughs around so it was no surprise, but I had hoped I wouldn't get it. As I came home from work one day the next week, the Downings invited me to their house for supper. When I finally went to my house after the meal, I found a note on my door inviting me to the Crossmans' for supper. By the time I told Marieanne Crossman that I had already eaten and we talked a bit more, I had no time for letters.

About one hundred children came to my children's class again. I gave out Sunday school papers to those who learned their verses, which I posted at my window during the week. As I was resting one day, some children passed by, and what a joy to hear them read and learn the verses. I prayed they would know God's strength to withstand temptations.

Children from Bible class

Those falling to temptation led to great sadness. A father of one of our medical girls told me his daughter was pregnant by one of the medical men. It was too sorrowful to think about. The man was a new graduate of last year's class in Nyankunde and had a wife and family. So after two evenings of meetings with the elders, we lost two more from the work. Having the oversight and leadership of our ten medical girls took prayer and wisdom. Leadership was a great challenge.

The next month brought 405 to baby clinic. Ella Shoemaker, Marieanne Crossman, Jean Schram, and some of the national staff helped me. We had polio vaccine for the first time in many months.

The station came alive when the children of the missionaries had school vacation. The Crossmans picked up the four Shoemakers and one of their own with the other coming in a few days. Ella Shoemaker's parents visited about the same time, and Ella came down with malaria.

Jean helped her with the children and was in her element having been the oldest of eleven. Diane Downing also came down with malaria and almost fainted in the pharmacy. We were busy.

At the end of July, I had some information on the state of Sudan. Abednego along with other church leaders had met with the President, and things were looking up a little. The government was open to relief agencies entering Sudan. Though missionaries were welcome, the work of proselytizing, as it was put, had not been cleared. All personnel reentering Sudan required clearance from the Sudanese Embassy and also through whatever category of work they would be engaged in. However, to return and actually work at a station was still a problem that hadn't been worked out. I saw great thought and foresight in Abednego's remarks, and it sounded like he had grown in the Lord. Our leaders needed prayer to be very sensitive to the Lord's voice and leading. Earthly things are real temptations, but may our eyes be upon the Lord.

A new challenge came before us at the hospital. A tree had fallen on a woman going for water and fractured her pelvis in four places and did some internal damage as well. Ted Crossman helped me rig up a type of Bradford frame using a pipe, and Barnaba and I made a canvas for it. We hoped it would work. Of course, the woman was with us for a long time. The frame was successful: she did develop pressure sores, but she eventually made a full recovery.

Barnaba, the man who helped in my house, learned to sew on my machine and worked on much of the sewing needs for the hospital. We almost ruined the machine in trying to sew the thick material of mattresses for the hospital. After I adjusted the tension, he was able to complete the task.

A new young doctor and his wife came for our scheduled doctor visit, which meant time for interpreting. He was studying Swahili and had been here before my furlough, though when I first heard his name, I couldn't picture what he looked like. The days during doctor visits stretched well past our usual quitting time. My hips and legs tired out from all the walking and standing. One time, I spent an hour trying to pull a broken tooth and couldn't get it out. We took him into surgery to remove it under anesthesia and had a time when he stopped breathing. We were able to revive him, and he went home the next day.

Our monthly baby clinic in August totaled 520. Although we had some faithful workers, handling the maternity cases and writing the monthly government reports left little time for other things. I should have had more help, but I didn't have the time to train more women. I still wrote to Mother and Daddy each week, but my correspondence with others lapsed during this time.

We had another thing to pray about when our medicine supply grew scarce. The Indian man who ran a reliable shop in Kampala planned to close it and leave, making it difficult to get enough for our large need. It was hard to know how things might work out. Dr. Becker urged us to be careful with the drugs we had. We kept our eyes on the Lord, for it is He who supplies. He would make a way in His time and His fashion.

One of the Greek men came to us, but he refused to stay as recommended, even when we begged. Three days later, he came back in a worse state than before. He had some kind of infection of the blood, a new problem that had just started showing up. Nyankunde also had a case. It was thought to be from ticks and presented as hemorrhage and pus in the skin. In this case, it was mostly in his hands. Benjamin helped me with the frequent debriding of the fingers.

Turns out, the man, Mr. Parnishe, was Italian, not Greek. He had a Zairean wife who cared for him well but was under a strain. She lit up when I showed her the Bible in the bedside drawer, and she bought a Swahili Bible for herself.

The man's hands were very painful, and he had a mind of his own (like so many men). He wouldn't use the bedpan and fainted on his wife more than once in trying to get up. After about thirty days, his hands were healed; however, he then contracted meningitis. Dr. Becker prescribed by radio but would have liked to have his chart in hand.

About this time, I began to feel more and more concern for Benjamin. He seemed to lack the desire to give himself completely to the Lord. He was like many—success in his work life but not in his family or his desire to serve the Lord. He was the head administrator of the hospital, and I appreciated the work he did. I upheld him in prayer.

Another problem arose when we began to see more and more women delivering on the path to the hospital. I suppose they waited too long to start out. One said to me, "but look, you had to help me the other two times and this one just came (quickly)." The girls wrote a fine if the women delivered on the path. I could have cut out the fine, but I didn't because so many were doing it. It just didn't seem necessary and it increased the chance for dirt and infection.

At the end of August, I consulted on some cases with Dr. Herb Atkinson over the radio. He would talk with me for a time, confer with the three other doctors sitting nearby, then come back on the radio to inform me of their decision. We kept it up for at least a half hour. A former Peace Corps man from Washington D.C. was also listening in on the session. My questions were mostly about female problems, but what could I do? The man had come out with the hope of learning about our setup. He wrote novels and had been to Ethiopia and other parts of the world, and now he wanted to see the Pygmies and planned to put them in his next book.

A new couple, Wendell and Faithe Zercher, arrived to teach in the secondary school. They were from the Mennonite Central Committee (MCC) and fit easily into station life.

An African medical student came along with Dr. Herb for our September visit. Dr. Muhindo, whose father had trained with Dr. Becker years earlier, would be at Nyankunde for six weeks, and they hoped to get him back for his internship. He was so humble and easy to talk to. I was glad to see some Christian men in training.

We began hearing of increasing difficulties at Kagando. After all these years, the government wanted $7,000 for the rights to the property. The country itself was in political turmoil. At the end of September, I received a note from Barb. "All well here—though uneasy." The Rineers came back from furlough just as the upset began, so they stayed in Kenya. The Allens were also in Kenya on vacation, so only Barb, Lois, and Dr. Keith were on the station. Of course, they were busy.

Zaire also had its problems. We had to hand in all foreign currency. Beef prices rose because they were no longer allowed to transport the beef on hoof, so it became too expensive to buy.

Word came that it would cost Z56,696 ($120,000) to use our radios, so we were ready to shut them down. No more calling the doctor for advice or radio contact for the plane (which meant limited flights). The next day, folks listened in just in case anything was said, and praise the Lord, word came that it didn't apply to missions. We had been off-air for only a day. It was good to be able to communicate again. Because things felt so uneasy, I asked my parents to be cautious in how they wrote and talked about our problems here.

We lost another girl from the work due to pregnancy. Then we found our night man Ofeni drunk. He was a good fellow, but the drink got hold of him, and I thought it might be the ruin of him.

The week of my birthday (fifty-one now) presented challenging maternity cases as well as an outbreak of measles. Our October baby clinic topped out at 619. By this time, our Italian man, Mr. Parnishe, had been with us seventy days. The meningitis seemed better, but at times he didn't appear to speak with full understanding. We had some folks come in and give blood for him. Then at eighty-five days he developed a kidney condition.

In November, our hospital was full and overflowing. Benjamin kept asking Yona to find more and more beds. I don't know where he found the beds, but Yona always came through. The measles epidemic was going strong. We were so busy that I began teaching some of the cleaning women how to take temperatures, and I hadn't been able to get out on the dispensary visits.

Eventually, the hospital numbers dropped. The Lord had spared so many of the very sick babies. Our Italian man seemed to be improving despite our lack of knowledge concerning the cause of his problems. He was shaving, eating well, and sitting up in a chair with his trousers on.

Once again, the news in a letter from Barb in Uganda was discouraging. The Lord knew, but I wouldn't have been surprised to see them our way one day soon, and I figured their things wouldn't be coming with them. I felt the time for giving forth the Word in real freedom might be short. Oh, that we would be faithful in proclaiming the good news of God's salvation.

Our December doctor visit was a full one, and we kept him working to the very end. The plane took off with two minutes to spare because of an emergency surgery at the last minute. Dr. Herb's family was with him that week, and they were already on the plane by the time he ran from the operating room to the car in his scrub suit. He jumped in as I handed him his clothes, watch, and glasses. His son David (a senior and heading home to the States in the summer) had helped him in surgery that day and was on the run in his scrub suit as well. Just then Dan, another son, rode by on his bike. The time was so short that I told him to get in the car and leave the bike.

Christmas neared, and I baked my usual cookies. Barnaba had planned to visit his mother in January, but she died mid-December so he left to go to her village.

Our station missionary family gathered together the Sunday before Christmas because Christmas day was devoted to a church service and games. The Zerchers had traveled to Nyankunde for Christmas to meet up with some of the other MCC workers and were not with us for the get-together.

I had many preparations during the Christmas season. I gave our patients gifts of cards with needles, pins, thread, and buttons. For the missionaries, I made up cans of cookies and gave other odd things I could find. My Bible club children received two cookies and two pieces of candy each. They were out 163 strong and were so happy with their treats. I also hosted the medical girls for tea, cookies and popcorn and gave them a gift of crochet cotton.

On Christmas day, I brought in two white rose buds from my bushes.

"Looking to Jesus"—A better motto could not have been found for those days.

1973

You will keep him in perfect peace, whose mind is stayed
on You, because he trusts in You. (Isaiah 26:3)

I finished evening rounds on the New Year's weekend, and as I left the hospital I inadvertently passed into the area of my *enemy*. Though I didn't see her, Benjamin's dog saw me and lit into my right leg. The blood flowed. Jean cleaned it and gave me a tetanus shot which hurt more than the bite itself. She took my call duty at work the next day while I sat at home with an elevated leg. Benjamin's dog had always been fierce but became more so with her two puppies. He moved them to a different area as she had bitten several others that same day.

We gathered for our conference in Rethy and had a blessed time together. That year, I stayed in the home of Bernetta Wambold, who was from Emmaus, PA which was near my hometown. I had a comfortable bed; however, Rethy was a mile long so I had a good fifteen–minute walk from house to chapel.

On the day we arrived back at Oicha, our Italian man, Mr. Parnishe, had a stroke, and he died a few days later. We had a male nurse with him for two nights, so I wasn't there when he died. The other Italian men came the next day. I had thought they would take him to Beni, but they wanted to bury him here. Of course there wasn't a grave ready, but our men worked quickly, and by 8 p.m. we were going to the cemetery. Pastor Daniel spoke as we buried him by lamplight. His wife was standing well, and the Lord enabled for all. About a month later, we received a letter from the Italian Embassy inquiring as to any debt from Mr. Parnishe. The other men had already paid, so nothing was owed to us.

Barnaba returned from his mother's village to report that his mother hadn't actually died but was very ill, and he needed to return to care for her. He stayed with us for several days and helped finish a few extra things then went to help with his mother.

I finished the monthly report and the drug order to the central government. We now sent a yearly order to the central government that supplied a goodly amount of drugs for our hospital. Though we received an order every six weeks from the medical center, it helped to have the government supply to fall back on. So it went, one thing and another. Dr. Atkinson's son was having health problems, and they eventually went home at the end of January. I didn't know what that would mean for our doctor visits, but the Lord knew our steps one by one and day by day. We went more and more just leaning on Him. Dr. Wilcke was also out with health problems. We heard of a possibility of another doctor arriving in spring.

David Downing and a Dutch doctor climbed Mt. Ruwenzori but didn't make it to the top because another person was ahead and delayed them. The next day was poor weather and they couldn't complete their climb. Dave would have to try again if he wanted to reach the very top.

At the end of January, Elsie Maier, a short-term nurse/midwife arrived from Aba to work at Oicha for a few weeks. She was wonderful and fit in well. I really should have stayed to teach her, but it was my only chance to get away. So after a week together, I headed for Nyankunde.

I happened to be there just in time to get in on a scheme of Vera Theissen and some others to take the Beckers out to dinner at a tourist place an hour and a half away. It was run by a Belgian couple who had been stuck at Oicha due to bad roads a few months earlier. Back in '64, they had fled Oicha with their daughter and her six-day-old baby.

The meal was so nice. They served soup, mushrooms on toast, antelope steak that just melted in our mouths, french fries, and salad. They ended the meal with cake and wouldn't let the girls pay.

We drove home by way of the waterfalls, and the Beckers told us they enjoyed the outing very much. The next day, Mrs. Becker fell in the pharmacy but thankfully wasn't injured in any way. Later that same day, Dr. Becker grabbed the car door to get in just as Mrs. Becker closed it, and he ended up with black and blue fingers.

A few days later, I caught a ride to Linga. Though I wasn't ready to travel, I couldn't turn down a direct ride. I had a nice rest at Linga, visiting Betty Wilson and Margaret Clapper. The beautiful flowers were in bloom, and I collected some seed thinking that perhaps Job, my garden helper, could get them to grow at my house.

Since it was so dry, young girls brought buckets of water to fill the drums. It worked out well—they got money and we got water. It felt like Sudan days. Since Oicha had a water system that had been working well, we didn't have to draw water by hand there. I continued to pray for Sudan and for Abednego as he led the work of reentry for the church to the area where we had been. His brother Nikolau and their families had all returned, though I didn't know how many of the local people were back. Pastor Andreya, who was aging and not well, had only visited thus far.

I was able to get to Rethy and thought I might catch a ride back to Oicha with the Crossmans if they drove up for parents' day. I didn't see how folks could afford all their travel, but it was none of my business. I actually rode back with the MacDowells whom I had cared for with Harold, their first baby, back in '49. That was the same Harold who gave Jewell the motorbike ride that injured her back. We arrived at Nyankunde by February 22, and I topped off my vacation with malaria.

Word came from the government that printing of Christian magazines was no longer allowed. That hit the Swahili and Bangala ones printed at Nyankunde. I prayed the Lord's will be done in the going forth of His precious Word.

How fast time flies in vacation. Fanweli began searching for a ride to Oicha for me, then suddenly another way opened. I quickly said my goodbyes, threw things into my suitcase and went down with some Greek men from Butembo. I missed a dinner with the Wattses (he in the pharmacy work and she a nurse). It was a rush, but the Greek men had a nice Datsun sedan, and I was quite sure Fanweli's ride would have been an uncomfortable truck.

The month I had been away from Oicha had been filled with cases, and Elsie was tired but so excited about all she had been able to do. She planned to stay for another three weeks, and I was glad because I knew I could use her help.

We had a terrible storm the day after I arrived home. It felt like the house would blow away, and part of my roof did. The Zerchers' roof flew into their garden. Part of the roof on maternity blew off. That in turn caused the mud ceilings to fall. Two babies were hit with mud, but they were not injured. We had to squeeze the beds together in one side of the building. The laboratory ceiling fell down as well. The roofs weren't just loose—they literally blew off. The twister got under them and they went sailing. Because it was night, fewer folks were around, but we had three victims from homes further out. We praised the Lord that the tile roofs didn't go because the heavy tiles would have been quite dangerous.

Everything was one mess of dirt. We had some things repaired by the time Dr. Becker came for the doctor visit a few days later, but we were crowded under the remaining roofed buildings.

Benjamin took a vacation. Ofeni came back to the work, repentant of the drink that had been his great temptation. I prayed he would seek the Lord for the victory, and I tried to encourage him. We lost two others from the work. Not nurses, but helpers, both for other women in their lives. I couldn't understand it all. Another of our workers had ten children, and yet I heard he had two other women and more children. How they thought they'd feed and educate them all, I didn't know. I'm afraid the job of finding enough food and gardens fell on the women.

The days felt different to me, and we never knew what another would bring forth from any and all different sources. We had to move slowly on the decrees that came from the government. Our information came from such a distance and with so many different interpretations that we found it best to wait and see what came of it before taking action. Mr. Brashler's report on meetings in Kinshasa gave some cause for thanksgiving, but not without the fact that in time we would be considered redundant by the government and no longer allowed to do our work. It might be long or it might be short until we needed to think about what the Lord had for us. I'm afraid my thoughts went to a good long rest before I would think of something new. These years had been heavy, but the Lord knew and gave strength for each day.

Jean Schram and Elsie Maier went to Kenya hoping to get Jean's Land Rover. Jean had a job to get all the necessary papers in order. We still couldn't pass through Uganda, but folks could come out to us. Catherine from Kagando came over and stayed a few days, so I caught up on some news from Uganda.

One evening, Nina Smith called me complaining of pain so great she thought she would fall over. I administered nitroglycerine and she soon felt better. The next afternoon, she called me again with severe pain and shortness of breath. The episode lasted a half hour and took a lot out of her. She had been to Nyankunde for a medical exam back in January, and they had thought her pain was not serious. She flew up again, and

Traveling in Africa

this time they definitely found heart damage. Dr. Becker didn't want to tell her she had to go home, but she did need to take it easy. She began working less, and because she didn't need her car as often, she let me use it around the station.

At the beginning of April, the Rift Valley Academy children came on a two-engine plane through Rwanda into Zaire instead of our MAF plane which would have had to make two trips for the large number of children. The plane dropped off David Crossman and the children of Oicha. We were really getting up in the world to have a two-engine plane land on our strip. With all the children home, our station was full and lively again

Tourists continued to come in all the time, and Vic Paul financed the building of a place for them to stay. April was filled with many happenings. Margaret Clapper came for a few days. Marieanne Crossman headed home for a month to celebrate her folks' fiftieth wedding anniversary. The Morrises came through with their son, a senior at Kijabe, and a group from "Youth with a Mission." Diane Downing began training Etienne for the pharmacy, and Benjamin came back from vacation.

I had 100 in my children's group, and that week we reenacted the Children of Israel at the Red Sea. I picked up a stick in the midst of the children to use as Moses' rod, and when all the folks were to have crossed the river, I said to one girl still sitting that she should move over too. She didn't move. Finally, the children got it across to me that she had a lame leg and that I had the stick she needed to walk. I immediately gave it back to her, and she crossed safely over the sea.

An Indian man came in for his cholera shot and then had to stay for a few days because he was so sick with malaria. He was a mechanic, and he helped us finally get lights back to the patient houses on the other side of the road. I was glad for his help as I had asked so often and couldn't get Ted Crossman to agree to hook them up. Our plant was small and gave trouble the more lights that were hooked up to it.

By the end of April, Jean and Elsie were back with the new Land Rover. They had had seven days of travel down through Tanzania and around the lower part of Lake Victoria then over through Rwanda into Goma. The Rover was nice and marked up as an ambulance, so I hoped that would help with customs. Elsie would be with us one more week then head back to Aba before going home. I told her she should go home, get rid of her job, and come back to us. I thought it would be nice if the Lord led her that way.

Dr. Ulrich came down, and we had fifty-one surgeries in the week. We worked until 8 p.m. every day. Elsie Maier and Dave Downing did two surgeries with Dr. Ulrich helping, and Benjamin did ten. We had my washing machine down at the hospital for the entire week.

After Elsie left for home, a bomb dropped on us—both Benjamin and Grafele were involved with other women and had to leave the work. They told the pastor they would leave quietly at the end of the month and not make a stir. I didn't know how things would work out.

Malona took over as Interim Director for our hospital and worked to sort out problems. He had found that people continued to get medicine even though their cards had not been paid. He also discovered the lack of payments for some of the special medicines. I tried to encourage him to work with the medical men so we could get things moving along well, and we reorganized our workers to fill all the positions. We also discussed the problem of folks coming on Sundays, not because of need, but for the sake of no lines.

At the beginning of May, we learned that Dave Mason, our laboratory man in the Nyankunde work, had to go home. His wife Marilyn had been in the States since January for medical treatment, and the doctor felt she shouldn't return to Africa. Dave planned to stay until the end of their children's school term. Then the Shoemakers would move to Nyankunde to take his place.

Things weren't great at Nyankunde. They had too few doctors for all their work. Dr. Ruth Dix was very tired and covered a wide range of work outside her specialty.

We went along. Maternity wasn't busy, but we had other problems. A man came in with a hernia which would, in times past, have been under Benjamin's care. Since he was out of the work, we had to send the man to Nyankunde. Times like these were hard because folks would get their ideas and stir up strife with their talk. It was too bad Benjamin had to leave. He was the local men's "man for the hour of need," and they had a difficult time accepting the change. It was hard on Dr. Becker. He had trained the men so well, yet they were not willing to follow the Lord and use their talents for Him. Eventually Yonama went for extra training and

312

took over for our emergency cesareans and hernia cases.

Towards the end of May, David Downing made another try for the top of Mt. Ruwenzori. Dave Mason decided to join him for the climb before he went home with his children to join his wife Marilyn in the States.

A few days later, my day began well. I listened to music on the radio while gathering fish, rice, and salt to take to the TB patients. Yona and I had just begun handing out the food when I saw a Roman Catholic priest walking rapidly up the path towards us. He came with a radio transmission from their mission work in Mutwanga at the foothills of Mt. Ruwenzori. The priest translated the message from the French—our David had been injured and David Mason was dead.

I went with the priest to inform Ted Crossman, and as I took the priest back to his motorcycle, the men radioed Nyankunde. As it turned out, they already knew because the park had somehow gotten word to Bukavu headquarters who then radioed the message to our pilot. The plane, grounded for some work, was quickly prepared and headed for the airstrip near the mountain while Ted Crossman, Yona, and Hank Shoemaker went by car. Marieanne Crossman and I went to tell Diane Downing, who was due with her third baby in a month. Thankfully, we were able to tell her before she heard it from others.

As soon as we heard the plane overhead, I picked up Diane and the children and we sped to the airstrip. We found that David Downing had not been injured physically, but he returned with a great heartache at having to bury his fellow worker there on the mountain.

David Mason had been thrilled to attempt the climb to the very top of Mt. Ruwenzori before he went home, and now his going home was to the Lord and not America. They had made it to the very top. On the descent, Dave Mason hit a rock slide and fell a great distance. Dave Downing climbed down and found the body where it had fallen. Unable to carry him out, he buried Dave Mason there on the mountain.

The Lord's ways are not our ways. We prayed for Marilyn as she received word at home and the three children still at our mission school in Rethy. Another missionary was going home shortly and would take the children to reunite them with their mother. We prayed for Dave Downing as this had been a hard experience, but he testified to the presence of the Lord and could report of the wonderful fellowship he and David Mason had had with each other and a tourist on the trip. In my missionary service, the Lord had given me many opportunities and responsibilities, and I praised Him for enabling every time. This day was another time of proving the Lord *all* sufficient.

David Scott Downing was born on June 5, three weeks early. He was a sweet little fellow, and dad was bursting at the seams at the birth of his son.

When we learned that Zaire was in the path of a solar eclipse, I cut out the dark sections of old x-ray films and gave them out so folks could look at the eclipse of the sun and not hurt their eyes. The crowd grew so thick that finally Etienne opened the pharmacy window and had the people line up. After we handed them all out, they still waited and waited, thinking I'd come with more. I did manage to keep one piece for myself. As the eclipse progressed, more children came by. I told them they could look with my piece but couldn't go away with it. They still begged for a piece to keep, telling me they wanted to be ready for when it would happen again in a few days. We were too far south to have a complete eclipse, but it covered about eighty-five percent of the sun.

In July, we had the usual mid-year–round of pay raises. I praised the Lord for the way Yonama undertook his job as director of the work. Hank and Ella Shoemaker were packing up to move to Nyankunde. Nina continued to have trouble with soreness and tightness, but she held her own. Jewell planned to return sometime in August. We had a busy load and the Lord enabled.

During school vacation time, many of the local boys came by asking me for work. I drew up a weekly rotating schedule of four boys each week so more of the children would have a chance to earn money. Then some girls also wanted work. I dug through my boxes and found patches of material donated by the Graterford Bible Fellowship church. I set them to the task of sewing little covers for the babies. Then I remembered I needed some *americani* (imported cotton cloth) for the backing or the raw edges would never hold up in the wash. These would end up being expensive covers, but I trusted the girls would learn to sew and have money to help in their schooling. I paid $1.50 (American dollars) for two finished quilts. They needed $12.00 to pay for secondary school.

I became more or less "Mama" for Yodita, one of our nurse/midwives when she married in mid-July. I had given her material for her dress, which someone else sewed. I ironed the dress using Diane Crossman's electric iron which was so much easier than mine. All the girls changed at my house, and what a time. She had three of her co-workers stand with her. She also had five little girls all with yellow dresses. After we got them dressed, I noticed the little ones didn't have slips. I dug through boxes and found four that someone had sent to me. Two of the older girls never showed up at the house and finally we discovered they were still at the tailor—waiting for their dresses. The dresses had been made short and tight and there wasn't anything we could do about it.

When we were ready to go to the church (almost two hours late), we discovered the bride didn't have any flowers. The maid of honor was supposed to get them from Diane Crossman but had never found her and then forgot to go back. I dashed into my storeroom and found a table centerpiece. After tying some ribbon around it, we had a bouquet.

The march down the aisle took thirty minutes. Jean told me the horn players went through the piece at least sixty times. The pastor gave a good message, and I prayed they might be a home for the Lord.

Five premature babies needed care in maternity that July. One weighed just two kilos. The littlest weighed one kilo (two pounds) and by two weeks old was gaining weight and doing nicely.

Yodita on her wedding day

At noon one day, a woman with a ruptured uterus was brought in from Mutwanga. I was amazed, first of all that she was alive to tell the tale, and secondly that she was lucid and not in shock. I radioed Nyankunde and learned that the plane was unavailable, so no doctor. Our first choice was the doctor in Beni, and second was for Yonama to do the surgery, but we needed written permission from the family. We found the woman had come to Oicha because there was no doctor in Beni. So, they signed their agreement and Yonama did the surgery with Manasee assisting. Of course, we lost the baby, but mother pulled through. Before the surgery, Yonama declared, "The Lord will help." How wonderful to trust the Lord.

Once the Downings left at the end of July, bookwork fell on me again with help from Yonama, who managed the pay books. I was back in charge of the account books and found problems with money disappearing. I tried to check it out and felt weak in the thought of the debt to the hospital once again. Companies in town had paid bills that had not been written up in a valid way. That caused me to check on other things, and I found more underhandedness. I thought my eyes would wear out working the records. Jean loaned me her adding machine that ran on four batteries which was so much faster than my own little machine.

One of our young men from the area had studied in France and met a Swiss girl there who came out to meet his people. The cultural background would be something for her, but it was good that she came out to see before stepping into marriage. While she was here, she joined our medical girls in the Bible study.

At that Bible study, we had tea, bananas, and popcorn. I stacked the dirty dishes after everyone departed. Before I could pick up the popcorn from the floor, the ants took care of it. I saw a large piece inching up the side of the wall, and they worked hard to get it in a hole there. Once I had killed a spider in my house and the ants took it away before I could dispose of it.

We had a man brought in from Mangina with a badly mangled leg from a falling tree. We gave him ether to clean the dirt and prepare him for transport to Nyankunde by plane. As we finished the case, I looked up and was surprised to see Musa, my cook from Nyabirongo. He was a neighbor of the man and had come along to care for him.

By the end of August, Jewell was back to the work. Jean's siblings, Beth and Tim, arrived safely on the same MAF plane from Goma right to the airfield in Oicha. Only one suitcase and a guitar were missing.

I was delivering a baby when the plane came in, then I decided to do rounds before going up to see Jewell. What do you know but another woman needed help, and I finally met up with the others at supper. Jewell was back in her old house. Jean moved to the Downings' house (originally the Beckers' home) to accommodate her brother and sister who were in Africa for short-term work.

I had 180 in children's class that month. On the whole it didn't go badly, but there were far too many to listen and really get something out of it. The next month, over 350 children came, many from a distance. Things swung out of control when I didn't have enough papers to give out and the children grew cross and mean. They ran around picking flowers, and then they went into Jewell's strawberry patch and told her we stole their papers. I wasn't sure what to do about it.

The Nyankunde training school had sent a student to work at Oicha for the summer. At the end of the previous school year, some students went on strike and responded disrespectfully to their leaders. If any of those second-year students wanted to go back for their third term, they had to prove their repentance through manual work. Kule, who also worked for us, couldn't go back because his marks were too low. I intervened with the doctor on behalf of Kule as he was a hard worker. In the end, Dr. Becker gave permission for him to return for his third year if he completed his manual work. Over the radio, I told the Dr. Becker that I was glad to be able to make Kule smile again, and Doctor told me to go quickly and tell him. I trusted these young men would grow to know the Lord and learn to trust Him and give Him first place.

Jewell was back, and what a blessing. Dr. Wescott did the surgeries during the doctor visit, and Jewell managed the OR. She had such a good way of handling things. She didn't get excited or upset or cry out about the work. They did fifty-two cases during the week.

Arabeni came to work for me because Barnaba went back to work for Jewell. A new female nurse started who was Alur and so tall compared to the other girls here. It had been a shock to see her at first. She proved to be a very good worker.

Sadraka visited from Uganda. He had helped me in the house and was now the hospital evangelist. He told me that Dr. Keith was working hard and now had been assigned by the government to go into the area's leprosy work. Lois Clark wasn't back yet which left Martha Hughell and Anny Rineer as nurses. I would have liked to visit Kagando if the border opened, but permits to go in and out of Zaire had to come from Kisangani now. I hated to have my passport out of hand so long.

I enjoyed all the birthday notes folks mailed to me. Jewell's birthday was close to mine, and I threw an indoor picnic for her (meant to be outdoors, but it rained). We had hot dogs on square rolls because I forgot to tell Arabeni to make the long rolls. Jewell and I discussed the work. She would be in charge of the OR, and I the books, and we would rotate the other duties by the month as we had done before.

News of the Israeli war reached us. Reports came through of the banning of oil for those standing with Israel. I trusted that those at home would have what they needed to keep warm in winter.

In October, Jerry and Anny Rineer stopped by on their way to deliver medicines to Nyankunde and brought excellent cheese and butter for us. They had never been to Nyankunde and were eager to see it. Anny thought our roads here were worse than our Sudan days. They brought a

Dispensary at Oicha

letter from Martha expressing a great desire to go back into Sudan; however, no visas had been granted to those who had been there before—no word one way or the other, just silence. We prayed that others might be willing to go.

Ray Stauffacher's daughter Sally Jo, a nurse and midwife, went into Sudan with two other British nurses under the ACROSS program (Association of Christian Resource Organizations Serving Sudan) newly formed by AIM, SUM, SIM and MAF. The women were sent from AIM but worked with the relief effort for the present. The country called for teachers as well, but not missionaries, although those in the ACROSS program were not denied to bear witness of their faith.

I learned from reports about the Africa Inland Church (AIC) that Abednego was traveling about and heading the work. Nikolau was in Torit, Yousfu in Katire/Gilo, Martin at Obo, Israel at Pajok, Thomas at Logotok, Jonas at Kapotea, and Andreya at Nimuli. They were hoping to begin a work in Juba sometime. Nikolau was the secretary-treasurer for the AIC work and had a bank account in his name because AIC (now fully autonomous) was not yet recognized by Sudan, and so they couldn't open the account in the name of the church.

Olive and Jewell

A month later, after Sid Langford visited Sudan, he told me that all that was left of my home in Katire Ayom was a cement slab. The Olsens' and Betty's brick places were standing though without roofs. The church was trying to go forward, and Lucepu was back at Katire Ayom. They were talking of a Bible school.

I took a quick trip to Rethy in mid-October with the Crossmans at mid-term weekend, hoping to repair my glasses. This time I stayed with Anne Cowell in the duplex she shared with Bernetta Wambold whom I had stayed with at conference time. Anne had been on the field since 1928 in Swahili translation work. She still did translation as well as teaching the language to new workers. Carolyn Saltenburger gave me the tour of the newly completed operating rooms, and Paul Buyse worked on my glasses trying to fix the bifocals. He couldn't get them right, so I ended up staying longer than I had planned. Ernie the pilot managed to fit us all in on the trip back to Nyankunde—two fracture patients, myself, another missionary, plus all the luggage.

By the beginning of November, I was back into the routine at Oicha. Jewell had had a busy time while I was gone. My week of relaxation quickly faded away once I tackled the books again. With Etienne on vacation, we had extra work in the pharmacy as well.

My concern for the work here increased in seeing so many coming for help yet the number of workers capable of such a job so slim. Even keeping track of drugs was not easy. I sent a bottle for injections to the autoclave, and it never returned. Of course, no one knew anything about it. Even in Nyankunde, the prayers at their medical prayer meeting showed concern for the lack of zeal in the students.

Dr. Wescott flew in early for the November visit along with our Thanksgiving turkeys. Richard and Dr. Ruth Dix, on a two-week vacation, were in Beni and joined us for our feast. Dr. Ruth had been carrying a heavy load, and once the two Dr. Woods had arrived at Nyankunde she took a much–needed break. Dr. Nancy Wood née Houser had been in Kampala one summer when I was still at Kagando. She had seen the work of the Center and had her heart set on it ever since. Now we had two doctors for the work. Dr. Helen Roseveare, also very worn out from her term, was at home looking after her aged Mother.

Churches often sent donations around the holidays. Two boxes that arrived from the Harrisburg Bible Fellowship church had both been opened. Not a piece of clothing, sheets, or blankets was in the boxes. The bandages, pill bottles, Bible puzzles, and toys were there, but no clothing. Two boxes of bandages from Sinking Spring Bible Fellowship church came through fine. I later received two more from Harrisburg with some clothing missing but with three new blanket sheets still in the boxes.

Our tourist camp was in full operation, and our third group occupied the house. They told me that it was great to have a place with an actual shower instead of just a bucket of water. This was a large group, and what cars, tents and setups they had. One of the men was a doctor from England who worked with leprosy patients there, so of course he was interested in our work here. I didn't have time to travel around with him, but Manasee helped out. They told us that Oicha was on the map even back in Britain. They had many questions about Dr. Becker and about me and how long I had been in Africa. It hardly seemed possible that twenty-five years had passed since I traveled to our Wissinoming church to meet with the mission board about their support to come out here.

By the beginning of December, I felt more in control of the bookwork, and I handed the ordering of drugs over to Jewell. Yonama and I took a trip to Beni to try and straighten out the mixed-up charges from earlier in the year. Yona, our light man, drove so I could relax in the back.

We found out that people had taken money and used it for themselves instead of bringing it in to pay the medical fees as they were supposed to do. The company paid us, and the folks would have it taken out of their pays. Our man was not without fault as he wrote up invalid bills, so we would no longer give him the money box. We would have to keep a closer watch on the writing up of charges and keep better check on things.

We heard that Margaret Clapper would come back to Oicha in July. I didn't know what would happen to me. Would I have to move? That depended on whether we had a couple to take the Crossmans' place when they left. The Africans wanted a man for overseeing the building. Time would tell.

Many of the area's Greek merchants were on their way out. I didn't know how we would get supplies after they were gone. We lacked kerosene (not because of the current problems in the Middle East, but because of those controlling the kerosene). The girls from Kagando wanted to visit sometime in January. If things kept up as they were, it didn't seem possible. We couldn't enter their land from this side, and there were road checks. I supposed the government was fearful of things being taken out of the country. I wondered if it would affect our conference. As it stood, we had permission to gather together. Step by step.

We celebrated Christmas with the Watts family from Rethy. I worked on finishing my cookies and sorting the clothing bundles. I finished the pays so Yonama could write up the books and I could get the money for the pay packets.

Jean was on call on Christmas day, and I went down to give patients the needle and button cards I still had. I took a tin of cookies along to give out to the children. Eighteen gathered for our station supper, which we ate in my backyard.

On the way to our conference in Rethy, I stopped in Nyankunde for a checkup with Dr. Dix which resulted in scheduling a D&C in the New Year. I would rather have been the nurse, but God had it different for me. I wanted to learn of Him in this time. We have a great and wonderful Lord.

1974

I would have lost heart, unless I had believed that I would
see the goodness of the LORD in the land of the living.
Wait on the LORD; be of good courage, and He shall
strengthen your heart; wait, I say, on the LORD!
(Psalm 27:13-14)

How good the Lord was in giving us time together with the richness of God's word. Over 110 missionaries plus their children attended. I stayed at Bernetta Wambold's home. The messages inspired, and we praised the Lord for our national pastors and leaders as we labored together to His glory.

Though my upcoming procedure remained on my mind during the

conference, all was well with my soul, and the Lord's ways are perfect. One morning Dr. Brashler, our field secretary, gave me Psalms 27:13-14 to take with me on the morning of the procedure. Those were the same verses which had meant so much to me when I had made the move to Logotok back in 1961.

On the day of my procedure, I recited those verses instead of counting when they administered the anesthesia. I went through once, then repeated, "Wait on the Lord," and I didn't remember anything else until I was finished. Dr. Dix told me that everything seemed benign to the eye, and in fact the lab report eventually confirmed her impression.

Faithe Zercher was due to deliver soon, so she stayed at Nyankunde after the conference to await the arrival while her husband Wendell went back to Oicha to work at the school. Though she spoke with Wendell on the radio and kept busy helping the Dixes' five-year-old Mary learn to write, Faithe was lonely. Stephanie Ruth arrived a few weeks later.

A half-hour flight and I was home at Oicha along with a large quantity of mangos that I had bought for only $3.00. I gave some away and my helpers canned the rest. After putting up eight pints and six quarts, we still had mangos left over.

I came home to bad news—no gas, kerosene, or diesel in town, and no one was sure of what the future might hold due to these shortages. We also heard there was no money in the bank. Usually all our allowances funneled through Kinshasa then to a bank in Bunia, but at this point, no money was moving.

Other things at Oicha were progressing smoothly. I checked through the books and found that Yonama had done well in

Araheni and Toma

keeping the money in order. Job had kept my garden going, frequently replanting to take advantage of the regular forest rains. Arabeni had kept all my in-house plants alive while I was gone. He carried on well with a new young fellow Toma helping. He and Job had kept guard on the place while we were all away from the station. One little fellow greeted me and told me, "We prayed for you when you all went away from us— we wanted you back again."

On February 1, over 103 folks gathered at Nyankunde to celebrate Dr. and Mrs. Becker's eightieth birthdays. Ruth Dix arranged the whole thing. Dr. Becker had told her he didn't want anything for his birthday, but she answered that it was too late—the invitations had been sent. To get back in his good graces, she promised no more parties until he turned ninety.

Mrs. Becker looked lovely in a long dress made just for the occasion. When she looked at Dr. Becker, you could see her adoration for him. Two men representing the Greek community gave them two gold cups and $300.00 to use for philanthropic purposes of their choice. Bernetta Wambold represented UEC, their home church. Margaret Clapper and Pastor Zephania spoke for Oicha days and Dr. Dix for Nyankunde. Malona, the hospital evangelist, prayed and related that if Dr. Becker had not come and taken an interest in him and his health, he would not have had the twenty-five years to serve the Lord. Harry Stam gave a message about a righteous man as a shining light and of how Mrs. Becker filled the post of the wife in Proverbs 31. The Beckers received the tributes with appreciation, and Dr. Becker enjoyed the evening more than he had expected.

At the end of January, Jewell decided to find a way to Bukavu to pick up her VW which had been brought there by some Baptist missionaries. It was stuck at the border and they wanted 100% customs. She didn't have the money and was hoping to get it lowered. She finally found the way in February.

I don't know how Jewell did what she did. She came back with her car a few weeks later, and it was typical Jewell in the way the Lord worked things out for her. She hopped rides here and there to get to Bukavu. When she arrived at customs they had a paper made out for the $2000.00. She informed them that she couldn't pay that much, but they insisted there was no other way. Finally she said, "Lets pray about it."

They looked shocked but she bowed her head and prayed aloud, not daring to look at what the men were doing. Then she told them she'd come back the next day with someone to buy the car. She went out the door but was soon called back in. They wondered how much she could pay. She told them half. By the next day things were arranged, and after the red tape to get the right papers and license plates (ten dollars each) she had her way. The little yellow bug sat in her backyard, and she drove it the next day on a dispensary trip.

When I talked with Dr. Becker, he was glad to hear she was home and had the car. When he wondered how it went, I told him, "Just the way things go for Jewell."

Ted Crossman was nearby the radio and said, "Tell him about her praying." Dr. Becker roared with laughter and said we'd continue to watch how the Lord led her and worked things out.

Once we had an American tourist who walked over the back path of Luanoli into Uganda. He was picked up and taken to a prison in Kampala for six days before they brought him back to the border to return the way he came in. Finding no cars traveling our direction, he walked the distance and arrived shaking and shivering with malaria. We treated him and accommodated him in the guest house instead of the "tourist court" so he could bathe in hot water and sleep in a real bed. He recovered and left a few days later so thankful for our help.

Our days seemed so different. Times were changing. Gas remained a problem. Supplies came in very slowly, and we had a challenge to be in line at the right time to find the things we needed. To conserve fuel, we reduced lights to three hours in the evening.

Jewell went shopping in Mangina and found many things we needed including milk, coffee, and fat. Flour wasn't available, but I could save my supply for later because Jewell found bread. If my flour became more alive with bugs, I could sift it.

The Greek merchants in town were down in the mouth. The hotel and one store in town had been taken over, and they expected other establishments to follow soon. Some of the Greeks didn't have enough money to return home. Plantations were as much as taken over because they couldn't sell their coffee anymore.

Our work continued in quietness, at least outwardly. Yonama had to give a talk about missing items and not from outside hands. It seemed that some were setting up work on the side. Oh that the Lord would get hold of hearts and lives for Himself.

Juneno, the Alur nurse, began teaching with me in the children's class along with Sari, one of our longtime helpers. During Yona's vacation, Jean's brother Tim took his place, handling maintenance and the lights.

News on the radio from the States was anything but encouraging. It was hard to know what to think about the impeachment of the president. Then there was a kidnapping in Georgia. What was the world coming to except preparing for the Lord's return.

We had a big feast with the medical workers at the end of February. Yonama liked to do things in a big way and brought in a whole cow for the festivities. I borrowed extra flour from Jean and made cookies.

The number of babies born in February reached 105. March started with difficulties, and I hoped the month wouldn't continue as it had begun. We lost a mother due to hemorrhaging. She must have been in a weakened condition because she went so quickly. The very next day, we lost another mother who came from the Catholic work for her thirteenth. I thought she seemed ready to deliver, but we couldn't get the baby. We went to surgery, but she died before we finished. She was infected and a bad risk, but we had to try.

I began to feel my advancing years when caring for difficult cases. I no longer had the strength in my hands and arms, and I straightened up slowly after working over patients. But I did finish the February books on time, and I felt good about that. I still planned to turn the task over to a local person and was praying for someone who had the capability and responsibility for such a task. The day for the mission to be in charge of such things was passing.

Though Benjamin did not repent, Grafele did and made things right at the church. He had his eye on working again, and Yonama offered him to Jean to take the place of Manasee, one of her helpers who was leaving for extra training in leprosy work.

Jean didn't want him. I didn't know what to think. First Corinthians 13 came to mind, and I wondered how to practice love in such cases and how or when to draw the line. Jewell had a soft heart towards Grafele, and don't we all when we have a hand in training and working together with someone through the years.

On March 22, my twenty-fifth anniversary of the day I left for Africa, I thought of how the Lord had blessed and led throughout all the years. He was faithful and never failed. How often had I been unfaithful and a failure, yet He was so loving and forgiving. Praise His name.

Plentiful rains were beneficial for the gardens but not for the roads. The plane was in Kinshasa for the yearly checkup, so Fanweli drove Dr. Wescott down in Dr. Becker's car. Dr. Wescott finished forty-one cases and then performed surgery on the Crossmans' dog to remove a tumor. He wanted to help if he could. Their children had one more vacation before furlough and they loved that dog.

Dr. Mark Buchanan, an internal medicine major going home for his internship in summer came along and helped on some medical cases. That was a relief for Dr. Wescott who enjoyed surgery more than the medical work. I never heard Dr. Mark's impressions but figured he left with an experience if nothing else.

Kerosene became scarcer. Though I still had enough for my fridge, Jean turned hers off. What would happen as the days moved on? So far we still had some gas and diesel. The Lord knew the need and would allow more in His timing.

April came upon us, and I thought how quickly the year was flying by. Jean's helper Manasee left the country to attend a three-month course in leprosy work. Jean began developing local clinics so people could stay in their home area and not live in a compound. Leprosy work was changing from the big colonies towards local care. Except for the most difficult cases, folks fared better caring for themselves.

One Saturday night as I was sewing uniforms for the medical helpers, two rats scrabbled in through a loose window. I shouted at them and one ran out, but apparently the other lost its way and stayed inside. After smelling something days later, I had a search party but never located the carcass.

The yellow uniforms for the girls in training needed adjustments. I marked the hems and Arabeni finished hemming while my other helpers ironed. I figured the girls would look dressed up for our doctor visit. I tried to make them short enough so they wouldn't feel a need to redo them, though I had suggested they leave them real long so they wouldn't have to wear the floor length wrap over top. Our female nurses wore wraps from the waist down most of the time because the government made a fuss, so they dared not wear short dresses or slacks. Not just short-short skirts, but even the women who wore a modest length were required to wear the floor length African dress. One Sunday, I noticed that the girls who were just old enough to begin wearing the long wrap had a new fad of draping it in such a way as to leave an open slit on the side.

Mid-April brought a new round of company to Oicha. We had two doctors for the monthly visit. Dr. Phillip Wood carried the surgery with Jewell assisting, and I assisted Dr. Nancy Wood seeing the medical patients. They were a lovely couple who loved the Lord and did good work at Nyankunde.

During the week the Woods were on station, a maternity case came that concerned me. I feared I might get into trouble with the repair work once she delivered that night, and Dr. Nancy told me she would come and help. At 10 p.m., I called Dr. Phillip because a different patient arrived from Beni with a ruptured uterus. We lost both the baby and mother. It is always hard to lose a patient, but this time was extra hard on

The Oicha women in training

the doctor because it happened at the end of a very long day. As we finished working on her, they called to tell me the first woman was about ready. I set things up and sent the girl to call Dr. Nancy, but we had a mix-up and Dr. Phillip came instead. He was brave and stayed to help, but it was 1:30 a.m. until he got to bed—poor fellow. He still performed surgeries the next morning until the plane left after lunch.

The Shoemakers visited with their children, who enjoyed being back. The Zerchers also had guests, and the men took several days off to climb the mountain.

The Crossmans' son David came to Oicha through Uganda and had found that land in a sorry state with not much left to it. Ted and Marieanne planned to fill in for the Amstutzes in Kampala before going home on furlough, and David didn't want his folks to go. Day by day, the Lord would open or close doors.

After having been out of the work for a time, Martha was back in Kagando. She had undergone a hysterectomy, and what they thought was a cyst had turned out to be more. But she was recovering.

The end of April marked my parents' fifty-seventh anniversary. I reflected on their faithfulness in prayer and in standing by me through the years of schooling, the field, and furloughs. They were so dedicated to writing each week (even though at this point, no letters had been delivered for two weeks.) They were my prayer warriors and my support.

I continued to pray for Grafele that he might have victory in his life. Many of our hospital staff wrestled with their testimony before others. Yonama gave a strong talk to the staff about the drinking and the need to throw themselves on the Lord for victory. In spite of a heart for the Lord, Ofeni, our night watchman, couldn't overcome his thirst for the drink. Alcohol flowed everywhere and put a burden on the wives to provide for their children.

In May, I thought a woman with a ruptured uterus wouldn't make it, but the Lord had other plans and she recovered after surgery. She had traveled from Beni in the back of a truck. Think of bumping on the road in that condition. The Lord made our bodies able to take a lot.

Jewell took the Mwenda and Lume dispensary trips in her VW and came back feeling she should charge the government for her work scraping the road for them. All I thought was that she must keep her wings up or something because she finished both places in less time than

I could finish one. I suppose I thought longer on each case. We were different and the Lord enabled for each of us. Jewel never tired, and from time to time it caused friction with the medical women working with her. Often when they had problems, they came to me instead of going to her. I didn't like to get in the middle of the people's problems and often suggested that we pray together and that each one pray on their own.

Jean's brother Tim headed home. The Ericksons and Margaret Clapper were planning to join the team here, and we also had a couple to take the Zerchers' place. I tried to think of what I might do about housing in order to stay on my own. Jewell had suggested I live with her. There were advantages to sharing a house, but I also liked my quiet time. When would I read books if I couldn't read during meal time?

Many sick folks came, and our May doctor's week was full. One morning we admitted two patients into our last two available beds.

That week, we learned of news that left me weak. Jean had sent a letter to all the heads saying she was resigning as of June. Everyone was surprised. I supposed we shouldn't have been, but it was hard to take. Once we straightened out the facts, we understood that Jean wasn't resigning from the mission, just as head of the leprosy work. She and one of the men in the work had been in conflict for years. Sure, we won't get along with everyone, but I had thought things like that would be fixed up between them if they allowed some love and sought to try. Not everyone is a leader. We prayed, and the Lord knew and cared for His own and His work. Thegbo (Manasee) was still in training, and when he finished he would probably be the one to step into charge.

Nina and Jewell returned from Nyankunde after dental work. The next day we went to Nina's for prayer meeting and found her on the floor. We took an x-ray and discovered a fracture at the radial head of her left wrist. Tim and Wendell took her back to Nyankunde in Jean's Land Rover along with medicines that had just come in from Kampala.

We invited an eye doctor to join Dr. Wescott on the June doctor visit. Dr. Wescott finished the major surgery, and as he left, Dr. Shannon the eye man came. What a time for him to come—on the weekend when everyone was tired from the big week. When we gave the invitation, we assumed both would be here at the same time, but Dr. Shannon had gone to Rethy instead.

The Zerchers left, and the Ericksons arrived. Hilda Erickson came to the station without her husband Glenn, who had to finish some work on a church he was building. Margaret was still at Linga and planned to stay to cover vacations. Nina took her arm out of the cast at four weeks, claiming the doctor told her she could. She kept it in the sling, but I was afraid she'd reinjure it because she intended to drive her car to the plane. She was a different person to guard, though I never had any broken bones to know what it was like.

With word that the Downings would move to Aba, we settled the housing issues. Jean and Beth Schram moved back to the house next to me. Margaret Clapper would use the Beckers' old house, and I could stay put.

Housing settled, but I thought ahead to furloughs and couldn't see where coverage would come from. We had a good national staff, but they didn't carry everything.

Maternity was crowded with difficult cases, and we lost two mothers. Because all the beds were taken, we moved several mothers with infections who had lost babies from maternity to hospital rooms. One young girl developed postpartum psychosis, and she was moved over as well.

After the Crossmans left, I picked up more responsibilities. The airfield needed checking, so I rode up and down the strip. A new pilot was flying, and he wouldn't know the holes and anthills to avoid. Previously, Ted Crossman inspected it every other month, but I didn't think that would be often enough, even though it cost $35 each time someone fixed the runway. The Lord enabled.

A few days before the Crossmans left Kampala for the States, Ted and an Ethiopian man were badly beaten by thieves. At first we heard that Ted had a fractured shoulder. We later learned that he was in the Kijabe hospital with a fractured jaw, shoulder, clavicle, ribs, and knee cap. The Ethiopian man who was heading to an Evangelism Seminar in Switzerland had his suitcase stolen and couldn't go.

Glenn Erickson finally joined his wife by plane but left his car and a load of things at Nyankunde until the roads cleared up. Margaret Clapper tried to come but couldn't make it past the thirty trucks stuck or lined up and waiting on the roadway.

Margaret made it through by the beginning of August, and we all ate supper together to celebrate. Most of the nationals were in Beni to see

President Mobutu that day. He showed up in his helicopter, which thrilled everyone with the way it hovered here and there. The folks were happy that their arrangements were not in vain.

About this time I hosted another wedding preparation, this time for Penina, one of our hospital workers, with her seven attendants and nine young girls. She was the adopted daughter of our school director Yakobo who was now in Aba and had worked for Jewell and I back in '49. As a rule, weddings were held in the groom's area, but they decided to hold it here. What a swaying good time they had marching down the aisle, and they managed it in a half hour, though the horn players were sweating by the end. Pastor Zephania (Kasale) led a very nice service, and Penina and her husband Kyabu moved to the Mbogo area where Kyabu taught school.

Our days were full of many things. Vic Paul was presently in Germany, and seven German young people connected with him visited us. Vic would be back in the fall, and they brought some of his things out for him. They also brought one hundred new horns he had had specially made in Germany just for Africa. The horns the fellows played here were tied with string and held together by all sorts of things, but they worked. The new ones were made stronger, but I didn't know how much they cost or who would buy them.

The German group traveled in Unimogs, a camper-like vehicle. Vic had one at Oicha that needed repair, and they soon had it in shape again using parts they had brought along. They did some things for Jewell's VW as well. The group also had a big truck which they told me carried a smaller Unimog for Nyankunde.

When the father of one of our hospital workers died the same time that another worker was on vacation, we had a shortage of help. Jewell called a married nurse who lived nearby to fill in for a few nights, and we now had a new wrinkle—a woman at work with her four-month-old baby on her hip. We did what we had to do—become a nursery for working mothers.

Nina's arm healed, then Margaret Clapper fell and broke her arm.

Barb Battye sent a letter catching me up on all the news. She wondered if I had any information from AIC (Africa Inland Church) in Sudan. Both she and Martha had told them that they would return if permits were granted and they had replacements. She wrote. "More and more, I have felt I should return if the way opens." The church in Sudan had contacted me, requesting that I prayerfully consider returning to reopen the dispensary at Katire Ayom.

In the same letter, Barb also asked for flour—anytime, any size, and at any price. Things were difficult there, but they survived. Our prices in Zaire continuously rose as well.

Mid-September, four Land Rovers filled with tourists drove into our station after having spent three days in our northern mud holes. They had traveled nine-tenths of a mile in one day. One of the men, an Indian doctor on his way back to Zambia, toured the hospital and then checked a case for me. He had a nice way with the child, gaining his confidence first, and all went well. He told me he preferred doctoring to making roads. The doctor's father had been a professor in Khartoum, Sudan, and I felt a kinship.

We had quite the mix-up of cars due to the road situation. Some of the holes were five feet deep and filled with water. Three cars for Oicha were stuck at Nyankunde, and one of theirs was at this end. The things of the Wikerds and Ericksons were up there, and the Downings' things were here. By mid-October, the road north had been repaired, and folks quickly traveled through before the big trucks spoiled it again.

David, a Zairean medical student, and Kambale, a medical student from our area but a year behind David in training, helped out during their vacation. The doctor, used to the experienced nurses in the OR, found the medical students a bit trying, particularly when he called for a suture and it wasn't ready. But they caught on quickly.

Mid-October, a message on the mission broadcast caught my ear. The plane would be flying empty to Nairobi on December 23 and back again on January 7, and they were looking for anyone who wanted to travel. I quickly reserved my place in order to visit Jean and Dan Olsen and the Gehmans. I couldn't do it cheaper by land. I sent my passport over for a Kenyan visa and looked forward to a phone call with my parents. We exchanged letters and tapes but hadn't spoken directly in three years. How good the Lord was to make such a flight available. Just the thought of a getaway made me feel different. It was a chance I couldn't miss taking. The Wikerds' parents were coming out for Christmas, but I figured they'd be around for a while. In reality, I only saw them get off the plane as I boarded. Zaire wasn't celebrating Christmas this year—

orders from the top, we learned. We could have a remembrance for the Lord without a great gathering.

We needed more properly trained staff. Oicha was a big work. Above all, our personnel needed a desire to live for the Lord and bear His testimony. Yonama brought in men and women and started a training school. The Center wanted him to close it, but it was hard for him to do so. We needed trained workers. I didn't know what would happen. I began to have Etienne (Musombe) of the pharmacy work take over making up the drug orders for the dispensaries. He began well, and I trusted it would continue so. I had no direction on anyone to take over the burdensome finance books. Just when I thought all added up nicely, I'd hit a snag. Though I improved in finishing them in a timely fashion each month, it was a long, hard job.

People from home supported me by sending boxes filled with many things, and I appreciated each one. Some folks sent uniforms, some Sunday school papers. To my great excitement, a box with eight bags of drapes arrived eleven months after it had been sent. We always welcomed bandages. Once when Thegbo (Manasee) came over from the leprosy work needing bandages, I was able to hand over an entire box. I told the folks at home to keep them coming. At least bandages weren't stolen.

I heard that the pilot Jack Spurlock had my visa for Kenya. He also had my passport because he took my papers to get the permit to leave and reenter Zaire. I prayed I would get them all back in time, and I had them in hand by the end of November.

Zaire celebrated the anniversary of the new regime on November 24. We scheduled church at 7 a.m. so folks could get to Mbau to be on hand for the big day. By the time I arrived to church at 7:45 after my rounds, Pastor was already closing in prayer (usually he preached for at least an hour). Many of the young medical fellows and lab workers who played horns missed work in the weeks leading up to the celebration because of the extra practice time. The people were so excited, and Yona chauffeured at least four trips to Mbau for the hospital folks.

Dr. Muhindo came with Dr. Wood for the November visits. Dr. Muhindo (whose father was a nurse trained by Dr. Becker years back) had finished his education and now worked at Nyankunde. Though he didn't have full granting from the government yet, we trusted, as the Lord willed, that he might be the man to nationalize the school and work at Nyankunde.

Fog delayed my departure for vacation. When the plane finally arrived, I was dispensing medicine to the last patient in line. Because my health issues had not been resolved by the previous year's procedure, I stopped at Nyankunde for a checkup. The doctor gave me medicine for the two weeks but then informed me that I'd have to come back for another D&C.

After an uneventful flight to Kenya I stayed with Dick and Flo Gehman and the Olsens and also met up with Vic Paul. We had great gatherings at the Olsens' with wonderful food—steaks one night and Grant's gazelle the next. During the course of vacation I visited with the Fonsecas, the Booths, and the Rineers. It was so nice to see their children, who were all so friendly and happy to see me.

I was taking medicine for malaria, which always seemed to show up when I was away from my usual surroundings. But I went to town anyway. After attending the English service at the African church across town, I visited Metasula and his wife at their home right next to the church. We had a short time together, but it was long enough to catch up on all the changes since we had worked together at Logotok.

When I called my parents, I couldn't get the international operator on my first try, but I connected the next day. How nice to hear my parents' voices on our three-minute phone call. Though that isn't much time to really talk, our voices came through clearly, and I thought it well worth the $8.15 for the station to station call.

I also took time while in town to renew my soon-to-expire passport and later went back to the Zairean Embassy to pick it up. I never liked to leave it out of hand because if someone lost my passport that would be bad for me. As I paged through my new American passport, I noticed they had stamped "cancelled" on some of the pages and managed to hit the pages for my return to Zaire. So that I wouldn't have trouble getting back in, they issued a three-month tourist visa. I wanted them to transfer my real visa over, but they said all they could do was the tourist visa. I went back to the American Embassy and asked to see the Vice-consul. I met with her, explained my problem, and requested that their folks be more careful in cancelling pages. She understood and apologized for the carelessness.

On New Year's Eve in Nairobi, I read late into the night and wondered what verse I could carry on for this year in a special way. I read all of I John that evening and then went back over it. Chapter four stood out to me. God is love, and perfect love casts out all fear.

1975

How precious also are Your thoughts to me, O God! How great is the sum of them! If I should count them, they would be more in number than the sand; when I awake, I am still with You. (Psalm 139:17-18)

I enjoyed my vacation in spite of the malaria. I couldn't believe how much money passed through my hands. With passports, shots, dentist, watch repair, and room and board, I spent over $300.00. Of course, I would get some of it back because I bought a number of things for other folks.

Before I ended my vacation, I heard a bit on the radio that our President of Zaire had more "fantastic" ideas since his return from a trip to the Far East. He was acting like he was a god and people should worship him. I prayed for the Christians. I feared we might see more changes. I later read more details in the Nairobi paper quoting President Mobutu that the National Party would have authority over all the schools. Unemployment would be no more. Agricultural schemes were in the works, and employers would clothe the children of the employees. The government also took over transportation. Time would tell what it all might mean.

My plane departed for Zaire at 8:30 a.m. on January 8. We had no real problems with customs, except that we had to hunt down the immigration and customs men. They only charged me for the car parts and never asked what I bought or opened any personal bags. Hank, the pilot, said we had the nice fellow. I busied myself at Nyankunde until the next morning and my scheduled appointment with Dr. Kyle.

How hard it is for a nurse to become the patient. My examination indicated the need for a hysterectomy. Dr. Kyle, Dr. Becker, and Dr. Wood all agreed, so my surgery was scheduled for the following Monday.

"When you pass through the waters, I will be with you; and through the rivers, they shall not overflow you. When you walk through the fire, you shall not be burned, nor shall the flame scorch you. For I am the LORD your God, the Holy One of Israel, your Savior." (Isaiah 43:2-3a)

An article in a Bible Club Movement newsletter highlighting these verses spoke to me. Trials are not to stop the believer's walk. "When you pass through the waters. . ." It does not say when you get to the waters you shall stop there. Neither does it say you should quicken your pace. Walking is the pace at which men go when nothing distresses or alarms them. Isaiah 28:16 tells us, "He that believeth shall not make haste." God has ordained that no troubles, however great, and no persecutions, however terrible, shall stop the onward walk of His child. The water may be deep and the current swift and the river wide, but it shall not overflow him, for God's presence is near.

I wasn't scared, but no human can ever say they are not anxious at times, and my anxiety showed up as a knot in my tummy.

I talked a long time with Vera Theissen. I wasn't blind to the seriousness of my surgery. Though I was in good health, more than one had been taken in such a time. I just had to declare that I knew the Lord and was ready for what He wanted. But I still desired a pastoral call. I felt I couldn't go to surgery without it. Dr. Kyle came in and was very patient and talked with me a long time. Finally he said, "Let's pray together." How my heart leaped for joy. He prayed for everything from the least to the greatest, from the known to the unknown and put it all into our Father's dear hands. After praying aloud, Dr. Kyle was silent for a time before he rose from quiet prayer. I was on wings of peace. The Lord gave me Psalm 139:17-18, and I wrote part of it on the palm of my hand. "When I awake I am still with You," whether here or in glory. We have a wonderful Lord.

Dear Yosobeti, the OR nurse, was by my side as they administered the anesthesia. The surgery took two hours, and I was told that Dr. Becker came into the room for a half hour saying he had promised me he would. Juneno, who had worked at Oicha for a year, was now at Nyankunde, and she stayed with me after the surgery until I came out from the anesthesia. How wonderful the Lord is to make our bodies heal. After two days of surprising pain, I was able to move again. Everyone was so good to me, and as far as I was concerned, Dr. Kyle was tops.

Nine days later, I was a discharged patient, though not permitted to work for another month. Deep Africa is not the worst place for surgery. I don't think I would have had the spiritual atmosphere at home. I did miss having my family nearby. After surgery, they had MAF contact Kinshasa to get a phone message to New York and from there to tell my parents that everything went well. I trusted they received the message. Due to slow mail, I never received get-well wishes until over a month later, and I sent several letters with much the same information about the surgery because I didn't know if my folks knew I was recovering. All those letters home caused my mother to cry. I asked her forgiveness for seeking so much sympathy. I think God had a plan in the loneliness of those weeks without word from loved ones at home. The Lord knew and cared.

Over the next weeks, I received many cards. I heard from Doug and Kim Reitsma, which was a pleasant surprise. Dr. Doug was teaching at the Hahnemann Medical School, and the children were all growing up.

Before I went home, I had dinner with Dr. and Mrs. Kyle. They had a daughter Joanna of about seven months and such a doll of a girl, so much like my nieces. They also had a son Andrew who was about four and a half. I tried to make friends before lunch, and soon we were playing games and using his building blocks. Then he came out with some people toys including an older woman with a bun on back of her head and said, "Look, you have a bun like my grandma here." Dr. Kyle overheard and groaned, but I told him I was happy to be granny to them.

I also met Dr. Muhindo's wife, a British woman. She was lovely and had real abilities to teach Bible studies. Because the Bible could no longer be taught in school, we had been praying for God's guidance to begin Bible study groups, and the Lord was answering that prayer. The needs were great.

On January 27, I flew home to Oicha and was quite ready for my own firm bed with its mattress on top of a board. I started back into the work slowly, beginning with the books. Jewell was great and covered maternity for me until March. I admit I felt selfish in having so much of a break, though it was terrific to have the time to work on the books. I began feeling more like myself and went to children's class to help but not yet to lead.

We celebrated Margaret Clapper's birthday with a feast. I made sweet and sour pork but used mostly beef. Beth, Jean's sister, made rice, Ella

Shoemaker did the rolls, and Nina Wikerd made cake and ice cream. I was so full after that meal.

I went down and began helping in the back office. I was feeling good although I quickly understood why I was told to start part-time. The first day, I felt a bit shaky but thought that some of the cause was due to a patient going bad. Dr. Becker came with Dr. Wescott for the monthly doctor visit. I think he was happy to be at Oicha again. While they were here, they fixed the door of our autoclave.

Mid-February, my attention turned to the furlough situation. I told my parents to keep praying because I really didn't know how to plan. Someone had to take over the books, and no one was in the offing.

Jean Schram was leaving for furlough in April. Nina Smith was to go in summer, and I trusted she'd get there. The problem of where to put the orphan children weighed heavily on her. Margaret Clapper was due furlough but feared things would change and she wouldn't be able to return. She wanted to work longer before retirement if possible. The Wikerds were leaving in July, and the Ericksons were up in the air because of the government takeover of the schools. We didn't know what would happen to teachers. We heard a doctor might be coming to Oicha, but nothing was certain. We needed another nurse for the work. My thoughts went round and round. I didn't know how to plan and prayed for His leading and knowledge.

Paperwork went well for the month, and I was feeling good—then we had a sadness. Our laboratory head man drank so much that he missed two days of work, so we lost him. He was such a young fellow being led by some still getting away with it. Yonama told me that he had been warned several times. So many spiritual needs. Grafele took the head position in the lab, and I prayed for him as he had only been back in the work a year.

March found me fully back into the work. One day during the week of the doctor visit, as I cared for the office patients, a maternity case came in from Beni. I tried to deliver her, but when it didn't happen quickly, I didn't waste time. I sent her to Dr. Wescott and Jewell. Then in the afternoon a paralyzed woman in labor came in, and I had to do all the work to deliver her, cutting the symphysis and using the extractor, but all went well. The baby was seven or eight pounds, which was a big baby for the women here. I hoped she would get better and be able to walk again.

Some doctors thought the paralysis was a result of the pregnancy, but no one really understood. All were happy it was over. Then at 5 p.m. that same day, I again did the same work and all went well. Miriam, our midwife, told me, "You are just someone that work comes to." She talked as though they hadn't had as many cases when I was out of the work, but I didn't really believe that Jewell just sat around.

Jewell continued doing the dispensary runs, and mid-March she came back to find us with a big mess. The autoclave had blown up. Not that it was all in pieces, but the pipes came apart and the door burst open from the pressure. Everything was out of whack, and I didn't know what we would do with all the sterilization work needed. We were so thankful no one was in the way or injured. The stuff inside blew out, and applicators, salve pads, syringes, and needles were all over the place. A patient in the office at the time knew of a man named Stevens who had worked on the autoclave in Beni and offered to ask him to come out and see what he thought of it all. Stevens was able to repair it but wouldn't give us a bill. He said he had helped the Roman Catholics and the local hospital and he wanted to help us too.

The morning after the autoclave mishap, I locked my key in the house. I climbed through a window to get it before anyone could see my mistake.

We were having some trouble with thieves. Tourists had things stolen, and the pump from Jewell's Land Rover went missing. She put a sign on the garage door—"Thieves will go to hell." At the women's prayer meeting, one of the girls said "Praise that even if they took the pump, they left the jeep!"

I heard from Martha Hughell in Uganda. She was doing well health wise. The Rineers would be going home in summer. Barb Battye kept busy and had a chance to visit Kuluva, her old station. She enjoyed seeing the place again. To get there, she flew to Kampala and then drove ten hours. Flying back took just one hour. That's the advantage of a plane.

Dennis Wikerd found cement in town for the hospital but couldn't find fuel, so I trusted we could continue to run our lights. Gas for the trucks could wait. We could run the truck less, or not sell gas to passersby who ran out. The folks couldn't understand when we had to keep the little we had for the water pump. A week later, word came that more gas had been delivered to town. Dennis went back for the gas and picked up the mail at the same time. The post master had sent word that our box was "suffering." That was the translation from his French. Our mail and packages overflowed the box.

We had a fun weekend early in May when the two Dr. Woods came down from Nyankunde with twenty-one other fellows to play soccer. We had some rain, but it cleared and the game went off as scheduled. Oicha won six to two. It was a good game, lots of folks around, but no fighting. The next day in church, many presented special songs and all did well. At the very end, the Nyankunde group sang a greeting and a farewell to the Oicha folks.

I was scheduled for maternity that weekend, and at midnight they called me with a confusing message. I went down and found that robbers had stolen a stethoscope and the clock in maternity. It was almost unimaginable to believe it happened. That clock had survived the rebellion, and now it was lost to a thief.

Pastor Kasali (Zephania) returned from a meeting in Kenya of the African Church leaders from various fields and shared news from some of the Sudanese men he had seen there. He and Pastor Andreya had been in school together back when their children were small. Pastor Kasali (Zephania) said, "They really want you to come back up there." (I already knew that and had written that I couldn't consider it until I had furlough.) Pastor went on to say, "But we want you back here to us too."

He brought back the Swahili minutes from the Administration Council meeting. They granted me furlough for January 1976 and welcomed me back as the Lord led. I realized in reading the minutes that I was back in the spot I had been in many times before—wanting to do the Lord's will, but fearful in what it would be. I always enjoyed my work wherever I was, but I never adjusted easily to a change.

Poor Jewell. She decided she needed more exercise (trouble with extra weight). Someone had sent her a skip rope in a package, so she began to use it each morning. Then she felt it in her back. Heat seemed to help, and she wore a hot water bottle on her two-day dispensary trip. One night at supper the hot water bottle leaked and dripped water everywhere she went. I loaned her mine. She had had back problems ever since she had that jar on a motorbike ride with young Harold MacDowell years back. She was brave and continued on with her work.

A few months later, she sold her old Land Rover and bought a motorbike instead. I hoped she would be able to use it considering her back problems. Of course, she kept her VW.

Mail from home indicated my mother was not well, and I implored her by letter to take care. She would try to do too much then become weak. I prayed for her. I knew she liked to get around, but I asked her to please not do it so much.

As in times past, news from Africa reached my parents and caused concern. I reassured them from afar that whatever they heard about the kidnapping affair, it had taken place hundreds of miles south of us. American and Dutch students had been abducted in Tanzania by Zairean rebels. We trusted they would soon be free, and in fact they were all eventually released. A Pentecostal missionary was also missing along with his plane for almost a year, and we hadn't news of him either. I trusted he was a witness to the rebellious people of the area.

I had been concerned about my cook Toma because he and his wife never had children. I had big decisions to make when a woman delivering in maternity told me it was Toma's baby. I hadn't known he had a woman on the side. We so quickly say we're not surprised because that's the way people live. I had prayed for them, and I didn't know what to think of my prayer life. I needed guidance anew and asked the Lord to keep me from bitterness. He had something to teach me, and I wanted to be clay in His hands.

I began to train Kasereka on the finance books. He was our nurse/dentist and very humble in his work. I thought he would do a good job, but of course he still needed help to understand all the work. Even with him taking over the books, I was still concerned about the load Jewell would carry when I went on furlough.

On a Thursday early in June, Mr. Stevens, the man who had repaired our autoclave, came in. We had treated his child for malaria the day before, but he hadn't seemed that ill. Now they were back with the boy in convulsions, and in spite of our efforts the convulsions continued. Since the father had the means for transportation, we sent them on to Nyankunde. The boy reminded me so much of Ricky Beatty back in '58. By Friday, we heard he was brighter and they had hope for full recovery.

Dr. Wescott finished four cases one morning before his plane took off and hit his 2,600th operation for the two years he had been in Africa. Dr.

Harris had been along that week checking the status of family contacts of the lepers. Thegbo (Manasee) carried the leprosy work for Oicha, and I praised the Lord for him.

Nina and Dennis Wikerd were preparing to leave for home at the end of the school term. They had replaced the Zerchers, but no one would be replacing them. Instead of a nice flight, Dennis had to fix up their car to drive to Goma because our plane was grounded with engine trouble. In truth, I was glad they were taking the car so we wouldn't have to care for it until someone picked it up. They took my parents' address since they would be at Dennis' parents in Allentown and thought they might drop in. They wanted to see the Zerchers in Harrisburg as well.

I had enjoyed the year with Dennis and Nina. The school director would have been happy for them to stay, and they had considered, but they felt they should go home at the end of their two years. Nina gave me one of her dishes, the covered kind that could go from the fridge to oven without thought. I hadn't a chance to use it before something fell on the lid and broke it.

Our tiny premature baby, less than two pounds at birth, was up to three pounds. The mother wanted so much to take the little girl home, but it wasn't time yet. We kept her in the new incubator—warmed by hot water bottle. Other babies had been in bed with the mother at this weight, but we tried to keep this one isolated so she

Our two pound premie

wouldn't get a cold and spoil the work done to keep her alive.

Yakobo (Job), Jewell's cook, who had also worked for me, lost his wife Roda after a cesarean at the Aba station. The surgery had gone well, and towards midnight she had told Yakobo of her happiness and began singing. Soon afterward, he noticed that she seemed too quiet, then realized she was gone. No real reason other than the Lord said this was her time. He traveled with his other son and the darling little two-week-old baby by plane to Bunia then by car to Oicha. Everyone stood ready to help, and we prayed for Yakobo to be drawn close to the Lord. Roda loved and followed the Lord. We don't understand these things, but we know the Lord doesn't make mistakes.

Nina Smith placed her orphans in homes, and on July 19 she and Margaret Clapper drove to Nyankunde and then flew to Nairobi. Nina traveled on home to retire, and Margaret stayed for a few weeks of vacation. I bought some of Nina's belongings—her bed, a cupboard, a table, and her little red VW.

One night as I made rounds, a maternity patient called to me and pleaded, "Please help me, I never take this long to deliver." My examination found a face and brow presentation, and I knew she required help. Fearing the baby would tire, we acted without delay and I cut the symphysis. That didn't help, so we went right into surgery. The baby cried quickly and well, and we were delighted by that. His face was swollen and out of shape from trying to push his way out, but it improved by the next day.

The remainder of that week in maternity rapidly filled with other cases. The next day, we had another cesarean. The following day brought a fight with the bedbugs in maternity. Sunday was a quiet day with the memorial service for Roda. Monday, my 5 a.m. call went quickly. I was called again at 9 a.m. and continued from one patient to the next until 12:30. Five cases altogether—one to remove a placenta, one to remove the remains of a miscarriage, two vacuum extractions, and one moral support—encouraging Safi as she delivered a patient. Tuesday had a difficult case, but all went well after a hard pull. I supervised Safi for another vacuum extraction, and in the afternoon we did a cesarean for another brow/face presentation. All went well. Wednesday during prenatal clinic, a case came from a dispensary. This was the woman's seventh baby, and though we delivered her without surgery, the baby was dead. The mother was so disappointed because this was her third dead baby in a row.

Thursday, a case came from Mutwanga. They had hunted for five hours to find a car to bring her in. We went to surgery but lost the mother the next day. With fifteen difficult cases in the week and thirty-nine deliveries all together, I wondered if the obstetricians at home could match our record.

Toma, my cook, left for a weekend, telling me he was sick, and never came back. I had kept him on after several problems, but now I heard a bad report about his wife. Apparently she had been beaten up and went home to her parents. With all these things, I let him go and managed on my own until furlough. I cooked more food at one time and made up TV trays to put in the fridge. Esau still worked for me, and even though he was a very slow worker, I didn't need to hire anyone else.

We had to dismiss a young fellow at the hospital for what might be called witch doctor's work. Some folks thought that if they touched their fingernail to the tonsil of a patient with a high fever, the fever would leave. There had been village children who had died from hemorrhage because of this practice. I caught the fellow red-handed and he was gone.

This wasn't the only problem on the station. Outside people passing through and causing a problem was one thing, but when I discovered local people stealing, folks who had attended classes and learned verses, I felt sick. Surely these were the last days, when men turn from the Lord.

Someone broke into the back window by my fridge and took a bag of bread and rolls right off the top. We no longer had the strawberries or fruit from our gardens. Someone even pulled up carrots from Jewell's garden just as they were getting big enough to eat. Yona told me he saw two boys wearing shirts made from curtains that had been taken from Jean's house—boys who lived here and whose fathers worked for us. One was the son of Job who worked in my garden. Even little ones ran when they saw us coming, so you know they were up to something.

New government decrees meant we could no longer order medicines from other countries as had been our practice. We now had to obtain our drugs through the government pharmacy, though in the past they never had enough to fill our needs. When the doctors first caught wind of the coming changes, they ordered a big supply before the deadline. We prayed they wouldn't be stolen before they reached us.

I booked my flights for furlough and planned to be home by Christmas. When we pray, the Lord says that there will be signs to show His plans. I continued to seek guidance and asked others to pray with me for my travel, my time at home, and His leading as to my return. I was wanted back, and I trusted the Lord to lead me back. But the days seemed different and unsure, almost like when I returned to Sudan within a year of my leaving. I now had a visa for Zaire that was indeterminate, which meant it could be used for a long time, but I was restricted to only eleven months out of the country to maintain its validity. So with all these things in my mind, I made plans to the extent I knew and allowed the Lord to work out things in His best time and way.

By September 1, our tiny two-pound preemie was up to five pounds and had gone home with her mother. We were happy to see her again at our baby clinic. We had another newborn just over two pounds. She was holding her own, so our hot water bottle incubator was still in use. We also had twins and three others who were less than four pounds and were fed with droppers, but they could stay near their mothers (though still with the hot water bottles).

Safi taught the children's class. Four mothers came to help, although they seemed at a loss as to how to keep the children still—they all just ran around. I prayed for the group that it might not die out when I left for furlough.

By the end of September, I was within three months of leaving and so began my passport paperwork. I also worked on correspondence with folks at home and some of the Sudanese who now lived in Kenya. Kasereka gained in his knowledge of the books and did well, even catching a mistake that Yonama had made. We celebrated my birthday and then Jewell's birthday with beautiful cakes decorated by Margaret with real flowers.

We had another theft—this time the scissors from the shoe shop. After discovering the thief and the one he sold them to, we recovered the scissors. They had been sold to Benjamin. Because he had no use for scissors that size, he had planned to resell them, but he hadn't found a buyer by the time we caught up to him. What was so hard about the affair was that the thief was one of the boys who had attended my children's class and had easily learned all the verses. Jewell suggested that though he learned them, they never reached his heart.

Yonama's faith found the scissors, not mine. He declared one morning that we would pray about it for the Lord could show us. After we found them, he praised the Lord and said, "SEE, I said the Lord would." He continued on, suggesting that the Lord kept buyers back from Benjamin so we could retrieve our scissors. My faith is so small.

By mid-October, with only six weeks to close down my role in the work, I hurried to finish last minute letters. I sorted through papers and belongings, deciding what to take home and hoping to keep it to one suitcase, a smaller bag, and my handbag. Daddy said I could use his typewriter, so I wouldn't need to haul mine home. I figured that since I'd be back in eleven months I'd hold on to the car.

Dr. Wescott told us that the Center would soon begin covering the Baptist work for surgery. Think of a range from Detroit to Washington D. C. and in this whole area, no other qualified surgeons. Many of the other doctors that were around, as in Beni, didn't have enough medicine. Our supplies were not plentiful as in years past, but to this point we had been able to carry on well.

By the beginning of November, with my bookings confirmed, my thoughts turned more and more towards home. I finished the last-minute duties. Kasereka had traveled to Nairobi for a month, so I worked out the pays for October, which were complicated because of government mandated pay raises. I turned over the station books to Margaret. I praised the Lord for Yona and encouraged him to keep good records to help Margaret stay on top of station needs.

The Shoemakers and Vera came down from Nyankunde, and we all had supper at Jewell's house, talking until the lights went out. Jewell and I discussed my return. As it stood, if I arrived back in 1976, Jewell planned to go home to her father to help him. Together, we cleaned the station storeroom and packed away my belongings.

On November 27, I went to town to sign out and send my final letter from Zaire. Maternity stayed busy until the end. Late on my last day, while I was still working, I handed over the books and keys to Kasereka. Dear Jewell was brave and took my leaving in stride, but she carried a great weight. I prayed for her and that the staff might step up and notice all the small things needing attention.

By November 30, I was on my way home. After the business of my last days at Oicha, I was glad for a rest at Nyankunde, although my thoughts often strayed back to Jewell and the work before her. Mother and Dad Becker were showing their age. They continued to be active in some parts of the work and still attended all the services, but I could see they were slowing down.

I moved on to Nairobi on December 4. By December 11, I was

347

visiting with Annie Punt, and I landed in New York on December 14. I flew the final leg to the new Allentown Airport by a smaller plane. My mother was unable to come to the airport, but Daddy and my brother met me along with a large group from the church. They handed me a bouquet of twelve red roses and sang *To God be the Glory*. A few from other churches were also there to greet me along with Bill Beatty who had been in the area and stayed a few extra days to greet me. All the young people were eager to see if I could recognize them, and I think I placed everyone in the correct family if not with the correct name. I even recognized my nephew with his beard. The children told me that I never changed. I looked forward to meeting the four new great-nieces and nephews and to a time of speaking face to face with family and friends instead of by letter.

The Lord had been so good to me in this term.

Furlough and Beyond

And the LORD, He is the One who goes before you. He
will be with you, He will not leave you nor forsake you; do
not fear nor be dismayed.
(Deuteronomy 31:8)

Aunt Olive, as she was known to everyone, entered into her furlough in her usual way—helping her parents, arranging speaking engagements, and collecting supplies to take with her when she returned to Africa. She spent some of her summer weeks at Camp Gilead in Florida. While there, she was able to visit the AIM retirees at the Media facility and also had time for fellowship with Bill and Phyllis Beatty.

The blessing and highlight of her summer came when she and the Beattys visited Abednego from Sudan. He was in the States reading the Bible in colloquial Arabic onto cassette tapes. They had a joyful reunion filled with questions about people and his work in Sudan. Abednego was so like his father Andreya in his voice and motions, and Aunt Olive rejoiced to see the growth in him. She learned that John Kute, Yunia's son, and James Okot, Monwelli Okuma's son, were studying in their second year at Scott Theological in Kenya. Nikolau and Tabita had a third son. Abednego, the Beattys, and Aunt Olive talked and shared pictures yet ended their time together still wanting more.

By October of 1976, Aunt Olive was deep in prayer for her next steps. Though her desire and heart pulled her to Africa, her mother's poor health called that return into question. After much prayer, she surrendered her will and desire to the Lord and delayed her return to the field. She testified that the Lord enabled and gave joy and peace in following His will day by day.

She took up her new role of cook and caregiver and appreciated the good things of being at home. She enjoyed all the conveniences we so take for granted—pure water from the faucet, twenty-four-hour-a-day electricity, and cooking on a gas stove instead of three stones and a fire as in her first years in Sudan. Though she grew used to it, she always returned prayers of gratitude to the Lord.

Aunt Olive kept up her large correspondence and became a prayer warrior on the home front, closely following news from Sudan and Zaire. She worked part-time in a nursing home and took night classes in Bible. Now that she was home, she could enter more fully into the lives of her nieces and nephews. She also took on responsibilities at her home church including teaching the children during prayer meeting and serving on the missions committee. She faithfully attended AIM conferences and visited with missionaries home on furlough.

Jewell left for furlough in 1977 and full responsibility for the Oicha hospital and a new operating room were turned over to African hospital staff. Aunt Olive sent out five barrels of hospital supplies, longing to be on the journey with them. By 1978, Martha Hughell and Barbara Battye were back in Logotok under the Voluntary Medical Services. John Moyi and James Okot finished their last year of Scott Seminary.

On June 8, 1978, Aunt Olive's mother and best friend, who had so faithfully prayed and so freely given support, was called home to Glory. Aunt Olive missed her greatly.

Through the next years, Aunt Olive continued to care for her father. She enjoyed times of fellowship at AIM meetings and kept up with the news of those in Africa. She was able to meet with the Beckers who by then were retired and living in Myerstown, PA. The Kagando, Uganda hospital managed to stay open through the Idi Amin years. (It would continue to grow and eventually was named as one of the top three hopitals in Uganda.) In 1980, Dr. Keith Waddell took more training and established Uganda's first eye service, performing eye surgery in outlying areas and training others. In 1988, Olive visited with Barbara Battye as well as Dr. Doug Reitsma. After Kim's death five years before, Dr. Doug returned to Sudan. There he met Gillian, and they had just married in "the wedding of the year" in Sudan.

By 1989, Olive's Daddy was in a nursing home, and he passed away in December of that year. In the new year, at the age of sixty-eight, Aunt Olive applied to return to the mission field—her home. Because of her age and the length of time off the field, the mission felt the adjustment would be too great; however, they eventually consented to her return to Oicha as a volunteer for one year. She stayed for four years. If asked how that came about, she would break into a small grin and with a twinkle in her eye reply, "Well, I was already there, so I just stayed." In September of 1994, she bid farewell and left Africa for the last time. The staff at Oicha gave her a big sendoff but couldn't see why she needed to leave, since she was still so able to help.

She took off in the MAF Cessna to Bunia, followed by the AIM DC3 to Nairobi, Kenya, then on to London in the company of Martha Hughell and Barbara Battye. There she connected with many AIM missionaries including Dr. Pete Williams (Dr. Ted Williams' brother) and the Reitsmas. Once home in the United States, she spent nine days visiting the AIM retirees in Florida and finally flew to Pennsylvania to settle into an apartment in Souderton. She continued serving at her home church and maintained her vast correspondence, faithfully praying for the needs of those near and far. Many people from Bethany, her home church in Hatfield, fondly recall her walking around at church and handing out birthday or anniversary notes. Others of her vast circle of relatives, friends, and colleagues received notes in the mail.

In August of 2016, Aunt Olive suffered a series of strokes, and her physical world shrank to the size of a room in a nursing home. As in times past, adjusting to the sudden change in circumstance was not easy. She felt the loss of her independence as she, the one who had always been the helper, became the one needing help. Her niece Karen faithfully coordinated and monitored her care.

Aunt Olive eagerly received family and friends stopping by her room for a chat. Once a month, the ladies from her AIM prayer group gathered in her room so she could continue to participate in their meetings. Visitors often arrived to find her sitting in her chair, Bible or prayer letters in her lap, with her head bowed (sometimes in prayer, sometimes in sleep).

On January 23, 2018, at the age of ninety-six, Aunt Olive stepped from time into eternity and into the presence of her precious Lord and Savior Jesus Christ.

"Well done, good and faithful servant . . . Enter into the joy of your Lord." (Matthew 25:21)

Acknowledgments

As any project this size, many have contributed to its completion. First and foremost, thanks be to our precious Lord and Savior Jesus Christ who planted the idea in the first place and nurtured it to completion.

Karen Fluck so generously allowed me to haul away letters, photos, and artifacts. She happily looked through slides and files to find more information each time I asked. Rebecca Armstrong took on the monumental task of initial editing. I don't know how I would have finished without her encouragement and suggestions. Several others also read through the manuscript and offered helpful comments and corrections including Karen Stull, Steve Heck, June Hersh, Thelma Heist, and Linda Hanes. Ruth Pastori tracked down formatting glitches and proofread the final manuscript. Any remaining errors are mine alone.

Mark Haines designed a cover far beyond anything I could have imagined. Meta Wells helped with formatting decisions and final reading of the proof. Meta and Howard Wells, Barb Surrey, Sheryl Gordon, Rita Parker, and so many others offered their encouragement along the way.

I am thankful to Lynn and Steve Wichmann, and Ed Surrey for help with all things connected to the photographs. Also thanks to Steve for being my go–to computer guy.

I am grateful to each of the missionaries and missionary kids whose stories overlap with Aunt Olive's. Each one of you has a tremendous story to tell, and I loved learning about your part in this one. Though I was unable to track down everyone, I must admit to being a bit awestruck in communicating with those I could find. Thanks to the families of the Beattys, Wilckes, Booths, Beckers, Reitsmas, DeYoungs, Olsens, and also Freida Atkinson, Dr. Waddell, Dr. Dix, Dr. Phillip and Dr. Nancy Woods, Dr. Kyle, and Russ and Lyn Noble. Thank you for your encouragement in this project and the specifics you contributed to the narrative. A special thanks to the ladies from the AIM prayer group (Margaret Rineer, Gillian Reitsma, and Linda Stiansen). I enjoyed our chats each time we crossed paths in Aunt Olive's room. You were so helpful in clarifying information on people and life in Africa.

To all those I can't list by name, but who named me and this project in their prayers, please know that I felt those prayers.

Finally, I again give thanks to our precious Lord and Savior Jesus Christ, in whom we live and move and have our being.

Building in Sudan

Walls ready to be filled with stones

Walls ready for the mud

More Photos

Meeting with the children

Carrying home the wood

Made in the USA
Middletown, DE
26 June 2019